In Darkest London:

The Manuscript Journal of

Joseph Oppenheimer, City Missionary

In Darkest London:

The Manuscript Journal of Joseph Oppenheimer, City Missionary

Donald M. Lewis

Regent College Publishing
www.regentpublishing.com

Regent College Publishing
5800 University Boulevard, Vancouver, BC V6T 2E4 Canada
Web: www.regentpublishing.com
E-mail: info@regentpublishing.com

Published 2018 by Regent College Publishing

Regent College Publishing is an imprint of the Regent Bookstore <www.regent-bookstore.com>. Views expressed in works published by Regent College Publishing are those of the author and do not necessarily represent the official position of Regent College <www.regent-college.edu>.

ISBN 978-1-57383-564-0

Cataloguing-in-Publication information is on file at Library and Archives Canada.

To

Mark Mayhew

Contents

Illustrations

Acknowledgments

It is my pleasure both to acknowledge and to thank those who have helped me in researching and writing this book. My sincere thanks needs, first and foremost, to be extended to the Board of Governors of Regent College, who provided me with the support to write this over the thirty years of its gestation, and their on-going support in providing research funds. I am also indebted to the librarians at Regent College and the University of British Columbia. I am indebted to the librarians of the Bodleian Library at the University of Oxford for their assistance in consulting the manuscripts of the London Society for Promoting Christianity Amongst the Jews and other manuscript collections. My gratitude needs to be expressed as well to the London City Mission which has been so generous in allowing access to its archives.

I am especially grateful to the Rev. Gordon C. Taylor, the former rector of St. Giles'-in-the-Fields, and to the Venerable Dr. William Jacob, the recently-retired rector, both for their giving me access to the Oppenheimer manuscript and for their permission to publish the manuscript in its entirety.

Professor David B. Green of the Department of Geography at King's College, the University of London, has been most helpful in sharing his expertise with me both through his publications on the rookeries of London and through correspondence and personal conversation. His long interest in the Oppenheimer manuscript has been a great encouragement. I am also indebted to Eoin Dunne for his research assistance in accessing the probate records for the wills of Joseph and Jane Oppenheimer, and for looking at the settlement records related to Dudley Street in the London Metropolitan Archives. My gratitude needs also to be expressed to Alexander Poole for his assistance in genealogical research who was helpful in tracking down descendants of the Oppenheimer family in New Zealand.

I am indebted to the work of several research assistants over the years, but particularly to Greg Cowley, who has been acquainted with the Oppenheimer material for well over a decade. I am also indebted to Benjamin Frederiksen and Paul Gutacker for their help. Special thanks needs to be expressed as well to Kathy Tyers, whose suggestions for editing the work have been most appreciated.

Finally, I am especially grateful to my colleague, Dr. Sarah C. Williams, for her support and advice in this project.

Abbreviations

LCM	London City Mission
LSJ	London Society for the Promotion of Christianity Amongst the Jews
RBM	Ranyard Bible Mission
SRA	Scripture Readers' Association

Introduction

> And he began again to teach by the sea side: and there was gathered unto him a great multitude, so that he entered into a ship, and sat in the sea; and the whole multitude was by the sea on the land. And he taught them many things by parables, and said unto them in his doctrine, Hearken; Behold, there went out a sower to sow: And it came to pass, as he sowed, some fell by the way side, and the fowls of the air came and devoured it up. And some fell on stony ground, where it had not much earth; and immediately it sprang up, because it had no depth of earth: But when the sun was up, it was scorched; and because it had no root, it withered away.
>
> And some fell among thorns, and the thorns grew up, and choked it, and it yielded no fruit. And other fell on good ground, and did yield fruit that sprang up and increased; and brought forth, some thirty, and some sixty, and some an hundred. And he said unto them, He that hath ears to hear, let him hear.
>
> Mark 4:1–9 KJV

In the year 1890 the famous journalist and African explorer Henry M. Stanley, best known to history for his greeting "Dr. Livingstone, I presume?", published an account of his exploits in the southern Sudan: *In Darkest Africa: or, The quest, rescue, and retreat of Emin, governor of Equatoria.* The title builds on an earlier work by Stanley, his *Through the Dark Continent* (1888). In the same year that *In Darkest Africa* appeared, William Booth, the founder of the Salvation Army, published his best-selling book *In Darkest England and the Way Out* in which he brought to the attention of late Victorian readers the terrible destitution existing in England and discussed both the challenges and short-comings of short-term "band-aid" solutions and considered more long-term remedies to the desperate problems created by the Industrial Revolution. The title of this book picks up on the allusions from Stanley and Booth, concerned as it is with the destitution close to home "in darkest London."

The area surrounding the church of St. Giles'-in-the-Fields was "darkest London" in the 1860s, as it was considered the worst slum in the British capital. Its cramped conditions and overwhelming poverty were matched by an overpowering stench. Not only was it ugly to the eye and revolting to the senses, it was also dangerous to life and limb. Crime and disease rendered it off-limits except to the poorest of the poor, and to a handful of outsiders such as Joseph Oppenheimer, a "city missionary" with the London City Mission, the sower in this story.

The field where he was to sow his seed was the slum or "rookery" located in the parish of St. Giles'-in-the Fields, just a few blocks south of the British Museum. Here were three distinct areas of abject poverty: the "Church Lane rookery" between Broad Street and Great Russell Street just to the north of St. Giles' church; the Seven Dials area in Covent Garden, immediately south of the church; and the streets and alleyways intersecting Drury Lane just to the east of Seven Dials.

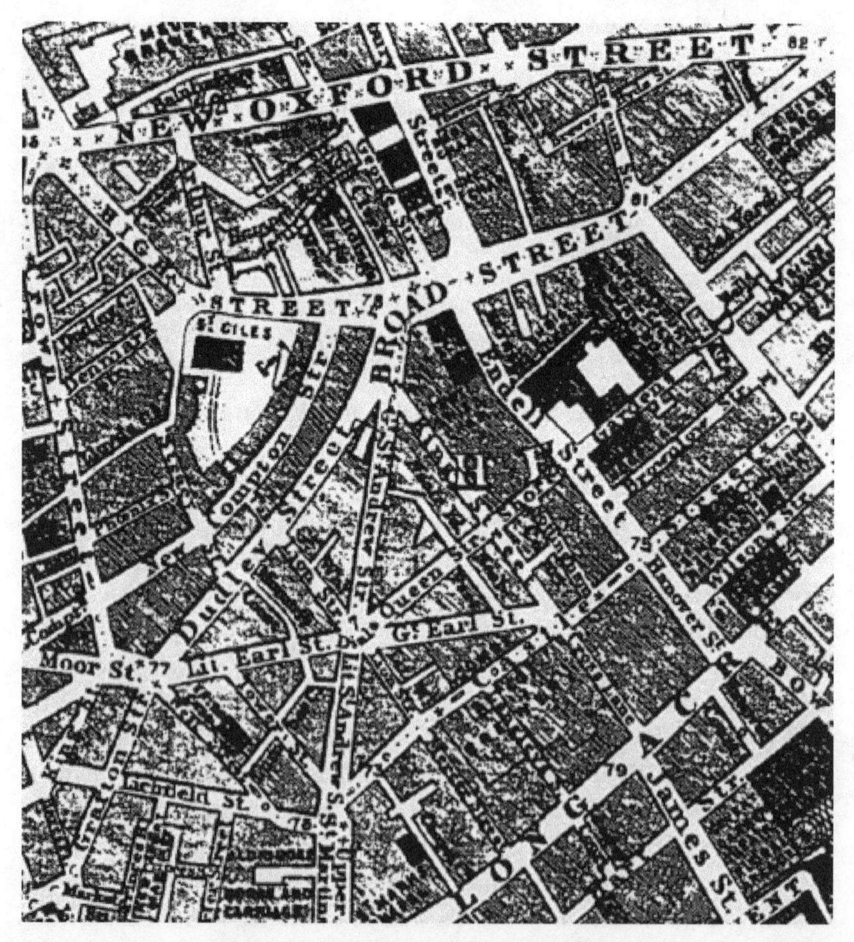

1. MAP OF ST. GILES' AND THE SEVEN DIALS
Dudley Street (formerly known as Monmouth Street) is where Oppenheimer worked.

The entire area was regarded as London's social and moral cesspool. During warmer months, it was also notorious for its putrid smell. In the mid-nineteenth century the common wisdom was that stench carried disease—malodorous "miasmas," as they were called. The miasmatic theory of disease argued that rotting organic matter such as sewage and decomposing corpses, both human and animal, created "bad air" which caused illness. This understanding was advocated by leading sanitation reformers such as Sir Edwin Chadwick, who once told a parliamentary committee that all smell is disease.[1] Only later in the century did people realize that while the smells were revolting, bacteria were the real enemy. The stench warned people off, but germs silently did their deadly work.

The rookery's alleys and lanes constituted a dense warren where pickpockets and prostitutes went unchallenged. Even the self-respecting poor sought to avoid it, yet the most desperate among them flocked to the area to sell rags and other detritus that self-respecting pawnshop owners refused to trade. The "dolly shops" were so named because of the distinctive brown-skinned dolls—a racist logo—hanging outside these shops that signified their place at the very bottom of the commercial hierarchy.

SEVEN DIALS. *(From an Original Sketch.)*

2. MID-NINETEENTH CENTURY SKETCH OF SEVEN DIALS
Little Earl Street would appear to be on the left by the street lamp; Lion Street the second from the left; Greater St. Andrew's Street, the third; and Queen Street, the fourth. Note the artist's use of light and darkness to highlight the fact that the narrow streets allowed for little direct sunlight in the streets.

3. SKETCH OF SEVEN DIALS
PERMISSION OF THE LONDON METROPOLITAN ARCHIVES, CITY OF LONDON
SC/P2/HB/01/218
The building on the right of this sketch appears to be the one on the left of the previous sketch. Little Earl Street would seem to be the street on the right with the street lamp; The street with the cab is Little St. Andrew Street; The southern end of Lion street would appear to be to the far left.

4. SEVEN DIALS STREET SCENE
"SKETCHES BY BOZ—SEVEN DIALS" BY GEORGE CRUIKSHANK—1835

This work is an in-depth study of the hand-written journal of Joseph M. Oppenheimer, a German-born Jewish convert to Christianity who between 1858 and 1862 was employed by the London City Mission to reach the poorest of the poor with the Christian message. While prepared for the eyes of his personal supervisor, it provides a rare first-hand account of this desperately poor area of the capital of the British Empire.

THE RELIGIOUS WORLD OF LONDON

Understanding Oppenheimer and his journal requires an appreciation of the religious world he inhabited, for in his mind the mission was first and foremost spiritual. A good deal of this work is thus given to explaining and making sense of Victorian evangelicalism, the religious worldview that Oppenheimer had embraced. Owen Chadwick, a leading historian of Victorian religion, has observed that "Throughout the mid-Victorian age, the evangelical movement was the strongest religious force in British life."[2] Yet ironically we know relatively little about it. A number of years ago, David Englander observed something that in large measure still holds: "The status of Evangelicalism in Victorian Britain, its role, structure, sociology and strategy have not been the subject of sustained study. Our ignorance of Victorian Evangelicalism is profound."[3]

Thus while Victorian evangelicalism's influence is widely acknowledged and can be clearly discerned in Oppenheimer's journal, it has been but little studied. The impetus for this book arose from my earlier work, *Lighten Their Darkness: The Evangelical Mission to Working-Class London, 1828–1860*. In it, I sought to uncover and make sense of the vast evangelical network developed in the Victorian era, devoted to encouraging the growth of popular Christian devotion in some of Britain's most barren soil: the ground inhabited by many of the poorest of London's poor. The Industrial Revolution drew the impoverished from Britain's rural areas and small towns in the hopes of a new promised land in the city—or, more realistically, the city was seen as a way of escaping the extreme poverty of the countryside. The rich harvest for which the evangelicals hoped among the urban poor never materialized, but in spite of great disappointment, they laboured on, undaunted. Religious observance in Victorian London—at least when measured in terms of church attendance—was closely linked to social class in the second half of the nineteenth century. The percentage of adult church attenders varied across the social scale but generally plummeted the further down one went. Well-to-do suburban areas had a median adult attendance of 37 percent, compared with 34 percent in the wealthy West End; middle-class areas came in at 24 per cent, lower middle-class at 18, upper working-class districts at 16 percent, the middle working-class at 13, and the poorest areas—such as where Oppenheimer worked—at 12 percent.[4]

Scholars are aware that evangelical Protestantism was the most powerful religious movement in the Victorian era, when religion was an important part of the social fabric of British society. Our knowledge of evangelicalism, such as it is, is more heavily weighted toward English Nonconformity than toward the evangelical movement within the Church of England. As long ago as 1962, Dr. Kitson Clark observed, "The Evangelical Movement [within the Church of England] is studied until the death of Wilberforce in 1833 or possibly that of [Charles] Simeon in 1836, after that no one knows what happened to the Evangelicals or much cares…."[5] Such studied neglect has led to an ignoring and/or dismissal of evangelicalism's role in shaping major aspects of Victorian social and political attitudes, although this is beginning to be corrected.[6]

Alongside the neglect of evangelicalism by scholars, there is the fact that little attention has been paid to the role that religion played in the lives of the poor. As John Walsh once observed, historians seem to be far more interested in what John Henry Newman said to Edward Bouverie Pusey as they walked across the quadrangle of Trinity College, Oxford, than in what was happening simultaneously among the poor in the overcrowded slums of Victorian England. What the poor heard or said about religion has been overlooked; their voices have been largely silent in the literature on Victorian religion. Because so much of the writing of church history has been dominated by high church Anglican historians, it is understandable that our picture of religion at a popular level has focused on the experience of Anglo-Catholic clergymen in the second half of the nineteenth century, rather than what was experienced by the poor in their daily life. As Geoffrey Best has noted, High Church Anglican historians have often written up the Anglo-Catholic Ritualists "as the only Christians who evangelized the slums" in nineteenth-century England.[7] A.D. Gilbert endorsed this view, writing that it was "the Ritualist clergy of the late Victorian era whose efforts contributed most to the modest achievements of the Church in the urban working-class parishes."[8] Kitson Clark further re-enforced this marginalizing of the evangelical Anglican clergy when he observed, "They became people on the periphery working in the dim streets of the provincial towns...."[9] The resulting impression has been that the urban mission to the poor was largely the work of Anglo-Catholic clergymen. This conception is still common at a popular level, although it is unfair to several generations of evangelicals, ignores the efforts of Roman Catholic missions, and fails to acknowledge the efforts of Broad Churchmen.[10]

In fact, while marginalized by historians, evangelical Anglicans did not disappear into the provincial towns in the mid-Victorian period, but rather were becoming dominant in the British capital. From the mid-1830s, evangelicals who had previously been largely shut out of Anglican churches in London began to be appointed by Bishop Blomfield—from 1828 the bishop of London—and by the mid-1840s, evangelicals were the dominant and most active group of Anglican clergy in the capital.[11]

The evangelical mission to the poor has also been greatly under-appreciated, the significance of its work having been ignored by many leading scholars. It is telling that Owen Chadwick, in his excellent study of *The Victorian Church,* had virtually nothing to say about the London City Mission and similar organizations throughout Britain. These were the missions that had the most direct and sustained contact with the poor throughout the Victorian age.

The whole religious enterprise represented by the city missions and similar organizations operating in the poorest areas of London—the sowing of so much seed in such apparently infertile soil—has been overlooked by historians to a surprising degree. It is arguable that the efforts of evangelicals in organizations such as their District Visiting Societies, the London City Mission, the Scripture Readers' Association and the Ranyard Bible Mission constituted—alongside the Sunday School movement—the most influential religious crusade to affect Victorian popular religion and to shape popular religious attitudes and mentalities among the poor.

My earlier work had a dual focus: the methods evangelicals used to communicate with the 'lower orders', and the ways in which this mission was shaped by, and in turn shaped the larger movement of Victorian evangelicalism. This study is different in that it seeks to look in-depth at the labours of one particular individual—Joseph Oppenheimer—to understand his locale and institutional context, and to examine the responses he received. In *Lighten Their Darkness,* a chapter is devoted to a consideration of Oppenheimer's journal; this work seeks to present readers with a transcription of the entire journal, so that they can evaluate it on its own merits and be aided by a fuller explanation of its context and background.

Oppenheimer's journal is remarkable in that it appears to be the only surviving manuscript journal of its kind from the nineteenth century. There were hundreds of lay evangelists working in the poorest areas of London who kept such journals. By 1860, there were 628 such workers labouring in London for three major evangelical societies—the interdenominational London City Mission (LCM) had 375, the (Anglican) Scripture Readers' Association (SRA) 119, and the Ranyard Bible Mission (RBM)—also interdenominational—had another 134. These figures rose through the rest of the century. By 1890 the figures had peaked, with 793 lay agents at work in London (500 for the LCM, 134 for the SRA, and 159 for the RBM). Oppenheimer's journal therefore represents a very small portion of the tip of a very large iceberg. Thousands of such diaries have been lost to historians, although selected portions were regularly published in the nineteenth century by the *London City Mission Magazine.*

The manuscript journal of Joseph Oppenheimer offers a unique view of this slum and its inhabitants over a nine-month period, beginning in September 1861 and ending in May 1862. It is a rare first-hand account of life among the poorest of Victorian England. In it, we encounter the names and voices of the poor as they interacted with a rather curious man. He must have seemed quite odd in terms of both his person and his mission, a young German Jewish convert urging Christian faith and practice among his (largely) Gentile hearers. We meet Irish costermongers, needlewomen, semptresses, glass cutters, manual labourers, tinkers, pub owners, shopkeepers, tailors and prostitutes. We hear the complaints of the poor, their objections to religion, the grievances of Irish Catholics, the indifference of many and the faith of a few.

These people are not all nameless, however. Oppenheimer often gives the names of those with whom he converses. This enables the historian to expand our understanding of their situation, and, in a sense, to bring them to life again. This is possible because a British census was taken on 7 April 1861, and thus we can identify some of Oppenheimer's conversation partners through the census record. We learn, for instance, that Mr Leighton of 14 Dudley Street with whom Oppenheimer conversed on 3 September 1861 was John Leighton, a 31 year-old-baker born in Norwich in Norfolk, married to a 29 year old London-born woman (only identified by her initials "M. A.") who worked as a shoebinder. They also had a 52 year-old female lodger living with them, Mary Bentley, born in Oxfordshire, who worked as a "monthly nurse."

5. 1861 CENSUS RECORD FOR 14 DUDLEY STREET

Oppenheimer's journal provides an unedited, first-hand account of life in the poorest of London's slums, written by a perceptive and well-educated outsider who was also a foreigner. Joseph Oppenheimer's only claim to fame is this journal, and it is hoped that this transcription will enable readers to form their own opinion of his words, his world, his work and his observations of some of the poorest of London's poor. Since he was a fairly recent convert to evangelical Christianity, his recently acquired religious attitudes well reflect the concerns of mid-Victorian evangelicalism. Further, the fact that Oppenheimer was a convert to an Anglican expression of evangelicalism is worthy of special consideration, insofar as it helps us understand the impact of evangelicalism within the English state church.

The journal of Joseph M. Oppenheimer enables us to understand several other phenomena, as well: first, the intensity of the evangelical efforts amongst the poor. Oppenheimer was assigned to visit "the Dudley Street district"— District Number 126, among the 350+ districts visited by City Missionaries at the time. It was a small area—only about six hundred yards long, or about two city blocks, including a narrow passageway between Dudley Street and a neighbouring street. Dudley Street was the northwestern border of the almost-rectangular "Seven Dials" area. (The short street had been called "Monmouth Street" until *circa* 1850 and is now the northern end of Shaftesbury Avenue.) He worked at this day-in and day-out for four years, often labouring seven days a week.

Second, the journal allows us to hear firsthand what the poor heard on a regular basis from the religious workers who had the most contact with them, the agents of various evangelical city missions operating in the major cities of Victorian Britain. For most of the poor urban dwellers, this was the face of Christianity that they most frequently encountered. These encounters undoubtedly shaped popular attitudes toward religion in general and Christianity in particular.

Third, it gives us an idea of what the people who were visited said to such agents: their concerns, objections, questions and the general reception that different groups gave to the lay evangelists. It also offers a unique window on the religion of the poor whom Oppenheimer visited in the Seven Dials area of London. The somber record of Oppenheimer's visits provides rare firsthand-evidence of the nature of religious discourse in mid-Victorian England, and it shows the influence of traditional Christian values in an era of economic and social turmoil.

Oppenheimer had converted to Christianity in London at about the age of 21. When employed by the London City Mission in 1858 he was only 24 years old, the minimum age set by the Mission for its workers. He was unmarried at this point. In 1859 he married Jane Charlotte Andrews at St. Giles' Church and by the time the manuscript begins, he was the father of a small daughter, Alice Ann. During the first few months of the journal, in the fall of 1861, his wife gave birth to a second daughter, Constance Lavinia.

Oppenheimer's manuscript journal accounts for only the last eight months of his four-year stint with the London City Mission, during which he was incapacitated for weeks at a time by illness. He was particularly good at summarizing the views of those whom he was assigned to visit, often recording their comments in their own words. Undoubtedly, as a German-speaking Jewish immigrant he was something of a curiosity to those whom he sought to engage. As a recent convert, he was and is an interesting representative of evangelicalism, having absorbed all that he knew of the faith as an adult.

The first chapter, entitled "The Sower's Work: The Mission in its Context", seeks to provide background material on the evangelical mission to London's poorest areas, explaining how the evangelical urban mission arose and the strategies employed. The second chapter, "The Sower: Joseph Oppenheimer, City Missionary" looks at what we know about the author of the journal. The third chapter—"The Sower's Field: Dudley Street, St. Giles'-in-the-Fields"—seeks to provide a thick social description of the area he visited, setting the mission and the man in the context in which he worked. The fourth chapter provides a transcription of the full text of the 150-page journal. This allows readers to make what they will of Oppenheimer's own words.

Chapters five through eight look at the different types of soil where he sowed his seed. The fifth chapter thus looks at the responses of Irish Catholics, who made up about a third of the people living in his district, to the work of this Protestant missionary. Chapter six examines his interactions with the handful of fellow Jews whom he encountered and with whom he seems to have established friendly relations. Chapter seven looks at his interactions with the prostitutes with whom he spoke. Chapter eight investigates the stony ground he often encountered and examines five categories of negative responses to his work: those who were overtly hostile; those whom he regarded as Christians in name only; those who were skeptics; those who were generally indifferent, and finally, those who were Sabbath breakers. The final chapter, "The Sower's Harvest," looks at the positive responses he records.

In these analyses of the journal along the lines of different constituencies, different themes emerge. The discussion seeks to juxtapose images of the raw journal alongside interpretive explanation, hoping to remind readers of both the complexity and the subjectivity of historical reconstruction, giving them some appreciation of both the nearness and the distance between history and source.

The apparent trivia that Oppenheimer records provides a consistent, daily record of the working of a lay evangelist and the operation of a routinized religious expression that worked to transform social relations and religious perceptions among the English working classes. Herein lies its importance. The chapters that precede and follow the journal are no substitute for it. They seek to provide an interpretation of it, a sort of exegesis. Based upon a close reading of the manuscript and supporting records, they attempt to open up Oppenheimer's book for the twenty-first century reader.

Oppenheimer's journal does not stand alone. A serious reading requires research in a wide range of sources, from the *London City Mission Magazine* to nineteenth-century descriptions of St. Giles and Doré's image of Dudley Street where Oppenheimer laboured. Wills, census records, baptismal certificates, and minutes of the board of the London City Mission provide additional documentation, as do Parliamentary reports, religious tracts and personal biographies. Still, the journal itself is central.

A word about the history of the journal: It was first brought to my attention in the early 1980s, when one of the anonymous reviewers of the manuscript that became *Lighten Their Darkness* suggested that I consult the journal in the process of revising the manuscript for publication. I took up this suggestion and wrote a chapter on the journal. When I first visited St. Giles'-in-the-Fields Church *circa* 1984, the church's verger showed me the journal and told me that it had been given to the church some time before—perhaps in the late 1960s—by a couple who came in off the street saying that the manuscript had been in their family for some time. They had no use for it, and thought it best if it were returned to the church that is mentioned frequently in the journal. The couple did not identify themselves, but only reported that they were from Vancouver, British Columbia.

For a number of years I assumed that Joseph Oppenheimer had eventually moved to Vancouver and was somehow associated with the four Oppenheimer brothers, German Jews, one of whom was Vancouver's first mayor, who played a leading role in the founding of Vancouver in the 1880s. They had a Portland, Oregon business associate by the name of Joseph Oppenheimer, who died in the interior of British Columbia in 1885; however, proving a clear link between the two Josephs was difficult.

Years later, I noticed that there is one page stitched into the end of the booklet. It is dated 1864 and 1865, and the City Missionary who reports statistics on that page is named as Hugh T. Monair, rather than Oppenheimer. The district number is still given as 126, and Monair appears to have replaced Oppenheimer in that district when he became ill in 1862. It would appear, therefore, that the journal was not given to the church by Oppenheimer's relatives; it would seem that Oppenheimer returned the journal to the London City Mission, where it was briefly used by his successor. It is likely that Monair's relatives, rather than Oppenheimer's, eventually made their way to Canada.

The survival of the journal allows us the opportunity to consider Oppenheimer in the broadest possible context, as that of one specialist in a larger religious economy. It represents a visible aspect of a comprehensive campaign to bring Christianity to the most desperately poor, and at the same time is an expression of popular religion. Oppenheimer's efforts, as represented in the journal, can be seen simultaneously as a mechanism of social control, as a strategy for the re-Christianization of the urban poor, and as a deeply personal calling. One might wish for more detail, for more open expression of the journalist's feelings, for fuller accounts of religious provision and more knowledge of Oppenheimer's training and reading, for more candour in describing figures such as his supervisor and rector, and for less circumspection in recording the destitution he faced. Yet for all its reticence, Oppenheimer's journal is an unparalleled document in Victorian religious history. It is powerful in part because it is so dense, so consistent in its daily-ness.

Notes

[1] Metropolitan Sewage Commission Proceedings. *Parliamentary Papers* 1846; 10: 651.
[2] Owen Chadwick, *The Victorian Church* (London: A. & C. Black, 1966), 1:5.
[3] D. Englander, "The Word and the World: Evangelicalism in the Victorian City," in G. Parsons (ed.), *Religion in Victorian Britain,* ii, *Controversies* (Manchester: Manchester University Press, 1988): 23.
[4] Hugh McLeod, *Piety and Poverty: Working-Class Religion in Berlin, London and New York 1870–1914* (London: Holmes & Meier, 1996), p.32.
[5] G.S.R. Kitson Clark, *The Making of Victorian England* (London: Methuen, 1962), p. 23.
[6] Next to the evangelicals' involvement in the movement to abolish slavery and the slave trade, their impact on international politics was felt in the rise of British support for a Jewish homeland which came to the fore in the Balfour declaration. See: D. M. Lewis, *The Origins of Christian Zionism: Lord Shaftesbury and Evangelical Support for a Jewish Homeland* (Cambridge University Press, 2009).
[7] Geoffrey Best, "Evangelicalism and the Victorians," in *The Victorian Crisis of Faith*, ed. Anthony Symondson (London: S.P.C.K, 1974), p. 54.
[8] A. D. Gilbert, *Religion and Society in Industrial England: Church, Chapel and Social Change, 1740–1914* (London: Longman, 1976), p. 135.
[9] Kitson Clark, *Making of Victorian England*, p. 23.
[10] A study of the Ritualists, Broad Churchmen and Evangelicals in East London makes the same point. See D. B. McIlhiney, 'A Gentleman in Every Slum: Church of England Missions in East London, 1837–1914,' Ph.D. thesis, Princeton University, 1977.
[11] This trend is clearly seen in a secret report prepared for the Editor of *The Times* in 1844. As he was anxious to have at hand a thumbnail sketch of the positions of the leading London clergy vis-à-vis the Tractarian issue, his reporters were instructed to analyze the eighty-nine leading clergy, the majority of whom were Evangelicals. Over two-thirds of the Evangelicals had been appointed after 1835, and of those appointed before that year, a significant number were incumbents of proprietary chapels.

Part 1

THE SOWER'S WORK,
THE SOWER,
&
THE SOWER'S FIELD

1

The Sower's Work: The Mission in its Context

'There have been at work among us,' a Nonconformist preacher told his people, 'three great social agencies: the London City Mission; the novels of Mr. Dickens; the cholera.'[1]

G.M. Young

Since the Reformation there were virtually no mediating institutions within the national Church which could engage the emotional, spontaneous, fervent spirituality of the poor on something like its own terms, while yet restraining it within the bounds of order and decency.... The Established Church offered almost nothing except its formal Sunday services, Mattins and Evensong, with a periodic Eucharist, often very thinly attended by the poor, who considered themselves unworthy to partake of a sacrament which they regarded as only on offer to the respectable.[2]

John Walsh

Victorian London was the wonder of its day, widely regarded as the world's first modern city. Its population seemed to be exploding in the nineteenth century, growing from under one million inhabitants in 1801 to just over two million by 1851 and then to over six-and-a-half million by 1901, making it almost twice the size of its nearest rival, New York City. Such rapid and massive growth was due to many factors: The Industrial Revolution had attracted many from the countryside to the emerging cities; a corresponding agricultural revolution enabled the feeding of a rapidly-growing population; sanitary improvements allowed people to live longer; changes in engineering enabled greater density of building and mass transit via train and subways; and of course, waves of migrants from rural England were joined by a veritable flood of Irish immigrants seeking to escape starvation in the late 1840s brought on by the repeated failure of the potato crop. The very poorest of the Irish were not among these immigrants, as they could not afford to pay even a shilling for the privilege of standing on board a ship crossing the Irish Sea. Immigrants from the farthest reaches of the British Empire also came—by the 1850s there was a growing East Indian population, along with the desperate poor of Eastern Europe.

Early in the nineteenth century, British Christians began to think of London as a new mission field, as challenging and needy as any that European missionaries had encountered in Africa, India or the West Indies. From the early 1790s British evangelicals had been recruiting and sending missionaries to spread the Christian faith in the South Seas, in British India, and in west Africa. In so doing, the British were not (as is often thought) the first Protestants in the field but were imitating what the German Lutheran Pietists had been doing since the early eighteenth century.

By the 1820s, the need for a strategy to re-evangelize the densely populated urban areas of London was being impressed on British Christians, and calls for innovative approaches to deal with the new urban reality were being voiced. The challenges of the care and cure of hundreds of thousands of the half-heathen poor were first met most rigorously by evangelical Protestants and by Roman Catholics—and then later in the century by "Anglo-Catholic" Anglicans. But the pioneers of this new urban mission were the evangelicals. As Sheridan Gilley has observed, the Roman Catholics in large measure used models originally developed by their evangelical counterparts: self-help and "friendly" societies, temperance organizations and even the techniques of revivalism.[3] The evangelicals, and especially evangelical Anglicans, were the most effective group working at the parish level in the Victorian slums. In 1860, one relentless critic of the evangelical Anglicans conceded that:

> The Evangelical party is redeemed by the working of its parishes. It is to its credit that it is foremost in united schemes of charity: it is to its credit, to some extent, that foreign missions have so increased and spread.... The Evangelical clergy, as a body, are indefatigable in ministerial duties, and devoted, heart and soul, to the manifold labours of Christian love. The school, the savings bank, the refuge, all the engines of parochial usefulness, find in them, for the most part, hearty supporters and friends. There is a positive literature of parish machinery, ... when the history of the Evangelical party is written, it will be told of them, that ... they ... worked manfully in the pestilent and heathen by-ways of our cities, and preached the gospel to the poor.[4]

A systematic response to the challenges of urban re-evangelization began with the development of "district-visiting societies" in the 1820s.

This approach involved lay people (often middle-class women) visiting the dwellings or hovels of the poor, inquiring about their physical condition and doling out alms and advice, offering consolation and care. It was first established on an organized basis in Glasgow by the evangelical Thomas Chalmers, leading clergyman in the (Presbyterian) Church of Scotland. The do-gooding of these volunteers often was pilloried in the literature of the nineteenth century, but it did constitute an important point of contact between social classes. Under Chalmers's scheme, visitors were to visit their charges once a week. Following his example, in the 1820s and 1830s district-visiting societies sprang up throughout England. Eventually in 1835, their efforts were brought together in the establishment of the General Society for the Promotion of District Visiting, which was reorganized in 1843 as the Metropolitan Visiting and Relief Association, an important forerunner in the emergence of the modern approach to social work.

These voluntary efforts soon proved inadequate to the challenges. The District Visiting Society struggled with a lack of financial resources and the recruitment of visitors. Another significant obstacle was the lack of clerical support in the early 1830s—until the translation of Bishop Blomfield in 1828 to the diocese of London, evangelicals were rarely appointed to Anglican churches in the capital. Blomfield, however, eagerly placed them in many parishes during his long episcopate. By the early 1840s, evangelical clergy were the dominant group among London's Anglican ministers. Given their great desire to reach the masses with the Christian gospel, the evangelical clergy became eager supporters of the emerging urban mission and eventually strongly supported the district-visiting approach.

However, the smell, squalor, danger and misery of the slums, combined with the social opprobrium connected with such visiting, deterred many. While still a layman, Edward Bickersteth (who was a leading evangelical Anglican minister in the 1830s) was discouraged by his parents from visiting the "sick poor," as they feared that familiarity with other visitors of lower social rank might cause him to "forget his position in society."[5] Others felt that the distributing of charity and the work of evangelization should be distinguished and separated in order to be better focused and more effective.

District visiting continued as an important part of nineteenth-century parish life. The approach was adopted by clergy of all shades of churchmanship as well as by Nonconformists, and was used in support of a host of philanthropic activities as well as evangelism. By 1850 virtually every Anglican parish church in London had a visiting society attached to it; only thirty-six Anglican churches were without one by then, and most of these were located in wealthy areas of the city where there were few poor people to be visited.[6] Promoted as a means of bridging class barriers, the societies normally consisted of middle-class "ladies"—the term "women" was used of females of a lower social rank—who by the end of the century handled much of "the regular distribution of money, food, and clothing" from the churches.[7]

The district-visiting strategy, while eventually judged by evangelicals to be inadequate in terms of its effectiveness in evangelism, did not disappear but gave birth to a novel approach employing full-time workers. The new pattern of evangelical urban mission was set by the London City Mission. This organization was established in 1835 by a rather eccentric Scot, David Nasmith, who had been associated with Thomas Chalmers while in Glasgow. Nasmith was determined to create an interdenominational society that would overcome narrow sectarian differences in order to reach London's poor.[8] He probably could not have chosen a less auspicious time for such a venture. The gulf between Anglicans and Nonconformists was broad and deep; many evangelicals within the Church of England hesitated to have anything to do with evangelicals outside the state church, partly out of a concern that such cooperation would be seen as disloyalty to the Church of England and make them odious to other Anglicans. The Bishop of London made clear his opposition to the London City Mission in the mid-1830s, which made life difficult for those of his evangelical clergy who were already publicly committed to working with Nasmith. Co-operation between evangelicals of all denominations occurred only in a few large societies, such as the Religious Tract Society and the British and Foreign Bible Society. However, these societies had constitutions that ensured effective Anglican control, guaranteeing that they would not be used in the emerging Voluntary controversy over the propriety of state churches, which raged throughout the nineteenth century.

Nasmith's dream for an interdenominational society became a reality in 1835. Within a decade, the London City Mission had over 120 full-time workers in place and had an annual donation income of £9,571. By 1858, when Joseph Oppenheimer began his work with the Mission, there were some 350 "City Missionaries" and the LCM was receiving donations of £32,230 a year, while its strictly Anglican counterpart, the Scripture Readers' Association (begun by evangelical Anglicans in 1845), had an income of £9,384 and a workforce of some 110 lay evangelists—all of them working in London. Clearly the cooperative interdenominational approach was winning the day among Victorian evangelicals, as is evidenced by the continued growth of the LCM's support over the rest of the century, while the SRA's support remained relatively static.

The basic approach of the LCM agents was simple: door-knocking, reading Scripture, and offering to pray with those they met. But there was a highly systematic organizational framework supporting this simple approach. It ensured that the same families were visited by the same agent in the normal course of things about every four to six weeks. Quickly the London City missionary became one of the most familiar faces in his district. They became so much part of the landscape that eventually the inhabitants of their districts often became protective of them. When the Salvation Army came along in 1880s, its workers often received a hostile reception from people in the poorest areas who saw the newcomers as usurpers of the LCM workers, trespassers on the religious turf established over several decades by the faithful persistence of the LCM's agents.

A "city missionary" was given a relatively small geographic area that he was to visit—normally a few streets in the crowded slums. Most agents were responsible for visiting between 500 and 550 families and were required to spend at least thirty-six hours a week in such work; in addition, they were to hold a minimum of two meetings a week for the poor in their districts. The missionaries were expected to keep detailed journals for the inspection of their clerical supervisors, and they were carefully instructed as to what they should say and do. Official "Instructions to Missionaries" were published in 1858, the same year in which Joseph Oppenheimer began as a city missionary with the London City Mission. These "instructions" were both a code of behaviour and a job description, developed during the previous twenty-three years of the society's existence and reflective of both evangelical theological distinctives and moral code.

Document A
London City Mission
Instructions to Missionaries
1858

1. Visit the inhabitants of the district assigned you for the purpose of bringing them to an acquaintance with salvation, through our Lord Jesus Christ, and of doing them good by every means in your power.
2. Read a portion of the Scriptures, and offer prayer, if practicable, in every house or room you visit; if impracticable, introduce into your conversation as much of the Scriptures as possible,

and see that the terms used are understood. In reading or speaking, let those portions that bear on the depravity of man, justification by faith alone, the necessity of a change of heart and of holiness of life, ever hold a prominent place.

3. Inculcate upon all persons the duty of searching the Scriptures as a revelation from God, and as the standard by which they will be judged at the last day.
4. Urge upon all persons you visit the necessity of attending the public worship of God. If they are neglecting it, point out to them the especial importance and duty of their attending the ministry of the Gospel. Specify no particular church or chapel, leaving to those you visit the selection of the place most accordant with their own views, provided that in that place the great doctrines of the Reformation are faithfully taught.
5. Inculcate upon parents the duty of training up their children in the way they should go, and the propriety of procuring for them week-day and Sunday-school instruction. Point out, as occasion may require, their relative duties, and faithfully but prudently reprove open vice, such as swearing, intemperance, and the profanation of the Sabbath.
6. See that those persons who have not the Scriptures are supplied with them.
7. Endeavour to hold two meetings every week in different parts of your district for the purpose of reading the Scriptures, exhortation, and prayer. Let those exercises be brief, the whole service not exceeding one hour, and do not undertake more than two meetings a week without the permission of the Committee.
8. Circulate no tract or book in your district which has not been approved and recommended by the Committee.
9. Avoid all unnecessary controversy upon religious subjects. Do not interfere with the peculiar tenets of any individual respecting Church government. Carefully avoid all topics of an irritating tendency, and seek by a simple manifestation of the truth to commend yourself to every man's conscience.
10. Studiously avoid entering upon subjects of a political nature, as altogether foreign from the purpose of your visit.
11. Devote yourself entirely to the objects of the mission, and abstain from all secular employment. Spend 36 hours every week in visiting from house to house, exclusive of meetings and other engagements. Give yourself to the study of the Scriptures and to prayer.
12. Write the journal of your daily proceedings with the strictest accuracy as to facts and circumstances, and submit it once a

week to the superintendent of the district for his inspection.

13. Conduct yourself in such a manner as will prove to all persons that you are in earnest in seeking their spiritual welfare. Be humble, courteous, and affectionate. Constantly realise your own obligations to the Saviour. Go to your district in a spirit of prayer, and with an earnest desire that every person you visit may be brought to a saving knowledge of the Lord Jesus Christ. Your work is awfully important; you have to deal with immortal souls, many of whom may never hear the Gospel but from you, and whose eternal condition may be determined by the reception or rejection of the message which you deliver to them. Be courageous, be faithful; keep the Lord Jesus continually before your own mind, and commend Him and his great salvation to the people. Be watchful and exemplary in every part of your conduct, public and private. "Owe no man any thing." Go forth daily to your work with your heart lifted up to God, for the assistance and direction of his Holy Spirit, and relying upon his promise for that wisdom and strength which all your adversaries shall not be able to gainsay or resist. Let the glory of God and the salvation of souls be your chief, your only end.[9]

David Bebbington has offered a four-fold definition of evangelicalism that has found a wide degree of acceptance among historians and is helpful in considering this document. Bebbington's definition focuses on four defining characteristics of evangelicalism: "*conversionism*, the belief that lives needed to be changed; *activism*, the expression of the gospel in effort; *biblicism*, a particular regard for the Bible; and what may be called *crucicentrism*, a stress on the sacrifice of Christ on the Cross."[10] The overriding concern of the LCM and its agents was clearly the personal conversion of individuals. Conversion, for the evangelicals, involved knowledge: first, knowledge of one's sinfulness (Item 2 above, "the depravity of man); second, acceptance of Christ's atonement for sin which alone could bring forgiveness (Item 2 "justification by faith alone"); and thirdly, a change of attitude and behaviour (Item 2 "a change of heart and of holiness of life"). Each of these three steps was for the evangelicals integral to the process of obtaining salvation, and each required considerable time and effort from the workers to explain to the people they visited.

A second characteristic of evangelicalism that is evident in the instructions is its "biblicism." This is clearly seen in that the chief task of the workers was to read Scriptural portions aloud to the people (Item 2), some of whom were illiterate; to urge their literate listeners to read the

Bible for themselves (Item 3); and to provide Scriptures for those interested in having them (Item 6). (By 1860 approximately 75% of British males and 65% of females were literate, and illiteracy was undoubtedly more prevalent lower down the social scale.) In the late 1830s, the London City Mission had undertaken a major initiative to provide the destitute poor of London with copies of the New Testament or a full Bible. Over 35,000 families had responded positively to the campaign.[11] Related to this concern with Scripture, of course, was the emphasis upon literacy. The workers strove to promote reading, trying to make sure that children in their districts attended Sunday schools (where learning to read was the top priority) and urging parents to enable their children to attend day schools.

The "crucicentric" focus of evangelicalism is implicit in its doctrine of conversion, but the "cross of Christ" is not directly mentioned in the instructions. The "activist" emphasis, however, is brought out in the final item (No. 13) in which the awesome responsibility placed on the agents' shoulders is underlined ("whose eternal condition may be determined by the reception or rejection of the message which you deliver to them").

Surprising, perhaps, in the LCM's approach is its sobriety and concern for order and decorum over against any emotional appeal, such as the sort associated with the Wesleyan revival or with American-style revivalism, or, indeed, with new highly emotional expressions of English Catholicism. Within English Catholicism in the 1840s, there was a struggle to shape a new Catholic approach to urban mission along the lines of the Continental Catholic mission. Ultramontane in orientation, it was emphatically loyal to the Papacy and to the person of His Holiness; however, it also eschewed both the class-consciousness of traditional English Catholicism and its reputation for emotional dryness. Championed by Nicholas Wiseman, from 1847 the Vicar Apostolic of the London District, and from 1850 the (Roman Catholic) Archbishop of Westminster, the radicals sought to introduce Ultramontane devotions in revival services in order to reclaim the poor, especially the Irish poor. Even emotional, Italian style street preaching was used to great effect by Catholic revivalists. As Sheridan Gilley has pointed out, these Catholic services "bore many of the marks of Protestant revivalism, for Evangelicals and Ultramontanes touched at a number of points, in their call of the agonized conscience to repentance in the midst of scenes of mass fervor, cathartically relieved in the ecstasy of promised forgiveness through the all-atoning Blood of the Lamb."[12]

Professor Gilley's assessment of the points of contact between the Methodist-style revivalism of 18th century Methodism and Primitive

Methodists of the early 19th century, and the emotionally laden Ultramontane approach, is correct. However, such an emotional approach was decidedly *not* characteristic of Anglican evangelicalism or of much of Nonconformist evangelicalism by the mid-nineteenth century. Even in the midst of the Prayer Meeting Revival of 1859–60, which had a significant impact in Northern Ireland and lesser effects in Wales and Scotland, there was a much more limited and much less emotional response in England. As a *Times* editorial put it in 1860: "A Church of England congregation's ... standard of conversion does not allow suddenness, or therefore give room to the action of sympathy. Three thousand of them might be undergoing conversion at once, and nobody would *see* anything; it would all be as noiseless and as invisible as thought itself."[13]

The London City Mission's approach was thus quintessentially Anglican and entirely different from the Ultramontane Catholic one. An emphasis upon an emotional appeal was allowed no home in the Mission. Its approach struck no chords of emotive or enthusiastic piety, popular among evangelicals in the revivalist strain: no emotional "camp" meetings, no lay preaching, no intense small group discipleship or "band" meetings as in Methodism, no "testimony" meetings where individuals could recount their personal conversion narratives as they did in Methodist "class" meetings. Instead, its approach was decidedly doctrinal and intentionally undramatic, a warm but not effusive piety that was closer to Anglicanism's *disciplina arcani*, a dignified restraint in devotion and theology. This conservatism was deeply indebted to the lingering effects of the revolutionary Commonwealth period of the mid-17th century: Following the Restoration of Charles II in 1660, High Churchmen had insisted on stiff devotion to the rubrics of the Anglican *Book of Common Prayer*, arising from a panic fear of proletarian "enthusiasm."

Frederick William Faber was a nephew of the leading evangelical writer, George Stanley Faber. Moving from evangelicalism to Anglo-Catholicism and eventually to Rome, even as a Catholic Faber said that he preferred "the pattern of the Wesleyans and Whitefieldians to the calm sobriety and subdued enthusiasm of the Protestant Establishment," and he considered the English poor better served by "the coarse tyranny" of sincere Methodism than by "the mild, considerate and good-natured rule of Anglicans," "because the one knew, and the other abhorred, 'the catholic view of the use of excitement in things spiritual.'"[14] Like William Booth of the Salvation Army after him, Faber held to his conviction that "all religious methods were right and good which won souls lost in the spiritual destitution of the great English cities."[15]

Still, the LCM approach was fashioned by cautious evangelicals, wary of emotional excess and anxious to work as closely as possible in a broad coalition with local evangelical churches, whether Anglican or Nonconformist. Furthermore, Anglican evangelicalism had undergone a prolonged crisis in the 1820s that continued to influence and shape the policy-making of evangelical societies, and particularly Anglican and Anglican-dominated organizations such as the LCM. In the first two decades of the 19th century, the evangelicals had laid the foundations of a philanthropic empire—a network of social and religious organizations that had been created to implement a series of social reforms and further a host of charitable causes. The presiding genius had been William Wilberforce, the leading Member of Parliament behind the effort to abolish the British slave trade. Wilberforce and his "kitchen cabinet" of highly talented colleagues (posthumously known as the "Clapham Sect") had sought to use all means and methods to further their cause, to commend a moderate and cultured evangelicalism to the middle and upper-classes of England, and to overcome the negative associations that were commonly made between Anglican evangelicalism and Methodism. In so doing, they hoped to capture the Church of England from within and see evangelical clergy promoted to high ecclesiastical office.

By the mid-1820s, however, a new generation of evangelical leaders had begun to emerge. These were profoundly influenced by the Romantic movement and increasingly restive under the leadership of the older generation. A feeling grew that the Claphamites had been too accommodating and had lost touch with the radical nature of the Christian message. In their attempt to live down their alleged connections with Methodism, and to be judged worthy of church appointments, the Claphamites were judged to have gone too far, to have compromised too much. The older generation's moderate, thoughtful evangelicalism had been profoundly influenced by the Enlightenment's emphasis on reason, order and moderation. They were accused of being too confident in their use of "means," by which the more radical evangelicals meant "organization."

This radical critique was most clearly articulated by Edward Irving, a fiery Scottish Presbyterian who in 1822 became pastor of a wealthy Church of Scotland congregation in London. Irving had served for a time with the famous Thomas Chalmers, a leading Scottish evangelical, and was regarded as a rising star in the evangelical firmament because of his astounding oratorical ability as a preacher. Soon, though, Irving was challenging "the complete Anglican Evangelical framework, its love of order, moderation, piety and prudence."[16] He began to espouse millennialism and believed fervently that God was about to restore the New Testament age; by the early 1830s, he moved off in a sectarian direction to begin a new denomination. A number of earnest radicals followed Irving; others associated with new groups such as the Plymouth Brethren. However, the mainstream of Anglican evangelicalism maintained the devotion to order, moderation and prudence of its Claphamite heritage, which helps account for the LCM's caution and moderation. Its workers were always to be under firm control, never to do anything that would be considered as usurping the authority of the local minister, and never were free to innovate, thanks to the clerical supervisor looking over their shoulders. The fervour and emotions of popular piety always threatened to unravel the Mission's commitment to order and decorum, and what the Mission could not share in, it could not exploit.

The fact that the LCM could not and would not allow its workers to exploit popular piety helps to account for its limited success. A concern with outward respectability on the part of the Mission and a fear of revivalist emotionalism hampered its effectiveness. Workers were strictly cautioned not to usurp the authority of the clergy: They could not preach, and they could not become slum pastors, although in effect many of them were *de facto* chaplains of the poor. Overall, these restrictions help both to explain and to reinforce Hugh McLeod's observation that in Victorian England, "involvement in the churches was limited both by class factors, and by the inability of English Protestantism to seize the imagination of the poor."[17] Perhaps the Salvation Army came closest to doing this, with its proletarian appeal, but most evangelical leaders feared that imaginations could run wild, and that "zeal without knowledge" could wreak havoc and do more harm than good. Many clearly felt that imaginations did run wild in the Salvation Army, but they were always constrained by General William Booth's military style and authoritative leadership.

While Catholics were urged to allow expressions of popular religion in the encouragement of cheap and gaudy church furniture in store-front city missions and other concessions to proletarian tastes: "Stations of the Cross, groups of the Holy Family, statues of the Blessed Virgin and St. Joseph, and everything else that may be a source of devotion or enjoyment to the poor"[18]—no such freedom was given to the LCM missioners. The real power in the Mission lay in the hands of the upper-middle class committee that ran the mission from above; popular expression had to be regulated in order to keep the mission neutral in the ecclesiastical wars of the time, or Anglican funding might quickly dry up.

The London City Mission sought to supplement the work of local churches, and often its workers functioned—in effect—as agents of local congregations. Such was the case with Oppenheimer. The LCM, rather than seeking to release workers who had the gifts and abilities to establish new congregations, always kept them subject to ministerial superiors who would see any such move as a threatening their positions. Few of the City Missionaries had the social status that would have ever allowed them to aspire to the office of Anglican clergy. The LCM might well provide religion "for the people" and even "by the people," but it could not allow for religion "of the people" in the sense of empowering the poor, nor even the City Missionaries, to own and shape its popular expression.

OPPENHEIMER'S PASTORAL LOCATION

It was Anthony W. Thorold, the rector of St. Giles'-in-the-Field, who recruited Oppenheimer and sponsored him as an LCM candidate. Thorold himself was only 33 years old and had only been rector of the parish for a year when the 24-year-old Oppenheimer began his work, Thorold having succeeded Robert Bickersteth as rector, following Bickersteth's elevation to the episcopacy in 1857.[19] Thorold was one of the most effective evangelical urban pastors in the Victorian age, ever willing to innovate and improvise. We know that Thorold's predecessor at St. Giles's had supervised three curates, five Scripture readers, and seven city missionaries—12 lay workers and 3 clergy. Thus, Oppenheimer was likely to have been only one among a dozen lay workers who worked under Thorold. Oppenheimer records monthly meetings with his direct supervisor and shared with him his detailed journal in a book provided by the LCM. In Oppenheimer's case, the supervision was delegated to the Revd H. Laudon Maud, the parish's curate. This is attested to by the fact that Laudon Maud's signature appears several times in Oppenheimer's journal. The rector of an important urban parish like St. Gile's had secular responsibilities to the Vestry and the Poor Law Board and relatively little time for pastoral work amongst the poor.

In terms of training, the LCM had a course of instruction "in the evidences of Christianity and the doctrines of the Gospel" for all its new recruits.[20] It was expected that those applying for work would have already proved their effectiveness in district visiting. Agents such as Oppenheimer were hired for a probationary period, during which time they were given on-the-job experience under a "training superintendent," while their ongoing work was supervised by interested evangelical clergy or laymen.

6. ST. GILES'-IN-THE-FIELDS
NINETEENTH CENTURY SKETCH

THE SPURGEON FACTOR

While the evangelical mission to the urban poor was constrained by many factors, this is not to suggest that mid-Victorian evangelicals in general, or the London City Mission in particular, were resistant to innovation. In the early 1850s a new phenomenon appeared on London's religious scene: Charles Haddon Spurgeon. Within a few months of the 19-year-old's arrival from Cambridgeshire, he was deemed the city's most powerful preacher and soon was addressing crowds of 5,000 to 6,000 twice each Sunday. His special services at the Crystal Palace drew upwards of 25,000. His arrival occurred at a time when leading evangelicals were complaining about the ineffectiveness of much evangelical preaching. John Hampden Gurney, writing in 1852, complained of *"a want of freedom in the pulpit,"* reasoning that preachers were out of touch with common folk.[21] The following year Lord Shaftesbury cautioned in a speech that if the clergy were to have any impact on the working classes, they must adopt a new style of preaching. It had to be "adapted to their tastes and apprehensions, and formed more on the primitive model of the early Christian preachers."[22] Spurgeon therefore was experimenting in a context in which innovation was welcome. By the late 1850s, evangelical Anglican clergy were attempting protracted mission church services that were geared to the unchurched.

MR. SPURGEON AT THE AGE OF TWENTY-THREE.

7. CHARLES HADDON SPURGEON AT THE AGE OF 23

8. INTERIOR OF ST. MARTIN'S HALL
Illustrated London News, February 16, 1850

9. EXTERIOR OF ST. MARTIN'S HALL
Illustrated London News, February 16, 1850

Controversy arose for the evangelical Anglicans, however, when some of the clergy sought to hold such meetings in unconsecrated locations such as theatres and music halls, taking their cue from Spurgeon's approach. There was a growing awareness that for many of the poor, their class-consciousness would never allow them to darken the door of a church. All the same, the thought of holding religious services in theatres or music halls created a furor. As the evangelicals had long been leading opponents of theatres, and associated as they were in the public mind with vulgar and lewd entertainment, it was a bold move to propose that such locales be hired as preaching venues. On the floor of the House of Lords, Lord Dungannon objected that such gatherings lowered the dignity of religious worship and were often accompanied by scenes of rowdy behavior.[23] As a result, evangelicals held special services in public venues designed to attract working-class attendees: places such as St. Martin's Hall at the corner of Long Acre Street and Endell Street, just east of the Seven Dials, two blocks southeast of Oppenheimer's Dudley Street.

Oppenheimer mentions St. Martin's Hall eight times in his journal, speaking of passing out "Handbills for the St. Martin's Hall special services for the working people" at both the 5 Dials and the 7 Dials (26 January 1862). His first mention of the services was on Sunday, the 5th of January 1862, when he reported that he "Was again engaged at St. Martin's Hall in the afternoon, at the Special service." Two weeks later he was "distributing tracts & handbills for the St. Martin's Hall special services. Attended at the evening service at the Hall," and again on four more Sundays (26 January, 2 February, 16 February, 23 February). Oppenheimer records that he had urged attendance at these meetings upon two men in particular:

Dudley St. February [1862]

Tuesday 11.

Hopeful case.

36. top front. poor old David Sauter[?] was glad to see me & I was again permitted to deliver my message to him, to which he listened attentively; promised me to attend the special services at St. Martin's Hall; reads the Bible I gave to him some time ago; accepted a tract.

Dudley Street. February

Tuesday 18.

Hopeful case.

57 2nd back. Called upon Mr Riley, an Irishman to whom I gave a Bible some time ago; told me to day that he reads it very frequently; attended twice St. Martin's Hall on Sunday evening since I saw him last & I think his case to be a hopeful one.

The real "proletarianisation" of the urban mission, however, had to await the emergence of the Salvation Army later in the century. The reaction of Lord Shaftesbury to the Salvation Army's adaptation to plebian tastes is indicative of why organizations like the LCM had not been willing or able to adapt to them in a similar manner. In an 1881 letter to Admiral Edmund Fishbourne, who had been urging his public support of the Salvation Army, Shaftesbury explained that he was not opposed to innovation or "abnormal modes of proceeding," and that he had spent his life in breaking down barriers and prejudices in order that the poorest of the poor might be evangelized. He had been willing to set aside external church forms in the effort. "But I endeavoured," he wrote to his friend, "and I hope I have succeeded, to keep within the limits of the New Testament and primitive Christianity. When, however, I look at the constitution, framework, and organisation of the Salvation Army, its military arrangements, its Hallelujah Lasses, its banners, their mottoes, and a thousand other original accompaniments, I ask what authority we have in Scripture, for such a system and such a discipline!"[24]

OPPENHEIMER AND THE RANYARD BIBLE MISSION

Shaftesbury could and did endorse other forms of innovation, as is seen in his early and fervent support for the Ranyard Bible Mission, begun in 1857, whose emergence directly impacted Joseph Oppenheimer. In September 1861 Oppenheimer recorded in his preliminary remarks the following enigmatic reference:

> I continue to addrefs the inmates of the Work Woman[']s Home 75 Dudley St though I cannot see that spiritual progrefs this quarter that I have reported in past quarters in this special field of labour yet I trust that a good work is going on in many; The most pleasing attention is given & thank[s] returned[.]

Undoubtedly this short entry would have made sense to Oppenheimer and his clerical supervisor, but a good deal of back story is needed to understand this reference.

The intensity of evangelical efforts to reach the desperately poor in London dramatically increased in 1857, with the founding by Mrs. Ellen Ranyard of her new Ranyard Bible Mission, which employed working-class women as evangelists who would also sell Bibles to their peers. Ellen Henrietta Ranyard (née White) had been born London in 1810, the daughter of a Nonconformist cement manufacturer. She came to an evangelical faith at the age of 16 through the influence of a young friend, Elizabeth Saunders, who gave herself to nursing the poor. While engaged in this work, Saunders contracted a fever and subsequently died; Ranyard also became ill, but survived and dedicated her life to the task of circulating cheap Bibles among the poor. In 1839 she married Benjamin Ranyard and soon was preoccupied with raising four children. In 1852 she began to discover her gift as a writer, penning *The Book and Its Story*, a history of the British and Foreign Bible Society for young people, a work that sold well. Two years later she published *The Bible Collectors,* in which she asserted that "30,000 British ladies are now engaged in the work of circulating the Scriptures"[25] in a voluntary capacity among the poor.[26] This Bible-selling activity was often linked with self-help initiatives undertaken by these women. These included arranging for needle work for poor women so they might become self-supporting; creating systematic savings schemes to allow poor children to acquire school supplies and clothing, with their savings being supplemented by a gift of 3 pence on the shilling; and beginning a program that enabled people to save for subsidized "food tickets."[27] Ranyard argued that "there is no better way of dispensing [help] … to our poor neighbours, so far as it concerns their temporal benefit, because it teaches them to help themselves, and to economize by method, which is a very valuable lesson."[28] Long active in canvassing for the Bible Society, in 1856 she continued popularizing the work of the Society in a periodical *The Book and Its Mission*, which expounded on the translation and publication work of the Bible Society.

In 1857, however, the family moved to London. Here, she became deeply distressed by the poverty she encountered in the streets near the family home in Hunter Street, Brunswick Square, near the rookeries of St. Giles'. Here, she drew upon her knowledge of the Bible Society's work abroad and the various self-help schemes developed in other areas of Britain, adapting them to the slums of London. She also devised a plan that employed pious, poor women to sell Bibles on penny subscriptions to other poor women and link these with self-help schemes. As has been noted, by mid-century many thousands of women were already at work throughout Britain in promoting the sale of Bibles amongst the poor, and some individuals and town missions had employed poor women as agents.[29]

Ranyard is often considered an innovator, but her significance—at least, when it comes to the use of "Biblewomen"—lies not so much in innovation as in her considerable abilities in organization, promotion and fund-raising. Lord Shaftesbury, who worked with her on many schemes, once commented that Ranyard had "directing and controlling administrative powers, such as few statesmen have possessed."[30] Her originality, courage and creativity were seen in 1868, when she began to train some of these Biblewomen as itinerant nurses in the wards of Guy's Hospital, calling these workers her "Bible-nurses." Armed with Florence Nightingale's *Notes on Nursing* and their Bibles, they soon became well known as evangelist-nurses in London's slums, giving "medicines and solace to patients with aliments ranging from bedsores to 'sloughs of despond.'"[31] Her influence on the history of nursing has been widely acknowledged by historians. F.K. Prochaska, the leading historian of Victorian philanthropy, has praised her medical work as "a gallant pioneering achievement" in the field of nursing.[32] Elaine Denny, an historian of nursing, has pointed out that by the end of the nineteenth century "the Ranyard mission was the largest nursing association for the sick poor of any city in the world."[33] The impact beyond Britain of her work in missionary nursing has only begun to be explored.[34]

Ranyard used her talents as a publicist to promote the efforts of the Biblewomen on a much more organized, comprehensive and systematic basis. Using postal districts as her starting point, she mapped out specific areas and streets where Biblewomen were to labour, in much the same way as the London City Mission had done from the 1830s. Her strategy was both personal and local: She was convinced that these working women were the "missing link" between the classes. They could promote Christianity amongst their peers while engaging these women in self-help projects that would eventually help lift them out of their desperate poverty. In this project, she worked closely with two well-known evangelical pastors: Anthony Thorold, the Anglican rector of St-Giles'-in-the-Field under whose oversight Oppenheimer worked; and William Brock, pastor of the Bloomsbury Baptist Chapel. Her interdenominational organization was first known as the London Bible and Domestic Female Mission, but soon changed its name to the Ranyard Bible Mission (RBM).

Ranyard's work began in the rookeries of St. Giles'-in-the-Fields with the efforts of "Marian," a woman hired by Ranyard to go from door to door seeking to sell Bibles on subscription to poor women. This proved remarkably successful until in June 1858, Marian contracted an illness while visiting at 75 Dudley Street, the very location which Oppenheimer reports visiting above. She recovered, and Ellen Ranyard determined to lease the same property for her mission. In the autumn of 1858 the rooming house was thoroughly cleaned and renovated to create a "Working Girls' Dormitory," with beds for 20 women and a room fitted out where the Biblewomen employed by the Mission could meet—all initially under the matronship of Marian.[35] This arrangement, Ranyard conceded in 1861, was ill-advised: Expecting one woman to be both an evangelist and the matron of the dormitory proved to be too much, and Marian retired to the countryside to recover her health. She was replaced by a woman who had managed a ward in Poplar Hospital, and whose reputation for efficiency and saintliness commended her. The aim of the dormitory was to rescue "Working Girls" from "their parents's over-crowded rooms." Ranyard explained in 1861: "It was supposed that if a quiet, cheerful home were provided for them in the centre of the district, they would gladly embrace the opportunity of escaping from their over-crowded rooms."[36]

In all of this, Ranyard managed to connect with some wealthy and powerful evangelicals. She was strongly supported by Lady Kinnaird (née Mary Jane Hoare), who was the wife of (Tenth Baron) Lord Arthur Kinnaird, a Scottish banker and Liberal MP; her father was William Henry Hoare, a wealthy English banker. Through her mother, Louisa Elizabeth Noel, she was connected to the aristocratic families of Lord Middleton and the Earl of Gainsborough, as well as to the Babingtons and Macaulays, names associated with the Clapham Sect and William Wilberforce. Lady Kinnaird had been one of two key founders of another evangelical society, the Young Women's Christian Association, which was formed in 1854 on the pattern of George Williams's Young Men's Christian Association, begun in 1844. Arthur Kinnaird as treasurer of the Ranyard Bible Mission was the money behind it, and his wife was a key member of the governing committee.

In the early years of the mission, Ranyard hoped that the idea of girls' dormitories would catch on, believing that "It is incalculable what might be effected by the wise multiplication of these Girls' Dormitories in over-crowded districts. It is not only the blessing of a quiet night in a peaceable house that is gained, though that is much; it is the motherly influence over them in their wild street life that gradually civilizes them, and we hope, in many cases will do more."[37] In the long run, however, the multiplication occurred under the umbrella of the YWCA. The dormitory in Dudley Street was originally intended for what Ranyard termed "steady and virtuous girls," but by 1861 the purpose had changed as "so many of another class have been brought to us by Missionary friends, that the association of the two had become undesirable, and we, therefore, now intend to set our former premises apart for a Rescue House, after a few alterations have been made in the premises."[38] The meeting room that had been the original headquarters of the mission was removed in order to accommodate ten more beds, in the hope that the added income would enable the dormitory to become self-sustaining financially and not require the annual outlay of about 100 pounds from the mission to keep it open. Although the term "dormitory" was continued, the location became essentially a short-term stopping place for women wanting to leave prostitution.

Ranyard's account was written in the second half of 1861, and the transition from "Dormitory" to "Rescue Home" may well account for the hesitancy about the apparent setback in "spiritual progress" that Oppenheimer mentions. The census record gives us a clear picture of the women who resided in the home a few months earlier, before the renovation. The census indicates that the matron was 38-year-old Harriet Hawkins from Warminster in Wiltshire. One woman, Mary Days, is listed as a servant (in relation to Hawkins as head)—she was 48 years old and from Aldgate in Middlesex. Twenty women are listed as residents, and it is clear that the women were hardly "girls"; the majority of them were mature women. Nineteen are listed as "lodgers" and one as a "visitor." Six of the 20 were widows ranging in age from 42 to 75, and the remaining 14 are listed as unmarried (age 19 to 54). Only four of the women were under the age of 25. As the majority of London's active prostitutes left the sex trade by their mid-20s, it would seem that the dormitory was at the time of the census (7 April 1861) still functioning as a dormitory and not a "rescue home." The women's occupations generally reflect the unskilled class from which they were drawn, which confirms Ranyard's description of them: "These girls either earn their living as servants in small places of all-work—as sellers of water-cresses, &c., in the streets—or as ill-paid sempstresses [seamstresses], flower-makers, &c." According to the census 7 were shirt makers, 7 were servants, 2 were dress makers, and the others included a governess, a mantlemaker, an upholsterer and a charwoman. Ten of the lodgers were from Middlesex in London, one from Scotland and one from

Ireland, and the remaining eight were from the rest of England.

The residents paid the matron nightly a shilling a day for their lodging, washing and food.[39] Ranyard acknowledged that they were used to paying 3 shillings a week for a space to sleep in a room in a lodging house, where they made do with the following diet: "Their general food is a small piece of meat, or a boiled egg, purchased as they go to their work—which, with the universal cup of tea, is their daily dietary."[40] She estimated that the most efficient women could earn 7 shillings a week in such occupations, but that 4 or 5 shillings was most common. She urged fellow women to help her create work that would allow the residents to supplement their income in order to afford their room and board, and she regretted that the dormitory at 75 Dudley Street was not large enough to allow for a work-room where such work could be undertaken. "Is it not time," she asked rhetorically, "that effort became more general to better the condition of our poor needle-slaves, and that it were made by women?"[41] Ranyard's novel approach caught on quickly with Victorian evangelicals, so that by 1860, there were some 137 women employed with her organization. Six of them were working in the area where Marian had pioneered in 1857–8, although it is interesting that there is no direct mention of them in Oppenheimer's journal.[42]

The systematic approach to the evangelization of London's poor developed by the large evangelical societies provided a stable framework and a comprehensive means of dealing with physical and spiritual destitution. It attracted significant amounts of funding from supporters throughout the British Isles, from the founding of the LCM through the end of the nineteenth century. It was remarkably effective in harnessing the energy of lay people in evangelism and in gaining the financial backing of a wide constituency. And it undoubtedly was the most important face of Christianity for the poorest of the poor in Victorian London. For one German immigrant to England in the 1850s, the structure provided by the London City Mission was the framework in which a young Jewish convert to Christianity could live, move, and have his being. Yet Oppenheimer's mission was constrained in many ways by the social and political context in which English evangelicalism operated by the early 1860s. He was in effect both an evangelist and a pastor, but given his social location, he could not aspire to Anglican ordination. He could sow his seed, watch it grow, and harvest it in, but he could never aspire to be a shepherd of a gathered flock.

Notes

[1] G.M. Young, *Portrait of an Age* (London: Oxford University Press, 1936), p. 55.
[2] John Walsh, "John Wesley and the Urban Poor," *Revue Française De Civilisation Britannique,* VI, no. 3, p. 22.
[3] Sheridan Gilley, "Catholic Faith of the Irish Slums, London, 1840–70," in *The Victorian City: Images and Realities,* edited by H. J. Dyos and Michael Wolff (London: Routledge and Kegan Paul, 1973) vol. 2, pp. 837–39.
[4] "The English Evangelical Clergy," *MacMillan's Magazine,* 3 (December 1860): 119–20.
[5] *Congregational Magazine,* n.s. 1 (February 1837):77.
[6] Sampson Low, *The Charities of London,* London, 1850, pp. 127–28. Cited by F. K. Prochaska, *Women and Philanthropy: In Nineteenth Century England* (Oxford: Clarendon Press, 1978), p. 104.
[7] Jeffery Cox, *The English Churches in a Secular Society: Lambeth 1870–1930* (Oxford, Oxford University Press, 1982), pp. 73–76.
[8] On Nasmith, see: D.M. Lewis, ed., *The Blackwell Dictionary of Evangelical Biography* 2 vols. (Oxford: Blackwell, 1995).
[9] *Parliamentary Papers, 1857–8, 9,* "Deficiency of the Means of Spiritual Instruction," Select Committee, House of Lords, Report, pp. 575–76.
[10] D. W. Bebbington, *Evangelicalism in Modern Britain. A History from the 1730s to the 1980s* (London: Unwin Hyman, 1989), p. 3.
[11] For details see: Donald M. Lewis, *Lighten Their Darkness: The Evangelical Mission to Working Class London, 1828–1860* (Westport, CT: Greenwood, 1985), pp. 60–63.
[12] Gilley, "Catholic Faith of the Irish Slums," p. 839.
[13] *Times,* Sept. 17, 1859, p. 6.
[14] Gilley, "Catholic Faith of the Irish Slums," p. 840.
[15] Ibid., p. 839.
[16] W. J. Clyde Ervine, "Anglican Evangelical Clergy, 1797–1837," Ph.D. thesis, Cambridge University, 1979, p. 2.
[17] Hugh McLeod, *Religion and Society in England, 1850–1914* (New York, St. Martin's Press, 1996), p. 2.
[18] John Kyne, "Appeal for the Saffron Hill Mission," *Tablet,* 10 June 1854, quoted in Gilley, "Catholic Faith of the Irish Slums," p. 846.
[19] For a fuller discussion of the Ranyard Mission see: Donald M. Lewis, *Lighten Their Darkness* (Greenwood, CT, 1986; 2nd edn. 2001), pp. 200–23 and F. K. Prochaska, *Women and Philanthropy in Nineteenth Century England* (Oxford, 1978).
[20] *LCM Magazine* (June 1847): 121.
[21] J. H. Gurney, *The Lost Chief and the Mourning People* (London: Nisbet, 1852), pp. 5–6.
[22] See Lord Shaftesbury's speech to the Blandford-mews ragged school in *Record,* Nov. 7, 1853.
[23] *Hansard Parliamentary Debates,* n.s. 156 (1860), col.s 1662–1668, Lord Dungannon's speech to the House of Lords on February 24, 1860.

[24] Lord Shaftesbury to Admiral Fishborne, 7 Nov. 1881 in Edwin Hodder, *The Life and Work of the Seventh Earl of Shaftesbury* (London: Cassell and Co., 1893), p. 728.
[25] Ellen Ranyard, *Bible Collectors* (London: Nisbet, 1854), p. 31.
[26] The Bible-selling approach was initially pioneered by Charles Stokes Dudley (1780–1862), an Irish-born London businessman and early supporter of the British and Foreign Bible Society. He developed a "System" of selling Bibles to the poor on a penny-a-week subscription basis and in 1820 published *An Analysis of the System of the Bible Society* to popularize the approach. Ranyard became personally acquainted with Dudley and acknowledged that her scheme had been anticipated much earlier in the nineteenth century.
[27] Ranyard, *Bible Collectors*, p. 21.
[28] *Bible Collectors*, p. 21.
[29] See Donald M. Lewis, "'Lights in Dark Places': Women Evangelists in Early Victorian Britain, 1838–1857," in *Women in the Church, Studies in Church History*, W. J. Shiels and Diana Wood, eds. (Oxford: Basil Blackwell, 1990), pp. 415–27.
[30] Hodder, *Shaftesbury*, p. 711.
[31] F. K. Prochaska, *Women and Philanthropy*, p. 129.
[32] Mary Stocks, *A Hundred Years of District Nursing*, London, 1960, p. 25. Quoted by Prochaska, *Women and Philanthropy*, p. 129.
[33] Elaine Denny, "The second missing link: Bible nursing in 19th century London," *Journal of Advanced Nursing*, 26: 1181.
[34] C. Chen, "Missionaries and the early development of nursing in China," *Nursing History Review* 4 (1996): 129–49.
[35] Well after the fact, Ranyard gave the name of the generous "Christian friend" who underwrote the expenses of the dormitory at 75 Dudley Street as James Alexander. *Missing Link Magazine* (April 1876): 99.
[36] L.N.R. [Ellen Ranyard], *Life Work: Or, The Link and the Rivet* (London, 1861), p. 249.
[37] Ranyard, *Life Work*, p. 251.
[38] Ranyard, *Life Work*, pp. 265–66.
[39] Ranyard, *Life Work*, p. 266.
[40] Ranyard, *Life Work*, p. 258.
[41] Ranyard, *Life Work*, p. 258.
[42] Ranyard, *Life Work*, p. 248. For details on the Ranyard Mission see: Donald M. Lewis, "A Sisterhood Powerful for Motherhood: Ellen Ranyard's 'Biblewomen' and 'Biblewomen Nurses'," in Marilyn Button and Jessica Sheertz-Nguyen (Eds.), *Victorians and the Case for Charity: Essays on Responses to English Poverty by the State, the Church, and the Literati* (Jefferson, NC: MacFarland and Co., 2013): 159–83.

2

The Sower: Joseph Oppenheimer, City Missionary in Darkest London

To open Oppenheimer's journal is to enter his life in mid-stream, at age twenty-seven. The reader is well served by engaging his experiences, without trying to remember all the details; still, being aware of what little we know about him allows the reader to read his journal with understanding and sympathy. Joseph Oppenheimer was a lay evangelist—and more. Between September 1861 and May 1862, he was simultaneously a lay evangelist, an amateur social worker, tract-distributor, apologist, and a husband and father. Furthermore, in the very act of recording his work, he became a chronicler of social and religious history in his area of London. The record he kept differs markedly from mainstream religious histories that deal with nineteenth-century England's great thinkers and church leaders, those who wrestled with questions thrown up by an era when many felt faith was receding. Oppenheimer's journal is first and foremost an eyewitness account of life "from below"—even, indeed, of life from "beneath below." It articulates the questions, concerns, hope and despair of the poorest of the poor, their objections to faith, and the acceptance of it by a few.

The most obvious difference is that it is an outsider's record. Oppenheimer was a German-born Jew who had not fully mastered English, his wordings and the spelling of names making this obvious. A German Jew trying to persuade Gentile nominal "Christians" to become "real Christians"—the irony would not have been lost on his listeners—must have seemed out of place in Victorian London, where the English regarded continentals with a certain degree of disdain.

To understand Oppenheimer's world we must approach it on its own terms, and Oppenheimer's journal reaches to the marrow of mid-Victorian life. He did not live in a golden age of evangelical influence—really, there never was such a time—and he was very aware of his minority status, in terms of his faith and ethnic identity. If one dwells for any length of time on Gustav Doré's sketch of Dudley Street (see Illustration 18, p. 62), where Joseph Oppenheimer laboured as a door-to-door evangelist, and sets that alongside the picture of Oppenheimer's work as it emerges in his journal, one is led to ask how is it that Joseph Oppenheimer could get up each morning to face his day. How could he spend a good part of each day knocking on doors in one of the poorest areas of London, endangering his health (and that of his wife and their children), while aware of the hostility or indifference that he would encounter—all for a pitiful wage? By the time the journal was started in 1861, he had done this steadily for three years, with intermittent breaks when his health had deteriorated so badly that he could not work, as it often did among London City Mission workers. Again, one marvels at his perseverance. One wonders what would motivate someone to do this rigorous work.

WHAT WE KNOW OF JOSEPH OPPENHEIMER: ORIGINS

His full name was Joseph Menco Oppenheimer. According to his adult baptismal record, he was born on 31 December 1833, the son of Joseph and Mirna (possibly Milna) Oppenheimer of the Duchy of Nassau in what is now southwestern Germany, near the city of Frankfurt on the Main. There are records of Jews living in the duchy from the thirteenth century; in 1865, there were some 6,995 Jews out of a population of 465,656, just over 1.5% of the population. In 1866 the duchy was absorbed into Prussia, becoming part of the province of Hesse-Nassau.

10. MAP OF THE DUCHY OF NASSAU NEAR FRANKFURT

His father was a shopkeeper, and Joseph was educated to be a teacher of ancient languages. He appears to have emigrated to Britain at about the age of 20 and converted to Christianity shortly thereafter (in 1854), and at that time was taken into the Jewish Converts Operative Institution, which housed and employed him. This Institution had been set up by the (Anglican) London Society for the Promotion of Christianity Amongst the Jews (LSJ) as a refuge for Jewish converts who were, upon their conversion, ostracized from the Jewish community. It provided them with a place to live and a means to earn their livelihood. He received Christian baptism on 10 May 1855.[1]

ASSOCIATION WITH THE CITY MISSION

The following is the record of his interview in 1858 with the Committee of the London City Mission:

Interview of Joseph Oppenheimer by the Board of Directors of the London City Mission in 1858

178

8.8.4 Petty Cash. [illegible]
20 - . . do [illegible]
2.13. . [illegible] [illegible]

Oppenheimer — The Exam.g Subcomm. reported that they had examined Joseph Abt. Oppenheimer of Palestine Place. This Candidate offers himself for Dudley Street, if approved by the Comm., at the request of the Rev. A. W. Herold, who desires to have him as supply there. He was originally a Jew at Frankfort on the Maine, but he was baptized 3 years since, & has been 4 years employed in the Jewish Converts Operative Institution. He is a single man, 26 years of age, & is a young man of some respectability & intelligence. His father was a shopkeeper, but he was educated, to gain his living as a teacher, especially of the ancient languages. The Subcomm. gave considerable time to the exam. of this Candidate. They were satisfied as to the soundness of his doctrinal views, & they believe him to be a true convert to Christianity, & [illegible] anxious to bring others to the knowledge of Christ. They consider he may be very useful in Dudley Street, under the Rev. A. W. Herold, & they agree to recommend that he be sent to the Exam.rs. The testimonials of Oppenheimer were then read, after which he was called

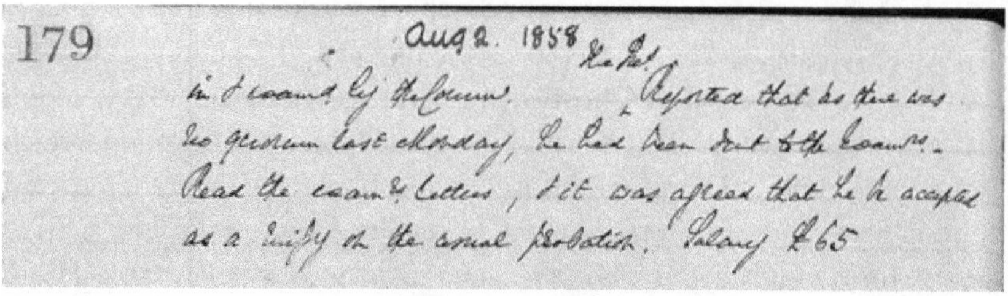

179 Aug 2. 1858

in & examd. by the Comm. Reported that as there was no quorum last Monday, he had been sent to the Examrs. Read the examrs letters, & it was agreed that he be accepted as a missy on the usual probation. Salary £65

11. EXTRACTS FROM LONDON CITY MISSION MINUTE BOOK, 2 AUGUST 1858

2 August 1858

Oppenheimer

The Examg SubComm^{e} reported that they had examined Joseph M. Oppenheimer of Palestine Place. This Candidate offers himself for Dudley Street, if approved by the Comm^{e}., at the request of the Revd. A. W. Thorold, who desires to have him as miss^{y} there. He is originally a Jew from Frankfort on the Main, but he was baptized 3 years since, & has been 4 years employed in the Jewish Converts Operative Institution. He is a single man, 26 years of age,[2] & is a young man of some respectability & intelligence. His father was a shopkeeper, but he was educated, to gain his living as a teacher, especially of the ancient languages. The Subcomm. gave considerable time to the esamination [sic] of this Candidate. They were satisfied as to the soundness of his doctrinal views, & they believe him to be a true convert to Christianity, & sincerely desirous to bring others to the knowledge of Christ. They consider he may be useful in Dudley Street, under the Revd. A. W. Thorold, & they agree to recommend that he be sent to the Examers. The testimonials of Oppenheimer were then read, after which he was called in & examd. by the Comm. The Sect. reported that as there was no quorum last Monday, he had been sent to the Examers. Read the examers letters, & it was agreed that he be accepted as a miss^{y} on the usual probation. Salary 65 pounds.[3]

There are only two more entries in the minutebook of the LCM Board of Directors related to Oppenheimer. The first is from 23 January 1860, when he first became ill:

Read a letter from Oppenheimer asking for leave of absence for 3 months without pay on the ground of the failure of his health. Agreed that "leave" be granted as requested and that

> he be allowed £1 per week from the Disabled Fund during the period of his absence.[4]

He was again very ill in the summer of 1861. He begins the journal with a summary statement in which he recalls this period of illness and reflects on his health:

> Through the mercy of God I am again permitted to give a short statement of my proceeding[s] during another quarter; The quarter opened upon me with fever in my district which thanks be to God did not prove fatal except in 4 cases; I was myself laid aside from labour for 4 or 5 weeks from something like fever which settled in my loins & unfitted me to crofs my own room for 3 weeks but blefsed be God fever & I might say all other disees [sic] has vanished from my district & my health has not been so good with me for the Past two years;

Bruce Haley, in *The Healthy Body and Victorian Culture,* makes the case that the Victorians were highly concerned about their personal health, aware that contagious diseases could slay tens of thousands of Britons in the course of a few months. The 1830s and 1840s had witnessed three massive waves of destruction: influenza, typhus, typhoid and cholera came to displace the threat of smallpox, which was diminishing with the advent of vaccination. Even the wealthy were not spared. On the 14th of December 1861, some three months after Oppenheimer started his journal, another German immigrant to London succumbed to typhoid fever: Prince Albert of Saxe-Coburg and Gotha, the consort of Queen Victoria.

Such illnesses were relatively common among lay workers in the slums. Daily contact with the poor gave city missionaries more than just a sympathetic concern for the unhealthy sanitary conditions of the London slums. As early as 1838, the London City Mission committee had reported that:

> some of the Missionaries have been seriously afflicted, as is to be expected from the crowded, and frequently infected, state of the houses of the poor. Three of them have suffered under Typhus Fever, and two of them have had the Small Pox, besides other cases of affliction .... In one case, the Small Pox spread in the family, and though the life of the father was spared, he had to weep over the loss of a beloved child through the ravages of that loathsome disease.[5]

R. W. Vanderkiste, who began working for the LCM in Clerkenwell in 1845, described some of the conditions he encountered:

> On my first appointment to the district, in 1845, I was called upon to encounter a severe trial. I was seized with violent itchings between the joints, accompanied with redness. I appeared to have caught the itch.... I was careful, however, to keep away from my friends in a room by myself, and after a few days the intolerable itching went off. A large amount of itch existed on the district.... Bugs and fleas, and other vermin, however, abound, and have tormented me sadly. I have been compelled to submit my apparel to diurnal examination. Whilst visiting at night, I have sometimes seen numbers of bugs coursing over my clothes and hat, and have had much trouble to get rid of them. The stenches have sometimes been so bad that my mouth has filled with water, and I have been compelled to retreat.[6]

One of the missionaries working in the "Church Lane" rookery in St. Giles a few hundred yards away from Oppenheimer's "Dudley Street" recorded his own experience in this regard:

> As many as 20 persons sometimes live in one room, in addition to dogs, cats, and rabbits. The filth and stench of some of these rooms renders them hardly endurable, and expose their inmates to fever and disease. The wonder is, that they are not more frequent. Often has the missionary been overpowered, and obliged to retreat into New Oxford-street for air, and, although he has been but a few months on the district, his health has been more affected during that short time, than it has been for several years previously; while the first missionary on the district lost his life through fever.[7]

Robert Bickersteth, the former rector of St. Giles'-in-the-Fields—the parish in which Oppenheimer served—told a House of Lords committee investigating popular religious observance in 1858 that during his five years as rector (1851–6), some nine or ten of his lay agents had suffered complete breakdowns in their health. Oppenheimer was eventually to add his own repeated health breakdowns to these statistics.

Deaths of missionaries and their family members were reported throughout the 1840s and 1850s, with perhaps the worst instance being the deaths of three missionaries in a single week in 1856, one from smallpox and two from typhus.[8] In fact, the very first missionary appointed by the LCM to work in the St. Giles' rookery in 1847 had died from fever.[9] The reality of such sufferings is seen clearly in the following appeal in the *London City Mission* in 1854 for support for its workers' orphaned offspring:

> "The Missionaries Orphan Children."
>
> Many of the friends of the Society having expressed a wish that

> the names of the children of their late missionaries, who are applying to obtain admission into Orphan Asylums, should be mentioned in our periodical from time to time, we beg now to state that the 3 following cases are deserving of their support:
>
> Thomas Ellis, aged 6 years, whose father died in his missionary work, after a few hours' suffering, from cholera, at Walworth, leaving behind him a widow, with 5 children dependent on her for support. This child applies for admission, in June next, into the New Infant Orphan Asylum, Stamford-hill.
>
> Eliza Nyhan, aged 7 years, in May last, whose father died, after 5 ½ years' labour as a city missionary, leaving behind him two children and a widow, who, a few days after his decease, was confined with twins, and all 4 children are now dependent on her for support. It is desired to obtain admission for the child into the Orphan Working School, Haverstock-hill, at the November election.
>
> John Saunders, aged 8 years. This child is a grandson of Mr. Higgins, who has been one of the city missionaries for 18 years, and, with 4 other children, without father and without mother, has been thrown on Mr H. for support. All 5 children are wholly dependant on him, through the death of the children's parents. It is desired to obtain admission for this child into the New Asylum for Fatherless children in the June election.
>
> The Committee will feel obliged if any of our readers can spare votes for either of these cases, and proxies will be thankfully received at the Mission House.[10]

When Oppenheimer was hired by the LCM in 1858, he was unmarried; he married Jane Charlotte Oppenheimer in 1859 at St. Giles'-in-the-Fields, and by the time of the writing of the journal, Oppenheimer was the father of a daughter, Alice Ann Oppenheimer, the first of seven children born to the couple.

OPPENHEIMER'S SOCIAL LOCATION AS A CITY MISSIONARY

Oppenheimer's elevated social status was obvious to the LCM Board, who observed that he was "a young man of some respectability & intelligence." The fact that he was the son of a shopkeeper and fluent in three languages set him apart from most of the other laymen employed by the LCM. An evaluation of the occupational background of LCM workers gives us a profile of the group's social status.

The question of LCM workers' relationship to an "aristocracy of labour," posited by Marxist historians, is an interesting one. Both Karl Marx and Friedrich Engels were deeply disappointed when British working classes failed to adopt a revolutionary stance, particularly after 1850, when improved economic conditions made the desperate, dark years of the 1840s fade from view. Instead of fomenting revolution, British workers developed trade unions and cooperatives. In order to make sense of this, Marxist writers developed the concept of a "labour aristocracy," an elite group that allegedly exerted a conservative influence in order to suppress and subvert the militancy of the workers. E.J. Hobsbawm sought to validate the concept in a 1954 article entitled "The Labour Aristocracy in Nineteenth Century Britain." Hobsbawm acknowledged the difficulty of setting criteria for membership and even conceded that it is doubtful whether such a group existed before 1840.

Yet even if one grants the existence of such a group at some point, others have argued that Marxist historians such as Dr. Hobsbawm "have completely got the wrong end of the stick: militancy was much more likely to be found among the better-off than among the poorer workers."[11] In other words, an aristocracy of labour, if it existed at all, was a force not for conservatism but for radicalism. Oppenheimer's journal offers no support for the idea of an aristocracy of labour among the poor whom he visited; his charges were so poor that radicalism appears to have had no impact among them, and he reports very little class resentment being voiced by those whom he visits.

The list of professions of LCM workers is somewhat sketchy, but two facts are clear. First, about a quarter of the workers were drawn from the lower middle class or above. Second, at least half of the agents came from the mainstream of the working class.[12] Thus the majority had known, in Hugh McLeod's words, "the stigmata of the manual worker—ingrained dirt, workman's clothes—and the contagion of a rough working environment."[13] Manual labourers lived on the bottom rung of the national social status system, clearly below the poorest clerk or shopkeeper, who might have had a similar standard of living. It was from this group that the greater portion of LCM agents appear to have been drawn.

Oppenheimer, the son of a shopkeeper and educated as a teacher, probably should be classified among the lower middle class. This ranked him among the most socially prominent of LCM agents.[14] In a number of ways, therefore, Oppenheimer was atypical of city missionaries: relatively well educated, fluent in both German and English, and able to write in Hebrew. As a German Jew and a recent convert to Christianity, he was hardly the most obvious candidate for work in a strongly Irish Roman Catholic area of London.

THE JOURNAL

We would know virtually nothing of Oppenheimer were it not for his journal which is the core of this study. The missionary's journal reflects the systematic nature of the LCM approach, showing that the agent made the rounds of all his assigned families every month or so.[15] Oppenheimer's journal is a small booklet made up of folded, hand-stitched pages approximately 11 inches (28 cm) by 5.75 inches (14.5 cm). The booklet has a thick black paper cover, and inside are lined pages on which he recorded the details of his visits. The individual pages have thin blue lines, and there is a feint red margin on the left-hand side of each page. In the margin column, Oppenheimer often has taken a few words to summarize or comment on his journal entry.

Stitched into the front of the journal are printed pages on which the agent was to record the statistics of his work (see illustration 12), with columns in which he could quantify his labours. The year and month are recorded at the top of the page, along with the number of the district (126), the name of the missionary and the name of his supervisor (A.W. Thorold), and the supervisor's address.

The column headings read:

Date.
No. of visitable families.
No. of ditto visited and called on during the month.
Hours spent in domiciliary visitation.
Visits.
Calls.
Total of visits and calls.
Of which to the afflicted.
Meetings held.
Average number of attendants
Tracts given away
Copies of Scriptures put into circulation.
Read the Scriptures.
Deaths of persons visited.
Interviews with superintendent.
No. of children sent to school.
No. of persons induced to attend public worship.
Ditto visited by the missionary only.

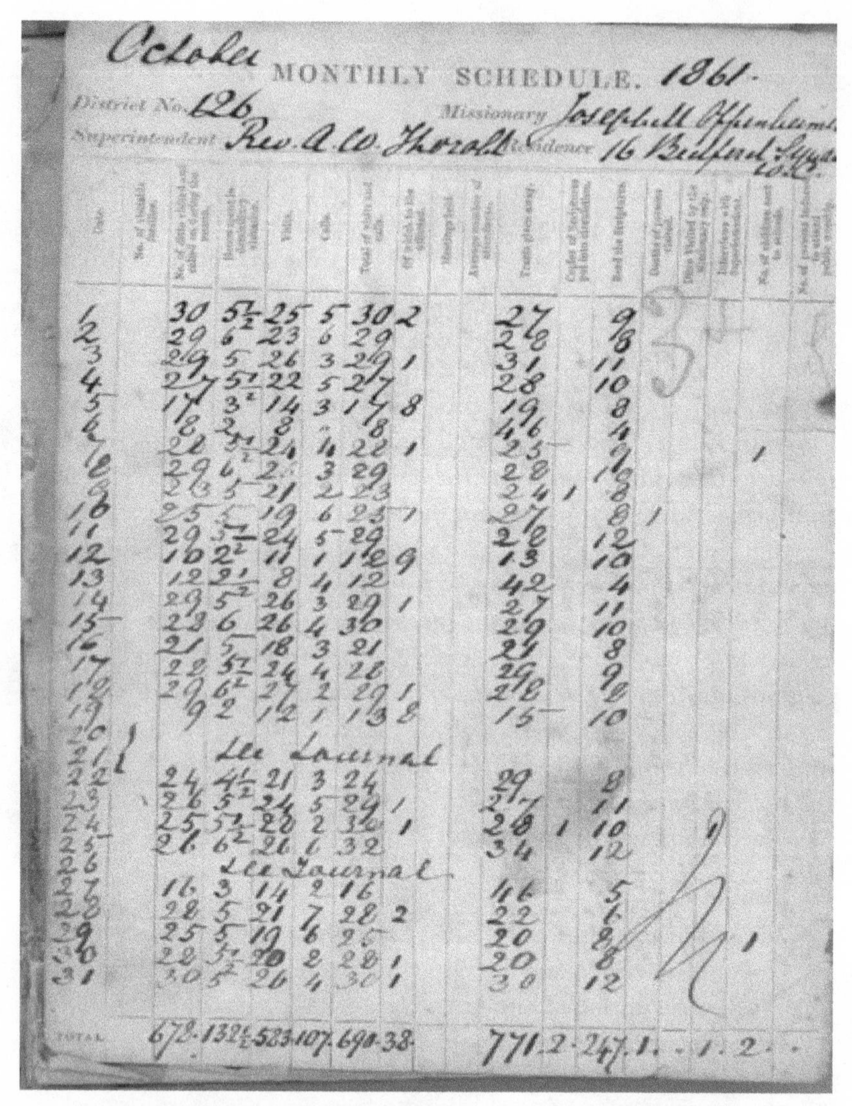

October MONTHLY SCHEDULE. 1861.

District No. 126 Missionary Joseph... Oppenheim...

Superintendent Rev. A. W. Thorold Residence 16 Bedford Sq... W.C.

Date										
1	30	5½	25	5	30	2	27		9	
2	29	6	23	6	29		28		8	
3	29	5	26	3	29	1	31		11	
4	27	5½	22	5	27		28		10	
5	17	3½	14	3	17	8	19		8	
6	18	2	8	"	18		46		4	
7	22	3½	24	4	22	1	25		9	1
8	29	6	23	3	29		28		18	
9	23	5	21	2	23		24	1	8	
10	25	5	19	6	25	1	27		8	1
11	29	5½	24	5	29		28		12	
12	10	2½	11	1	12	9	13		10	
13	12	2½	8	4	12		42		4	
14	29	5½	26	3	29	1	27		11	
15	23	6	26	4	30		29		10	
16	21	5	18	3	21		24		8	
17	22	5½	24	4	26		29		9	
18	29	6½	27	2	29	1	28		9	
19	9	2	12	1	13	8	15		10	
20	See Journal									
21										
22	24	4½	21	3	24		29		8	
23	26	5	24	5	29	1	27		11	
24	25	5½	20	2	36	1	28	1	10	9
25	26	6	26	6	32		34		12	
26	See Journal									
27	16	3	14	2	16		46		5	
28	28	5	21	7	28	2	22		6	
29	25	5	19	6	25		20		8	1
30	22	3½	20	2	28	1	20		8	
31	30	5	26	4	30	1	30		12	
TOTAL	678	132½	583	107	690	38	771	2	247	1 · · 1 · 2 · ·

12. OPPENHEIMER MS: STATISTICAL SUMMARY FOR OCTOBER 1861

In looking at Oppenheimer's reporting for the month of October 1861, one can observe that he worked every day of that month save for two days of illness (20th and 21st) and that on the one other day when he recorded no visits, he was attending a divisional meeting of missionaries at the London City Mission headquarters. He records spending between five and six hours in house-to-house visitation on Mondays through Fridays, and about 3 hours each Saturday and Sunday.

13. SAMPLE PAGE FROM OPPENHEIMER DIARY

The booklet was in fact used for two different purposes. First, Oppenheimer was to record his daily visits; 151 pages are devoted to these journal entries. Second, the booklet was used for a related exercise: A 24-page section records Oppenheimer's visits to the families of children in a local Sunday school—perhaps the St. Giles' Ragged School—all of whom were between the ages of 4 and 8 years old. It would seem that the London City Mission also directed him to visit the families of these children, many of whom did not reside in the very small district where he worked, to ascertain the spiritual state of each family and to discern any impact the Sunday school was having.

The manuscript journal covers a nine-month period, during which

Oppenheimer was healthy enough to work for about five months. The first section is dated September and October 1861, followed by two months of illness; the second section is from January and February 1862. He was then ill again from the 1st of March through to the 8th of May. The third and final section covers his brief return to work from 9 to 25 May, at which point the last few lines become illegible. The following day, 26 May 1862, the following entry appears in the minute book of the Board of Directors of the LCM:

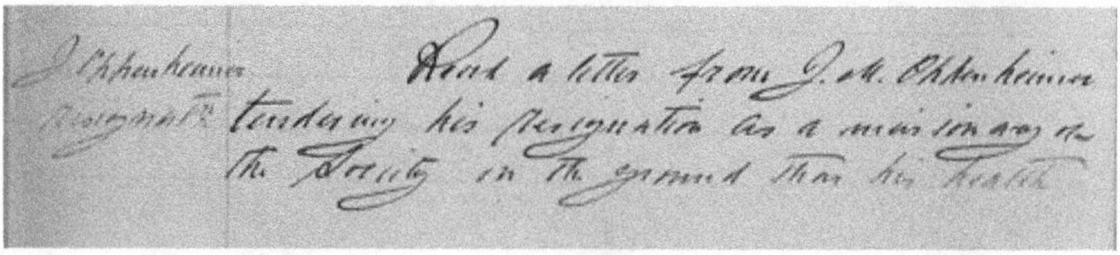
J. Oppenheimer
Resignation
Read a letter from J. M. Oppenheimer tendering his resignation as a missionary of the Society on the ground that his health

14. LONDON CITY MISSION MINUTE BOOK, 26 MAY 1862

> 26 May 1862
>
> Read a letter from J. M. Oppenheimer tendering his resignation as a Missy of the Society on the grounds that his health required that he should live in the country; requesting also that he may be allowed to leave at the earliest convenient time. Agreed that his resignation be accepted & that he be allowed to leave at such time as might be convenient to himself. [16]

This final breakdown in Oppenheimer's health thus brought about his sudden departure from the Mission. It appears that the journal was retained by his supervisor and then used briefly by the city missionary who succeeded him. At this point, Oppenheimer disappears from LCM records.

WHATEVER BECAME OF OPPENHEIMER?

What became of Oppenheimer has long been a mystery. Only two Joseph Oppenheimers are listed in the 1861 census for the whole of England, and only one has the middle initial of M; the census places him in the county of Middlesex, an area of London that included St. Giles. He is identified as German-born and a naturalized British subject. Marriage records indicate that in the fall of 1859, he had married Jane Charlotte Andrews of Middlesex. Alice Ann Oppenheimer (b. 1860, d. 1876) was the first of their seven children. Their second child, Constance Lavinia Oppenheimer (b. 1861, d. after 1907), married a man by the last name of Bell, but no record of her death has been found, nor any indication that she bore children. In addition, the family had a 16-year-old servant girl, Eliza Rutherford, whom the census lists as living with the family.

After leaving the London City Mission in May 1862, Joseph Oppenheimer recovered his health and became a successful shopkeeper, following the profession of his father. He went into tobacco retailing, at the time an occupation that was very much the preserve of Jews in London, and became a very wealthy man. When the next census was conducted in 1871 the Oppenheimers were still living in London, but their address was now 57 Waterloo Road in Lambeth, just across from Waterloo train station on the south side of the Thames. It is likely that the Oppenheimers lived above their tobacco shop, its location opposite a busy train station being ideal for such a business. It appears that they had made the move to Lambeth by 1865; by 1871, the family had three more children—two more daughters and a son—all born in Lambeth. The third child was Jane Amalia Oppenheimer (b. 1865, died 1958, age 93), who married Robert Benjamin Vince (b. 1864, d. 1911). It appears that Jane Oppenheimer and Robert Vince married about 1890 in Winnipeg, Manitoba but in 1895 returned to Britain. The Vinces gave birth to four Oppenheimer grandchildren: (1) Cyril Oscar Allan Vince (b. 1895 at sea on the family's return trip to Britain), d. unknown; (2) Edith May Vince (b. 1896, death date unknown) who married Jesse Albert G. Moore (1899–1984) in 1920; (3) Alice Vince, b. Chelsea, c. 1987, d. unknown; and (4) Maude Beatrice Vince, b. Marylebone, 1908, d. 1958.

These are the only four Oppenheimer grandchildren that we know of, and it appears that only Cyril Oscar Allan Vince, the son of Jane Amelia (née Oppenheimer) and Robert Vince, married and had offspring. He and his wife and firstborn appear to have emigrated to Australia circa 1921. Cyril married Edith Worrall, and together they had two sons: (1) Alan Vince (b. in Bolton, Lancashire in 1921, and died in Tauranga, Bay of Plenty, New Zealand in 1985); and (2) William Robert Vince (b. 24 August 1922 in Australia, and died in 2009 in Kati Kati, Bay of Plenty, New Zealand). Alan Vince married Lucia Fragiacomo and had two children. William Robert Vince married Tresna Herbert and had six children.

The Oppenheimers' fourth child was their only son: Edgar J. A. Oppenheimer, b. in Lambeth ca. 1867, d. Oct. 1890. There followed three daughters, none of whom appear to have married: (1) Gertrude Victoria Oppenheimer, b. Lambeth, c. 1870, d. 1941; (2) Rosalia Florence Oppenheimer, b. 1873, d. Dec. 1934.; and (3) Maude Bertha Evelyn Oppenheimer, b. 1877, d. 1954. It would appear, therefore, that the only other grandchild of the Oppenheimers who might have continued the family line was Edith May Vince, who married J.A.G. Moore in 1920. It is not known whether they had any offspring.

According to the 1871 census, the family also had two female servants, aged 18 and 14. In the 1880s the Oppenheimers moved to Brentford, Middlesex—about ten miles west of Lambeth. Joseph Oppenheimer died at 2 Williams Terrace, Chiswick in Middlesex on 7 March 1890 at the age of 56. His wife, Jane Charlotte Oppenheimer, died at 5 Prebend Gardens, Chiswick, age 72 on 7 November 1907. When Oppenheimer died in 1890, he bequeathed his entire estate to his wife; she left the remains of the estate to her four surviving daughters seventeen years later. The estate was valued at 5,148 pounds in 1907, which constituted a considerable fortune in its day. It would appear that Oppenheimer's career as a city missionary was succeeded by that of a very successful businessman.

Notes

[1] MSS Dep. Church Mission to the Jews, The Bodleian Library, Oxford. C. 63. Entry 696.
[2] The date on his baptismal certificate would indicate that he was 24 years old at this time.
[3] MSS LCM Minute Book, 2 August 1858.
[4] MSS LCM Minute Book.
[5] *LCM Third Annual Report,* London, 1838, p. 5.
[6] R. W. Vanderkiste, *Narrative of a Six Years' Mission* (London: Nisbet, 1852), p. 5.
[7] *LCM Mag.* (Nov. 1847): 242–43.
[8] MSS LCM Minute Book, July 28, 1856. For other examples, see: *LCM Mag.* (June 1849):110 for the death of two missionaries from fever and one from a recurrent cold; *Ibid., (Aug 1849):156* for the death of Mr Henry Clark from Asiastic cholera, *Ibid., (Oct 1848): 199 ff.* for the death of another missionary from cholera and the deaths among families of missionaries, including the two children of one missionary.
[9] *LCM Mag.* (Nov. 1847): 242 for the death of the first St. Giles missionary from fever.
[10] *LCM Mag.* (March 1854): 53–54.
[11] Henry Pelling, *Popular Politics and Society in Late Victorian Britain* (London: Macmillan, 1968), p. 61.
[12] I am indebted to Dr. Graeme Wynn of the University of British Columbia for his help on the difficult and controversial subject of trying to classify these workers. See *Lighten Their Darkness,* pp. 280–82.
[13] Hugh McLeod, "Class, Community and Region," *A Sociological Yearbook of Religion in Britain* (London: SCM Press, 1972), vol 6, p. 34.
[14] For a detailed analysis of the social background of the LCM agents see: *Lighten Their Darkness,* pp. 280–82.
[15] For an instance of this, Mr. Cook of 13 Dudley Street, top back, was visited on 3 September, and then again on 2 October 1861, in the regular course of Oppenheimer's visiting.
[16] MSS LCM Minute Book. 26 May 1862.

3

The Sower's Field: Dudley Street, St. Giles's

> In common parlance, St. Giles's and Billingsgate are types—the one, of the lowest conditions under which human life is possible,—the other, of the lowest point to which the English language can descend: ...[1]
>
> Thomas Beames, *Rookeries of London, 1852*

Joseph Oppenheimer sowed his seed in a very specific and limited field. The street where he worked was known as Dudley Street, only two blocks long, located on the northern side of an area known as the Seven Dials, in the parish of St. Giles'-in-the-Fields. In 1835 Charles Dickens had brought attention to this street in his *Sketches By Boz* with his humorous description of the two-block section that was then known as "Monmouth Street":[2]

> We have always entertained a particular attachment towards Monmouth-street, as the only true and real emporium for second-hand wearing apparel. Monmouth-street is venerable from its antiquity, and respectable from its usefulness. Holywell-street we despise; the red-headed and red-whiskered Jews who forcibly haul you into their squalid houses, and thrust you into a suit of clothers, whether you will or not, we detest.
>
> The inhabitants of Monmouth-street are a distinct class; a peaceable and retiring race, who immure themselves for the most part in deep cellars, or small back parlours, and who seldom come forth into the world, except in the dusk and coolness of the evening, when they may be seen seated, in chairs on the pavement, smoking their pipes, or watching the gambols of their engaging children as they revel in the gutter, a happy troop of infantine scavengers. Their countenances bear a thoughtful and a dirty cast, certain indications of their love of traffic; and their habitations are distinguished by that disregard of outward appearance and neglect of personal comfort, so common among people who are constantly immersed in profound speculations, and deeply engaged in sedentary pursuits.[3]

15. ILLUSTRATION OF MONMOUTH STREET
(FROM 1858 KNOWN AS DUDLEY STREET)
FROM
SKETCHES BY BOZ (CHARLES DICKENS)
1835

What follows in this chapter is an attempt to consider this sowing field from five angles or vantage points. We will look at the lay of the land by examining it in depth from five contemporary sources: The first is a study of the parish of St. Giles'-in-the-Fields published by the London City Mission in 1855; the second is an in-depth examination of Dudley Street in the Seven Dials area where Oppenheimer was to work three years later, again produced by the City Mission; the third is the first-hand report on Dudley Street by investigative journalist James Greenwood, written in 1873; the fourth source is a series of visual images by French illustrator Gustav Doré, and the accompanying description of the area by British newspaper editor Blanchard Jerrold, published alongside Doré's drawings in 1872. Significantly, in one of Doré's most famous woodcuts he gives us a sketch of what Dudley Street actually looked like in Oppenheimer's time. The fifth and final angle is that of Oppenheimer's own comments about the desperate poverty he encountered.

We begin, however, with a discussion of the larger social context in which all this needs to be set; after discussing the five angles, we will conclude with a discussion of other factors such as patterns of immigration and slum clearances that influenced the locale, ending with an assessment of popular religion and the effectiveness of the work of people such Oppenheimer on the same. It will be argued throughout that the City Missionaries' first-hand knowledge of the daily life of London's desperately poor played a major role in drawing the attention of British society to the social problems of the age.

THE LARGER SOCIAL CONTEXT

In 1839, Thomas Carlyle's essay *Chartism,* brought what came to be known as the "Condition of England Question" to the forefront of British public life. For Carlyle, this involved a series of complex social issues created by *laissez-faire* capitalism: appalling working conditions in British factories, dreadful housing in densely populated urban areas, and the decline of religion and morality among the emerging proletariat. Central to his concern was the matter of "pauperization," the deep impoverishment of the lowest social strata—a cycle of poverty in which people seemed trapped. Carlyle argued that such poverty differed from traditional forms of poverty in that it was a mass phenomenon, a condition built into the way in which the Industrial Revolution was unfolding, instead of being dependent upon personal contingencies; it also was permanent instead of seasonal. Further, it had the potential to expand to include social groups that had previously been regarded as secure.

The economic storm clouds steadily gathered in the early 1840s, not only in Britain but across Europe, as conditions worsened and crop failures aggravated the downturn. While the English debated the "Condition of England" question, in Prussia a similar moral panic was felt among the literati, bringing the deepening poverty to the attention of the ruling classes, just as Thomas Carlyle and Charles Dickens had done in England. In a work published in 1843, the Prussian situation was presented to the reading public by Heinrich Grunholzer, a young Swiss student who wrote movingly of the desperate poverty he had encountered in the most degraded tenements of Berlin. Grunholzer's exposé included not merely descriptions or the citing of cruel statistics, but was interwoven with accounts of his personal dialogues with the poorest of the poor.

A similar work was Friedrich Wilhelm Wolff's widely circulated November 1843 piece on the "vaults of Breslau," detailing life in the shanty-town that had grown up on the outskirts of the Silesian capital. A parallel phenomenon occurred in France with the publication of Eugène Sue's ten-volume novel detailing the Parisian underworld, *Les Mystères de Paris* (1842–3), which was widely read across Europe. As Christopher Clark has observed, "There was doubtless an element of voyeuristic pleasure in the consumption of such texts by bourgeois readers," and it is clear that in both Britain and Europe there was a "bourgeoning literature of social thick description" that mixed accounts of personal interactions with the poor with vivid and poignant portraits of their conditions.[4]

In Britain, one of the first organizations that began to call the public's attention to the dreadful state of the lodgings of the poor was the London City Mission. From its foundation in 1835, the Mission began to raise the level of public awareness of slum conditions through the accounts of its missionaries at work in the "rookeries"—a term coined in England comparing these poor, densely-populated areas with the noisy, filthy abodes of rooks (a type of crow).

In 1837, well before Carlyle's essay and the parliamentary inquiries of the early 1840s, it published first-hand accounts such as the following, written by one its workers, in a fashion that became typical of others throughout the period:

> In some of the districts large numbers of families reside under ground in cellars. In many of these I have found, crowded together in one small room, as many as seven families, and in one instance thirty-eight families were residing under one roof. In such places I have often been shocked at the immorality and vice I have witnessed, though my surprise has immediately abated, when I reflected upon the way in which they were forced to live.[5]

In 1841, *London City Mission Magazine* published an article that decried the miserable lodgings of the poor and attacked the squalor and poverty that were made worse by the subletting system. It warned that unless something was done, country youths migrating to the city would take "their ranks amongst the dangerous classes."[6]

Four years later the same publication, at the end of a detailed study of lodging houses, unleashed a blistering attack upon wealthy landlords who made exorbitant profits from their tenements while the poor lived in moral depravity, which was caused in part by the overcrowded and unsanitary conditions. So strong was the exposé that the governing committee of the Mission determined not to offend its constituency further "as different opinions had been expressed as to the propriety of publishing some of the more offensive evils connected with such places."[7] In a wide variety of ways, British evangelicals both highlighted and responded to the social problems raised by the "Condition of England" debate.[8] We turn now to the five angles from which we will view the specific area where Oppenheimer worked.

THE FIRST ANGLE: THE PARISH OF ST. GILES'-IN-THE-FIELDS

The ways in which evangelical organizations played a major role in drawing the attention of British society to the social problems of the age can be seen in the London City Mission's highlighting of the problems of the area in which Oppenheimer worked. In the 1850s, the *London City Mission Magazine* published a series of articles focused on specific areas of London; in 1855, the magazine printed an article on the Parish of St. Giles'-in-the-Fields. It constitutes an interesting original source document:

Report on the parish of St. Giles'-in-the-Fields in the *London City Mission Magazine* (December 1855): 277–78.

ST. GILES'S

'The very name of this parish is proverbial; and there are probably a few persons who do not associate with the mention of St. Giles'-in-the-Fields, the idea of pauperism, wretchedness, and crime.' Such are the words of the worthy Rector of the parish, the Rev. Robert Bickersteth, in a lecture delivered by him before the Church of England Young Men's Society, in St. Martin's Hall, on February 26th of the present year. And although he adds, 'in justice to the parish at large, I believe it has a worse reputation than it deserves,' he still asserts, 'be this as it may, certain it is, that no one need wander beyond the limits of St. Giles's, to find examples of misery the most appalling, penury the most heartrending, and vice the most degrading.' The following pages will abundantly confirm the latter statement.

Till about a century and a quarter since St. Giles's-in-the-Fields and St. George, Bloomsbury, were one parish, and they still continue as united for all secular purposes. They together form an area of ground which is nearly equilateral, and deviates but in a trifling degree from the form of a square. But in 1731 St. George's was taken out of St. Giles's, and made a district parish for all ecclesiastical purposes. The portion left to St. Giles's is a long and narrow strip of ground on the west and the south sides of the original square. St. Giles in shape has since resembled the letter L, the perpendicular and the horizontal parts of the letter being inhabited by a class as different as it is almost possible to conceive. The arm of the parish running north and south includes Bedford-square, Gower-street, and places of a like description, and there is no population sufficiently poor to be visited in the entire of that part of St. Giles, except a few mews, and the small portions of one or two poor streets cut in twain by New Oxford-street, and a fraction of which still remains north of that great thoroughfare. But the arm of the parish running west and east, except Holborn and Lincoln's-inn-fields, is almost one dense mass of poor of a low order in which the Irish are most numerous.

In this latter part of St. Giles there is probably more paid lay agency at work than in any other part of London containing the same amount of population. The London City Mission has 9 missionaries there, and a tenth, who had been removed for want of funds from one of its districts, is about to be appointed to another of its districts. The Scripture-readers' Association has also 5 Scripture-readers, and the Church Pastoral-Aid Society has 1 lay assistant, in addition to a curate. There is, moreover, a missionary unconnected with any of the Societies, supported by the congregation of Bloomsbury Chapel, under the superintendence of the Rev. William Brock. Both that chapel and Bedford Chapel, although situated in St. George's parish, make St. Giles's their sphere of action in benevolent efforts for the poor. There are, consequently, 17 paid lay-agents in this southern part of St. Giles's. But, in estimating the fruit of this agency, it must be borne in mind, that almost the entire of it has been newly appointed, and that little time has been yet afforded for large results. The entire parish is now visited, the Scripture-readers all occupying distinct districts to the City missionaries, and the two meeting together periodically for prayer and conference.

The population of St. Giles's in 1851 was 37,407, and it then only varied by 57 from the population of 1841. The people reside in only 2,702 houses; so that each house is tenanted, on an average, by 14 persons. The population is very crowded in the poorer parts of the parish, and has become still more so since the formation of New Oxford-street, as is ordinarily the case where a low population is cleared away, and no provision made for its future accommodation. The population of St. Giles' in 1851 was found living in 174 fewer houses than in 1841.

Brayley, in his 'Typographical and Historical Description of London and Middlesex,' published some years since, states St. Giles's even then to be improved from what it was. His statement is this, —'Passing through some excellent streets, we come to a very different part of the town, long known as one of the greatest nuisances of the metropolis. I allude to the wretched precincts of St. Giles'-in-the-Fields, where misery and depravity in all their various forms are exhibited beyond description. And yet even this part is much improved and improving. It has sometimes been called 'Little Dublin,' on account of the number of low and vulgar Irish who reside in this neighbourhood, but this appellation is extremely illiberal and unjust; for St. Giles's certainly bears no greater resemblance to Dublin in general than does Saffron-hill, Petticoat-lane, or the worst parts of St. George's Fields to the Cities of London and Westminster.'

The improvement since then has become more marked, and we feel assured that the good seed now so largely scattered in every part of the parish cannot be without its ultimate effect. Nevertheless, at present the condition of the people physically, morally, and religiously, is most distressing to the Christian mind.

The following are the districts of St. Giles's visited by the London City Mission. They are arranged, as they lie, from west to east.

CLOSE YET REMOTE

The *Magazine's* account of the parish is noteworthy on several counts. First, the remarkable juxtaposing of social classes in such a small area of London was often an occasion of comment among social observers: The poorest of the poor lived within a few thousand yards of some of the wealthiest people in London, but the very rich and the very poor seemingly functioned with little knowledge or awareness of each other. The two were at once both close and remote. Victorian Britain seems to have had an unbounded capacity to be shocked by the urban destitution that the Industrial Revolution had created, yet polite society preferred to ignore it.

Lord Ashley (from 1851 known as the Earl of Shaftesbury) had made the same point succinctly to an evangelical audience at Exeter Hall in 1848. In his first public address on behalf of the LCM, he paid tribute to the ways in which its workers had brought slum conditions to light: "I am here to bear my testimony to the very great debt which the public owes you, and to your missionaries, for having developed to the world a state of things, of which nineteen-twentieths of the educated and easy part of this great metropolis were just as ignorant as they are of what is going on upon the left horn of the moon." Developing the exploration theme, Ashley continued: "Why, talk of journeying to Timbuctoo, or penetrating into the interior of New Holland! I will venture to say that your missionaries have made discoveries quite as curious, and to us ten times more interesting, than were ever made by all the travellers that have roamed over the habitable globe." Their inner city work had revealed that "there are thousands and tens of thousands living in the courts and alleys of this great metropolis, in a condition so disgusting to every sense, and ten times more fearful when contemplated in a spiritual aspect." Deeply aware that rigid class distinctions and social isolation had served to distance the middle-classes from these scenes, Ashley challenged his listeners in saying, "...I dare say there may be, even in this present assembly, very many persons who may not know that within half an hour's walk of their own comfortable dwellings there are thousands and thousands of human beings who would furnish ten times more occupation for all their curiosity, all their intelligence, all their zeal, and all their prayers, than if they were to wander over the plains of Tartary, and the deserts of north and south Africa. This is a state of things which has been brought to our knowledge by the exertions of the City Missionaries."[9]

THE CITY MISSIONARIES' ROLE IN AWAKENING A SOCIAL CONSCIENCE

> Indeed it is difficult to exaggerate the City Mission's social importance. ... [The London City Mission] was undoubtedly responsible, more than any other body, for the multiplication of Evangelical social agencies of all kinds in the 1840s, especially Ragged Schools, and the Ragged School Union, which was founded under the Mission's auspices in 1844, while the journal reports gave the Victorian religious public a wealthy of information hitherto unavailable, on new sorts of urban destitution, and thereby aroused a new enthusiasm to succour the poor while saving souls.[10]
>
> Sheridan Gilley

Novelists like Charles Dickens and Charlotte Elizabeth and evangelical workers like Joseph Oppenheimer played a major role in bridging this social gap and familiarizing the middle-classes, and Parliament, with the realities of slum life. Norris Pope has written that "from the mid-1840s though the

1860s it is arguable that evangelical charitable propaganda supplied the single most important source of information on slum conditions excluding [Henry] Mayhew's justly celebrated investigations for the *Morning Chronicle*"[11] which produced his famous *London Labour and the London Poor* (1851). Pope's assessment needs to be qualified, in that Henry Mayhew and many other social observers were guided thorough London's rookeries by London City Missionaries.[12] Mayhew, who had a "decided grudge" against evangelicals in general and Lord Shaftesbury in particular,[13] nevertheless was only able to gather his facts with the invaluable assistance gained by one in the LCM's employ.[14] As Mayhew himself acknowledged in his work, "It is principally owing to the city missionaries that the other portions of society have known what they now do of the practices and habits of the poor..."[15]

Oppenheimer's journal offers confirmation of this important role of the city missionaries, in that he reports that one day he was accompanied on his rounds by Lord Burghley (1825–1895), a Conservative MP who eventually became the 3rd Marquess of Exeter and Privy Council member. Burghley joined Oppenheimer because he was eager to see first-hand how the desperately poor lived within a short distance of the Houses of Parliament. There is no evidence that Burghley had any particular religious sympathies with evangelicals or that he ever was a supporter of the London City Mission.

Because of their familiarity with the poorest of the poor, LCM agents were invaluable to government information gatherers, to politicians, and to those who made their reputations by familiarizing the Victorian public with the London slums. Before the extension of the franchise, "Parliament tended to obtain its information from religious bodies, missions, prison chaplains and reforming societies," and thus the better-educated missionary was often called on as "one of the few educated observers, apart from the doctor, to enter the slum."[16] Reliance on such sources for accounts of working-class opinion tended to strengthen the hands of the evangelicals in their social reform campaigns; few parliamentarians had any personal knowledge of the habits and dwellings of the classes for which they legislated.

This sort of information gathering had been requested of the mission from its founding in 1835; in August 1835, the society was asked to allow its workers to provide evidence for a House of Lords Committee on prison discipline.[17] Similar appeals continued to be received by the mission and were often related to metropolitan sanitation. It was Lord Ashley (later Lord Shaftesbury) who continually brought the LCM to public prominence by using its magazine's statistics in Parliament and by his repeated references to the mission's agents, who had led him through the worst and most dangerous of London's rookeries, familiarizing him with all aspects of working-class life and culture. Such knowledge was essential to Ashley's parliamentary campaigns for sanitation reform, his battle against low common-lodging houses,[18] and a host of other philanthropic concerns. The growing awareness on the part of evangelicals such as Ashley of the important role of environmental factors in causing poverty challenged older attitudes, which were rooted in Malthusian economics about the inevitability of poverty, and which undermined religious arguments (accepted by many of an earlier generation of English evangelicals) linking poverty with vice.[19]

THE SECOND ANGLE: THE REPORT ON DUDLEY STREET, THE SEVEN DIALS

At the center of the St. Giles rookery was The Seven Dials, a square section intersected by seven streets so that on the map the area looked like a clock. Located just a few hundred yards from St. Giles' Church, it included the "Dudley Street district" that Oppenheimer was expected to visit on a regular basis.

His regular visits were confined to both sides of two-block-long Dudley Street (about 800 feet long); to the several hundred foot-long extension of Dudley Street on the north, known as Broad Street; and to Monmouth Court, which connected Dudley Street to Little Earl Street (one of the seven streets intersecting the "Seven Dials." Today what was known as "Dudley Street" is the northern end of Shaftesbury Avenue in London's theatre district. (This portion of Shaftesbury Avenue was known as Monmouth Street prior to 1858 and then as Dudley-Street.) This short street was known, as Oppenheimer himself records, for the fact that the poorest of the poor "come to sell or 'dolly' their undergarments for drink; these 'Dolly shops' as they are called is [sic] the bane of my district." A "dolly shop" sold rags and refuse, and they were so-called because they traditionally were identified by the symbol of a black doll that was hung outside to denote the sale of muslins and silks made by East Indians.

The following is an in-depth study of the "Dudley-street" district in which Joseph Oppenheimer worked, written some three years before he began as a "City Missionary" and published in the *London City Mission Magazine* (December 1855): 283–85.

DUDLEY-STREET DISTRICT.

1. Ethnic make-up [headings not in original]

Dudley-street is the new name given to a street far better known as Monmouth-street, and the district comprehends chiefly the population of this one street. Dudley-street and Monmouth-court are the entire district, which contains 95 visitable houses, 89 of which are shops, 4 publichouses, and 2 common lodging-house. In these 95 houses live 697 families, of which 303 are Roman Catholic, 17 Jewish, and the remainder, with few exceptions, Infidels, sceptics, or mere nominal Christians. All these families, with the exception of 20, receive the missionary in his visitation. The occupations and migratory and other habits of the people are thus described in his report:—

2. Occupations

The occupations of the people are so extremely varied that the whole scene may be looked upon as forming a little world in itself. The majority of the shopkeepers and those who occupy the kitchens are receivers of stolen goods, and also what is termed leaving-shops, or places where articles of too small a value to be received by the licensed pawnbrokers are left, by paying *3d.* in the shilling interest for the loan of money thus obtained. Mrs. —, the owner of one of these shops, has informed me that by far the larger proportion of money lent by her was borrowed for no other purpose than obtaining intoxicating drinks. Another section of the people, chiefly women, are employed in making soldiers' clothing, with regard to whom it has often struck me with considerable force, that if our brave armies in the East could hear the moans of the hungry, and listen to the bitter exclamations of the suffering thousands who are doomed to eke out their miserable existence in preparing the showy and comfortable garments they are wearing, it would tend to blight their boasted courage, and bring disappointment instead of victory in our contest. Another section of the people are employed in boot and shoe making, the majority of whom are what is termed translators. There is also a considerable number of bricklayers' labourers, costermongers, beggars, thieves, and fallen females.

3. Rapid turnover of population

The migratory habits of the people form so peculiar and prominent a feature, that I feel it my duty to call particular attention to it, feeling assured that the broad fact itself will at least serve to counterbalance that which otherwise might have been attributed to a want of energy on the part of the missionary. *It is not an unfrequent occurrence to meet with from 2 to 6 fresh families in many of the houses on each time of passing through them. I kept a daily account during two circuits round the district, which occupied nearly 6 months, of all new comers, and found that during that period no less a number than 536 families had left, and a similar number of fresh families had entered the boundaries of the district.* [Emphasis in original.]

4. Sabbatarianism
Sunday trading forms here a prominent and painful feature. Nearly every shop and kitchen is open for business on the Lord's-day, on the morning of which day large numbers of working people may be observed recruiting their scanty wardrobes. During the year I have been made instrumental in closing one shop on the Sabbath, and fear that that small number will not be much increased until accomplished by the strong arm of the law. Shopkeepers are by no means anxious to keep open their shops, but, on the contrary, are crying aloud for help, that they may obtain rest as well as profit. Some have expressed a desire to attend my Sabbath evening meeting, but plead as an excuse for their absence the smitings of a guilty conscience.

5. Intemperance and links with Temperance organizations
Nearly two-thirds of the poverty, misery, crime, and disease which have come under my notice is produced by habits of intemperance. In every house, nay, more, in almost every room, some footprints of that fearful monster may be clearly traced. Seeing the enormity of this evil, I have been induced during the last nine months to become a total abstainer, with the earnest hope that, by God's assistance, I may be the better prepared by a living example to induce others to follow in my steps. My humble effort has not been fruitless, inasmuch as no less than 10 confirmed drunkards have been induced to abandon their evil course, some of whom are constant attendants at my Sunday night meetings; and who can doubt but their attendance upon a means of grace will, under the blessing of God, prove a blessing not only to themselves, but also to their families and the district in which they live? Upwards of 600 copies of the "Band of Hope Review" and "Band of Hope Journal" have been carefully circulated, and as eagerly sought. I may also notice, as a pleasing feature, that nearly 600 working people signed my petition for the closing of publichouses on the Lord's-day.

6. Business
Dudley-street may be regarded as the Rag Fair of the West. It is the

great Sunday market in that part of London for cheap coats, shoes, bonnets, and all articles of dress. The very pavements are converted into counters, and the very cellars are shops.

7. Record of City Missionary's activity
It is eminently a district for the Christian missionary. Nor has our missionary here laboured in vain, notwithstanding the enormous evils which yet exist. He is supported by the generous contributions of 2 anonymous country friends, who have just remitted us 210*l.* for the next 3 years, and he is superintended by the Rev. Robert Bickersteth.

A very vigorous missionary has just left this district for labour in another department of Christian enterprise. His place has, however, been already supplied. He has been a little more than 2 years at work in the district, and on leaving he thus enumerates his labours:—

"Since the commencement of my endeavours here I have spent 3,310 hours in domiciliary visitation, and made 9,447 visits, 1,291 of which were to the beds of the sick and dying. During these visits I have read the Word of God 5,021 times, and have held 125 Meetings for the exposition of the Word of God and prayer. 17,547 religious tracts have been distributed by me, beside large quantities of 'Band of Hope,' and other publications. 45 copies of Holy Writ have been carefully distributed amongst Papists, and others who were anxious to obtain and unable to purchase them. 139 children have been led or carried to Sabbath and day schools, where their tender minds will be moulded and shapen, under God's blessing, after the fashion of Him who said, 'Suffer little children to come unto me, and forbid them not.' In addition to the above, I may also add, that many drunkards have been reclaimed. Boys, destitute and criminal, have been introduced to asylums, and fallen females restored to honourable positions in society.
"The cases appended will but serve to illustrate the character and results of these operations."

Then follow a variety of cases, which we regret our space will not allow us to insert.[20]

THE THIRD ANGLE: THE INVESTIGATIVE JOURNALIST

A report from another source confirms the dire picture of Dudley Street sketched in the reports of the City Mission. In 1873 the investigative journalist, James Greenwood, undertook to investigate the effectiveness of the Metropolis Local Management Act of 1855 in dealing with the revelation a year earlier that "no less than a hundred and seventy of the notorious St. Giles's cellars were still in use as human habitations, and that, after the manner of rats and other burrowing animals, as many families, consisting of mother, father, and a more or less numerous swarm of big and little children, passed their lives in these dismal holes under the houses, working, eating, drinking, and sleeping all in the damp and dirt and dark."[21] Having read a newspaper report by the Medical Officer of Health, that "to his knowledge, not a single underground room in the district is now illegally occupied," he determined to investigate for himself. The result is a remarkable description of Dudley Street, which had changed very little since the time that Oppenheimer had visited it about a decade before:

> It was about seven o'clock, and the gas was alight—the gas and the oil and the paraffin and the naphtha. St. Giles's of 1873 is pretty much what it was a quarter of a century ago. A big brewery and three or four new streets have shorn its skirts somewhat, but it is heartwhole still, and as dirty and draggletailed as ever. The only "enlightenment" that modern customs and usages have brought it appears is in the increased brilliancy of its public houses, which are especially rich in plate-glass and gas glitter. There are the same ragged women, some with babies in their arms—some mere girls—and some with backs bent with age; and there are, as of old, the groups of lanky, ill-dressed youth, with a sharp look-out from under the peaks of their caps; the same knots of hulking men of mature age, too lazy even to support with their fingers the short pipe which hangs all aslant from their mouths, while their hands are plunged wrist-deep in the pockets of their trousers. The stalls are the same, so are the shops, the awful little dens—and there are scores of them—inside and out of which are exposed for sale scraps of household furniture, which, by a jocular fiction of the "trade," is termed "second-hand," although it must be twenty-second hand at the very least, and bedding, mattresses, and beds, and bolsters and pillows, the sickening complexion of which should be sufficient warrant for a sanitary inspector to seize them at once and consign them without delay to the flames.
>
> I purposely fixed on the Dudley-street quarter of the St. Giles's district, because it was within my recollection that, in the disgraceful old times, the dwellers in cellars mustered very strong there. There used to be scarcely a house in the front of which there was not a hole in the pavement and a ladder by which the underground lodgers used to descend to their lairs. Used to! why there they were now! I could scarcely believe the evidence of my eyes. I had

cut the comforting paragraph from the newspaper, and at that moment had it in my pocket. By the light of a street lamp I took it therefrom and once more perused it. No, there was no mistake-on my part, that is to say. There it stood in fair print. "The medical officer of health for the district of St. Giles now reports that, to his knowledge, not a single underground room in the district is now illegally occupied." And there, from where I stood, I glanced into Dudley-street, and left and right, within thirty yards, I could see the open mouths of several cellars luridly lit by the fire and candlelight below. As though to put the matter beyond a doubt, at that moment there slowly emerged from the jaws of the nearest gulf a male lodger with a pair of deplorably ragged trousers slouched about his legs, and wearing a shirt horribly dirty and so full of rents that his hairy chest and shoulders were almost bare. His face was dirty, too, and sickly white, and to prevent his lank black hair from falling over his eyes—which blinked and winked as do those of a miner who comes up in the cage after many hours' labour in the gloomy pit—he had encircling his head a fillet of cobler's "waxed end." With his dangling shirt-sleeve he administered a refreshing wipe to his face and throat, and seated himself at the edge of his hole, with the evident intention of enjoying a few mouthfuls of the comparatively pure air of Dudley-street.

So emphatic a contradiction of my newspaper paragraph demanded further investigation. I crossed the road, and, as an excuse for lingering long enough at the mouth of the cellar to obtain a peep at the interior, made inquiry of the man as to the place of abode of an imaginary tailor.

"It can't be in Dudley-street, I should think," he replied, "there ain't no tailors here that I knows of; we are nearly all translators."

This was startling. Was it possible that individuals whose pursuits were literary could be brought so low as this?

"Are *you* a translator?" I asked him.

"Ah!" he replied, "anybody might know that with arf a hi in his head;" and as he spoke he jerked with his thumb in the direction of the cellar's depths. My eyes followed the movement, and presently in the steamy haze were enabled to make out a cobbler's seat in the midst of a heap—a couple of bushel, at least—of old boots and shoes, apparently in the last stages of mildew and decay.

"There's what I translates," explained the ragged cobbler, with a grin that showed how neatly the stem of his short clay pipe fitted into the hollow it had worn for itself in the side teeth of his upper and lower jaw; "I translates 'em into sound uns."

"Is it good pay?" I ventured.

"It's starvegut pay," growled the poor translator, most unpleasantly scratching himself; "it ain't taturs and salt hardly for a cove's wife and kids."

"Especially with rents so high!" I remarked.

"Well you may say it, mister," he replied, ruefully; "fancy! four bob [shillings] a week for that!" and once again, with a backward movement of his thumb, he indicated the underground den.

The excavations under the ancient houses of Dudley Street possess no windows at all, and the only way in which light and ventilation can be conveyed to the wretched inhabitants is through a hole in the pavement—a narrow opening, no larger than might be made by removing an ordinary paving-stone.

Leading down into the cellar is a ladder or a flight of wooden steps protected by a handrail. The roof of the cellar is level with the common roadway, and its floor must be several feet below the sewage and gas pipes. A wooden flap is hinged by the side of the gap at the head of the ladder, and is, I imagine closed at night time, and when the weather is unendurably inclement; though how, at such times, the benighted lodgers contrive to breathe is a mystery.

"D'ye hear?" exclaimed the translator, calling down to his wife; "there's the doctor goin' to see Mother Simmons's gal agin."

"Ah! poor thing," came up the hoarse though sympathetic response of the translator's wife; "she'll snuff it, you may depend."

By which I believe the good soul—a mother herself—meant that it was her belief that the existence of the girl Simmons would shortly be extinguished. But just imagine any one man, woman, or child lying ill abed in such a pestiferous, dingy den! Should the bedstead happen to stand at a far corner of the cellar, the doctor, even though it were noon in sultry summertime, would be compelled to examine his patient by candlelight. And the minister would have to read the dying words of blessed consolation by the flickering tallow flame, which would afterwards show a light for the undertaker with his measuring tape. But how about the coffin? It is not difficult to slide an empty box down a ladder. But a burdened box? To bring it to the surface as a shoulder-load in the ordinary way would, under the circumstances, be impossible; there could be nothing for it but to haul it up with a rope, tearful mourners clambering up in the wake and lending a steadying hand.

As I turned away from the hole in which the translator and his family resided, my impression was that the medical officer of health for the district of St. Giles had made a mistake. He had said that there was now not one of the ancient cellars improperly occupied. Here, without doubt, was one. Were there others? Were there! At every step I took in dark Dudley Street I grew more and more amazed. Surely the medical officer of health for the district of St. Giles must have been shamefully imposed on. Here was another inhabited cellar of precisely the same pattern as that already described, and next door another, and again next door still another, this time with half-a-dozen nearly nude and hideously dirty children wriggling up and down the ladder, and larking in and out of the cellar darkness below, like rabbits in a warren. More inhabited cellars on the right hand side, on the left hand side—sometimes two and three together, sometimes with half-a-dozen houses between. From one end to the other of Dudley Street, which be it borne in mind, is but a small portion of the district of St. Giles, I counted thirty of these underground dens, all alive with human life. Besides these there were eight others, which though inhabited, could scarcely be said to be lively. In these a solitary cobbler toiled, the flames of his tallow candle disclosing him deep down in the dingy hole, hammering and stitching with desperate energy in the midst of heaps of mildewed wreckage of souls and upper leathers. In these eight instances I could not see any one down in the cellars but the cobblers themselves though for that matter there was so little light that there may have been in each case a wife and a large family of children stowed away in the background. But, as regards the other thirty instances, they made no secret of their existence as human dwelling-places. There they were, with their mouths open, gaping on the highway, and there was nothing to prevent the passer-by from looking down their dingy throats. There were the fires in the places, and the pots and kettles on the fires, and there were the mothers, and there were the babies, the elder children hauling refractory youngsters down the ladder, at the same time threatening them in forcible language with what they would "ketch" if they didn't "come indoors and go to bed." It may perhaps be objected that the words used in the report were that no underground cellar was now "illegally" occupied, and that by illegal occupation was meant the using of the said cellars as sleeping rooms. I am bound to confess that I am not in a position to prove incontestably that the law is outraged to this extent. I can declare that in two cases I caught sight of the legs of a bedstead, festooned with a ragged bed-quilt; but, for all that I can show convincingly to the contrary, the bedstead might in each case have been the family dining-table, and the ragged quilt the tablecloth. At the same time it strikes me as being in the last degree improbable that these wretched ill-paid patchers of old boots rent other apartments besides that in which, all day long and far into the evening, they reside, and work, and take their meals, and that at a certain hour of the night they bundle up the ladder, and into the street, with their sleepy children, and proceed to a dormitory,

> the healthfulness of which is officially certified. Maybe it is taken for granted that because everything in the shape of sleeping convenience is absent from a cellar, the inhabitants by day do not pass the night there. This, however, is a view of the matter scarcely likely to be taken by the authorities of a district hundreds of the population of which sleep in their rags and on the bare boards as many nights in the year as they are not more decently lodged in prison or the casual ward of a workhouse. Besides, if it comes to that, what is gained to public decency and public health by drawing the line, as it would seem the officials of St. Giles's now draw it, and by which it is declared legal and unobjectionable for human beings to herd from early morning till late at night in dungeon damp and darkness, breathing foul air and breeding fever and all manner of disease, provided they turn out and go somewhere else to pass the hours between midnight and daybreak. It is no less marvellous than monstrous that such an appalling condition of things should have been permitted to exist so long, especially when, as is evident, the sanitary authorities have long had the matter in hand. I did not pursue my investigation beyond Dudley Street, but it is fair to assume that in the surrounding vile courts and alleys—Dudley Street is a broad and busy thoroughfare—the evil is just as prevalent. I must be permitted to say in conclusion that the picture here given is not a bit overdrawn or exaggerated. There, to-day as yesterday, are to be seen in Dudley Street, Seven Dials, the deep black cellars, reached through a gap in the pavement, and by means of a steep ladder, and in each, at a greater depth in the earth than the sewers and the nests of the sewer rats, families of human beings—fathers, mothers, and little children—live and eat and drink, and make themselves at home.[22]

Greenwood's description is that of an astute observer, but not of one who lived or worked in the rookeries. As Oppenheimer walked each day from his home on Bedford Square, several streets to the north of the St. Giles rookery, he must have dreaded what new scenes of destitution were awaiting him on his rounds, what illnesses he might encounter (and possibly contract), and the physical and verbal challenges he might meet with.

THE FOURTH ANGLE: DORÉ AND JERROLD—THE ILLUSTRATOR AND THE SOCIAL COMMENTATOR

What Oppenheimer actually saw is probably best conveyed by Gustave Doré, whose sketches of London have become symbols of Victorian culture.

In 1872 *London: A Pilgrimage* appeared, presenting Victorians with 180 images of the capital of the empire; Doré's work has been called "one of the century's most extraordinary works of art—a meticulous and lurid record of late Victorian London."[23] The work was criticized by contemporaries for focusing too heavily on the darker sides of London, particularly its poverty. Three of his sketches from the work are particularly striking. The first is his "Over London by Rail" which brings into focus "a vision of grubby back-to-back housing, with tiny backyards in which washing hanging out to dry is besmirched by the soot of the trains on the giant viaduct."[24]

16. GUSTAV DORÉ, "OVER LONDON BY RAIL"

The image actually represents a somewhat more up-scale area than that of Dudley Street, with its broken-down buildings and ramshackle tenements. Doré had been led through the slums by Blanchard Jerrold, editor of the mass-circulation *Lloyd's Weekly Newspaper,* whose colourful text was placed alongside Doré's sketches and helped to illumine Doré's drawings.

The second image that is frequently cited is his drawing of a Scripture Reader in a night refuge, which Jerrold informs us was the Cow Cross mission refuge run by Mr. Catlin. This is the sort of work that Oppenheimer would have done at the women's refuge at 75 Dudley Street.

17. GUSTAV DORÉ'S "SCRIPTURE READER"

18. GUSTAV DORÉ, "DUDLEY STREET"

This image of Dudley Street is one of Doré's most famous, for it captures so well the desperation and grinding poverty, providing the combination of "eyewitness observation and meticulous execution" that give his pictures such a troubling effect. As Paxton commented: "These are real people, and yet their weary, woebegone faces become groteseques. You can feel the gloom and the gaslight, hear the mass of hungry children, see the sullen glares of the adults and almost smell the filth. There is the man who collects clothes cast off by the wealthy, accompanied by his tribe of feral children."[25] Doré sought to sketch from the shadows, preferring to remain as anonymous as possible.

THE FIFTH ANGLE: OPPENHEIMER'S ENCOUNTERS WITH DESTITUTION AND HIS RESPONSES

The final angle is provided by Oppenheimer, in his accounts of the destitution he encountered. The following seven excerpts are taken chronologically from Oppenheimer's journal and bring home the utter poverty he met with, confirming the account that Greenwood was to pen a decade later. Several entries indicate what resources he was able to call upon to help these people, or which parish authorities would be able to assist them:

4 September 1861
19 Dudley Street

A sad case.

19 Top front. An Irish family extremely poor, no Scriptures, attend occasionally St Patrick[']s chapel their children 5 in number are not going to school at all, for they are all but nacked [sic], two of them were running about the room with nothing about them but an old rags [sic] in a shape of a shirt; "I wish we were all dead["], said the mother, ["]I don't care we could not be worse of[f] than we are now, I don't believe that there is a God at all, if there is He don't care much for us, I know; Maybe we have not tried him, but I don't think it would be any use, I wish he would send us a loaf of Bread now.["]

11 September 1861
49 Dudley Street

back attic; Another Lee, but no relation to the above [James Lee], has four children ill, the poor little creatures are laying on the floor, there being no bed in the room, they seem more in want of food than aught else, the father having no work they are all but starving. Read the word & explained it; & promised to recommend their case to the proper quarters.

12 September 1861
52 Dudley Street

Poverty

Thursday 12
52. 1st back. Called upon Mrs I. Lee, who was glad to see me & was permitted to deliver my message; the poor woman is near [?] confinement & being in extreme poverty, I promised to intercede for her to get the loan of a box of Linen from the church; endeavoured to impress upon her the duty & priviledge of prayer.

11 October 1861
49 Dudley Street

A sad case.

49 Kitchen. A woman whose husband has deserted & left her with 5 little children in the most distressing circumstances, she expecting shortly to be confined & there is not a particle of furniture & anything else in the place; After I had spoken to her of the merciful & sympathising Saviour & endeavoured to impress upon her to go to him &.c. I advised her to go into the Union wh[ich] she promised to do so.

23 October 1861
83 Dudley Street

Temporal & spiritual destitution.

83 2nd back. An elderly man refused me admittance at first, but after a few minutes conversation I succeeded to enter his room where I was astonished to find 4 children in a perfect state of nudity, the eldest 7 & the youngest not quite 2 years old; not a particle of furniture or bedding is in the room & the windows being shut the smell is most offensive; after inquiry I learned that the children don't belong to him but to another family with whom the old man is living, both parents go out in the morning & come home at night what they do, he said he did not know. I spoke to the old man about his soul but I might just as well have spoken to the very wall, I could not get a single sentence out of him, besides "Yes" or "no". Left a tract.

14 January 1862
22 Dudley Street

22 2nd back; found a poor woman whose husband has deserted her in a most distressing condition, two of her children are ill & she has not been able to get any work for some time; more Complete destitution I hardly ever saw, the poor children were crying for bread, the want of which I believe to be the cause of their illness; for they look half starved. I endeavoured to impress upon the poor woman "the one thing needful" above all others, she listened attentively & cried very much when I offered up a prayer. I urged upon her to go with her poor children in the workhouse & I think I shall succeed.

12 February 1862
40 Dudley Street

Wednesday 12.
40. 2nd back; An Irish family in great distress; the husband, a cobbler, told me he had not broken his fast all day; (being 12 o clock) his children are out seeing where they can get something to eat;—the poor fellow seemed really to be half starved; whether or no it is a genuine case I cannot say, for it is the first time I saw them, but certain it is that there is extreme poverty.
I promised to apply for him to the relieving officer of the Parish & at the same endeavoured to impress upon the poor man the urgent necessity of going to Jesus, the friend & Saviour of the poor; read and explained a portion of the word, left a tract & promised to call again.

Oppenheimer's response to the extreme destitution that he encountered was two-fold. On the one hand, he offered advice and practical aid, promising to connect them with the "relieving officer of the Parish," interceding for them with "the proper authorities," urging some to avail themselves of the Poor Law Union and its Work House, obtaining the loan of a box of linens from the church. On the other, he also urged them "the urgent necessity of going to Jesus, the friend & Saviour of the poor," and of approaching "the merciful & sympathising Saviour."

THE ADMINISTRATIVE RESPONSE: SLUM CLEARANCES

The most popular solution to the problem of the slums was "slum clearances"—the wholesale destruction of an area and its subsequent reconstruction. Urban renewal this was not. Some of the worst accommodation was destroyed in the process, but this only increased densification. In 1850 Thomas Beames had warned, "The conclusion is obvious: if Rookeries are pulled down, you must build habitable dwellings for the population that you have displaced, otherwise, you will not merely have typhus, but plague; some fearful pestilence worse than cholera or Irish fever, which will rage, as the periodical miasmata of other times were wont to do, numbering its victims by tens of thousands!"[26] Beames's warning came on the heels of just such a clearance. Between 1842 and 1847, New Oxford Street (about 100 yards north of Dudley Street) was created in order both to improve communication between the West-end and the City and to obliterate the Church Lane rookery, one of the more notorious slums in London. The impact was that "the main concentration of paupers shifted away from Church Lane and into the streets and courts leading off Seven Dials." As Professor David Green has observed, "Far from eradicating the problem of poverty, street improvements merely forced the poor to shift their immediate area of residence and if anything helped to worsen the conditions with which they had to contend."[27] The uprooted poor simply moved elsewhere in the parish of St. Giles, thus driving up rents and further enriching the anonymous and absent slum landlords who collected their rents through middle-men, agents who acted on their behalf to garner the increased revenue. As will be seen, moving within the parish was the only realistic option for the poor because of the way the Poor Law of 1832 operated.

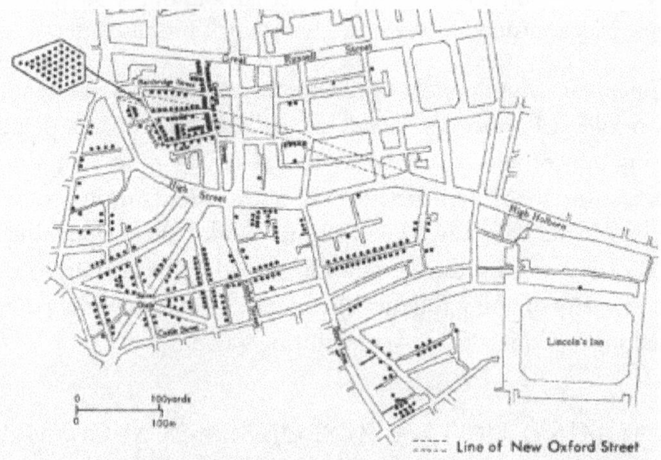

Source: St. Giles and St. Georges Directors of the Poor, settlement and examination books, 1840 – 49. [1 in 20 sample]

19. DISTRIBUTION OF PAUPERS IN ST. GILES 1840–9 (ABOVE) COMPARED TO DISTRIBUTION 1850–9 AFTER CREATION OF NEW OXFORD STREET
SOURCE: DAVID R. GREEN, "PEOPLE OF THE ROOKERY", PP. 39–40.

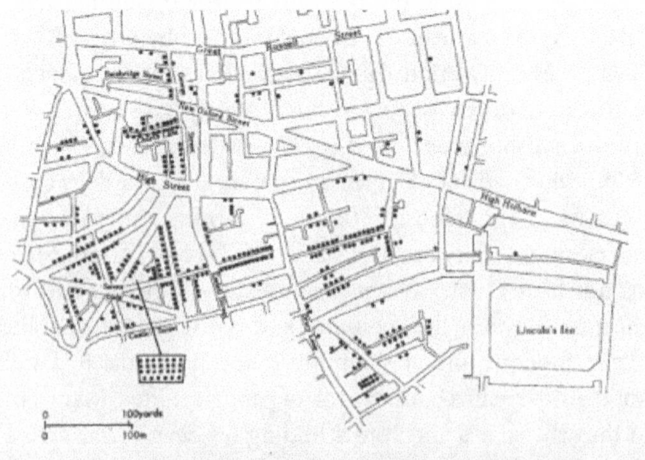

Source: St. Giles and St. Georges Directors of the Poor, settlement and examination books, 1850 – 59 [1 in 20 sample]

20. MAP OF ST. GILES, DUDLEY STREET AND SEVEN DIALS

THE PEOPLE

The great majority of the people approached by agents like Oppenheimer were women, as they were far more likely to be at home during the hours of the agents' visiting. It would appear from the testimony of the agents that they often encountered opposition when first entering a new district, especially from "infidels and socialists," but that quite quickly they were accepted as a standard feature of slum life in Victorian London. The fact that they were sometimes regarded as intrusive reflects the treatment received by government officials later in the nineteenth century, when they attempted to enter the slums to effect legislation designed to improve the conditions of the poor. In this respect, health inspectors, truant officers and evangelical lay agents like Oppenheimer often received similar receptions.

THE FUNCTIONING OF THE POOR LAW AND THE ROLE OF SETTLEMENT RECORDS

In 1832 the British "Poor Law" was revised. It was one of the most controversial pieces of legislation in the nineteenth century and bitterly resented by the poor, who found its operation harsh and demeaning. The system was based upon the traditional Anglican parish system, as the state church from the middle ages had been the primary social agency. Under the new provisions, individuals who could prove that they had lived continuously for four years (this was reduced to three in the early 1850s) in a specific parish could apply for relief from the parish poor law board, if their need was acute. The Poor Laws were intended to provide relief for the most destitute of British society and to act as a rudimentary social safety net, preventing the poorest of the poor from starving. Everyone in the rookeries knew that if they fell into desperate straits, they had the right to minimal support to keep the wolf from the door. Urban parishes each had a poor law board that determined eligibility, but individuals and families had to meet a three-year minimum residency requirement—otherwise, they would have to return to the previous parish where they had lived and where they would qualify. Those who were eligible were entitled to work in the "poor house," where food, clothing and lodging would be provided. It was this requirement to perform menial work that was so deeply resented by those receiving relief, and the social humiliation attached to such relief was acute.

The English poor (less so the Irish) often regarded this as a fate worse than death; the social stigma associated with the Poor House undoubtedly kept some away. If destitution struck before three years, local officials could direct applicants to apply to the parish where they had previously lived. Sometimes desperate people who could not establish residency were shunted from one set of parish officials to another; some died of starvation on London's streets in the process. Thus the British class system even pervaded the rookeries where amongst the desperately poor there were gradations of social respectability. One writer has characterized this as "the aristocracy of straw": the desperately poor could not afford straw to sleep on; their social betters could, hence their superiors were distinguished by the fact that they slept on straw. Even cellars and sections of the low crawl spaces under buildings were rented out to the desperately poor. But to many such an existence was preferable to the workhouse.

21. "THE ROOKERY, ST. GILES'S"
THOMAS MILLER, *PICTURESQUE SKETCHES OF LONDON,* 1852

Those whom Oppenheimer visited would all have been anxious to prove that they had been resident in the parish of St. Giles' for three years. The legal stipulation that one had to be resident in the same parish for three years meant that although the poor were clearly very mobile—something that Oppenheimer and other city missionaries often comment on—they were usually mobile only within the same parish. Therefore the slum clearances involved in the building of New Oxford Street necessitated that those displaced find alternate accommodation elsewhere in the parish; otherwise, they would lose their entitlement to poor law relief. This created huge pressure on the housing of the poor and meant that overcrowding was inevitable in such circumstances.

The Poor Law Board kept "settlement records" related to those residing within the parish who had applied for relief. Being able to prove residence was enormously important to the poor in order to be eligible for relief. The records of those who applied for relief are a great asset to historians tasked with trying to recreate the conditions of the poor. Here is a sample entry from 1862:

> Margaret Sullivan, examined after her admission to the workhouse on 15 July 1861. Aged 81, born in Bantry, Ireland but living in 4 Neals Yard for the period 1856 to 1861. Prior to that had lived at Marr's Building from 1853 to 1856; arrived in London c. 1851. Had lived with her son in law who was in the country looking for work. Applied for relief on account of old age.

In the period between 1861 and 1862 there were between 400 and 600 paupers in the St. Giles' parish who applied for relief, the very sort of people whom Oppenheimer encountered on his daily rounds in Dudley Street.

CHARACTERISTICS OF THE FIELD'S SOIL: ATTITUDES TO RELIGION AMONG THE POOR

In the early years of the London City Mission, at least until the early 1850s, what struck the workers most was the overwhelming degree of ignorance of the basic tenets of Christianity, in what was regarded by many Protestants as the centre of Christendom. The following account from a city missionary writing in 1852 puts it well:

> Missionaries who have just entered the Mission, and who have been sent to visit with me, have repeatedly been astonished. Visiting a sick man [an illiterate chimney sweep] with one new Missionary, I requested him to read and instruct him, which he did, detailing to him our fallen condition, our need of salvation, and the redemption purchased for us, in a very correct manner, and then reading a portion of a chapter in the Gospels in proof of what he had said, he replied "Certainly, sir;" or, "in course, sir." My companion appeared pleased with the man's attention to instruction, and I thought it time to undeceive him. "Mr. —," I said, "My friend has been taking much pains to instruct you, and now I will ask you a few questions. Do you know who Jesus Christ was?" "Well, no," said he, after a pause, "I should say that's werry hard to tell." "Do you know whether He was St. John's brother?" "No, that I don't." "Can you tell me who the Trinity are?" "No, sir." "Are you a sinner?" "Oh, certainly, sir, we are all sinners." —A pause. "Have you ever done anything wrong?" "Why no, I don't consider as I ever did." "Did you never commit sin?" "Why, no, I don't consider as ever I did." "But do you think you're a sinner?"

"Oh, certainly, sir, we're all sinners." "What is a sinner?" "Well, I'm *blest* if I know rightly; I never had no head-piece."[28]

Even among those who had had some contact with churches, many persons' conception of Christianity was mingled with superstition or a vague belief that religious observances would bring "luck" to the participants. Lay agents were surprised to find some of the poor attributing almost magical powers to the sacrament of baptism, such as the woman who declared to a city missionary "that before her child was christened it was very sickly, but that through being baptized it had throve amazingly." Another mother explained that she had had her baby baptized because it was her understanding "that unless a child is christened, it cannot go to heaven."[29] Such persistence in maintaining sacramental rites of passage such as christening and church weddings has long interested historians. At the same time, it has often frustrated clergy who have realized that "in the popular mind the Christian sacraments were associated with 'luck' more than with anything resembling Christian devotion."[30] That the city missionaries heard these views expressed by the mothers rather than by the fathers bears out Jeffrey Cox's view that "Women were almost always responsible for a family's practice of these rites of passage, which were part of an attempt to maintain a minimal level of respectability for the family."[31] Attitudes toward religious observances such as prayer were also of interest to lay agents such as Oppenheimer, as they were very concerned to encourage families to maintain daily family prayers. Among the very poor and illiterate, R.W. Vanderkiste found that in general children in his district were taught no prayers, although a few parents ventured to say to him: "Oh! I teach them the 'Our Father' and 'Matthew, Mark, Luke and John.'" The first prayer alluded to is of course the Lord's Prayer—the last is a Romish doggrel for saintly intercession—"Matthew, Mark, Luke, and John, Bless the bed that I lay on."[32] Unbeknownst to the city missionary, the latter prayer, the so-called "White Paternoster," has a long history in English folklore.[33]

Ignorance of basic Christian doctrine often went hand in hand with a second feature of popular attitudes, a strong anticlericalism that the lay agents encountered. The thoughts of one "infidel" on the subject fairly adequately represent the views of many of his peers: This religious business was "the parson's trade, just the same as painting's ours, only there's no work attached to it, and the pay's a bloody sight better than ours is."[34] The lay agents constantly emphasized the view that their work was important in overcoming this pervasive sentiment. Evangelical clergymen tended to argue that lay agency was necessary to overcome popular hostility, if the poor were ever to be evangelized. One cleric testified to a House of Lords committee in 1858, which was investigating religious conditions among the poor, that the lay agents were most effective in "breaking up the hard ground" and thereby prepared the way for the clergy to minister.[35] It is important to recall that in Victorian England, especially in rural villages, Anglican clergy occupied an important position in the social landscape. Even in larger towns, the Anglican vicar was closely associated with the social elite and enjoyed considerable influence and prestige. This prestige was related to a host of factors: They exercised real power through their connections, offering references for their parishioners for jobs and access to hospitals, as distributors of charity and relief, as advice-givers, as those who would "put in a good word" for those they favoured. The Anglican clergy were often the best-educated persons in their parishes; in the period from 1834–1843, we know that 89 per cent of the Anglican clergy were university graduates, almost all being graduates of Oxford or Cambridge. Although the proportion of non-graduates grew to about 35 per cent by the early twentieth century, an Oxbridge education defined the majority of Anglican clergy through to 1914. Throughout the period it was rare for a non-university graduate to serve in London. An Oxbridge education automatically set a man apart as a "gentleman," and in spite of valiant efforts by many clergy to identify with the poor through their visiting, personal care, and at times amazing efforts at self-sacrifice, it was difficult to throw off the image of one who was more comfortable with the social elite than with the average parishioner.[36]

A third aspect of popular religious attitudes is the strong identification of class with religious indifference. Although many Victorians feared that churches were losing their hold on the lower classes, it is doubtful they had any such grip in the first place. Organized religion was often seen by many of the poor, especially by the very poor, as the preserve of those of a different social rank—although this may have been less the case with poor Catholics. In Victorian England, at least on the Protestant side of things, churchgoing rose with social status. Hugh McLeod has observed, "nonconformity often represented a middle-class rejection of the politics and cultural values of the gentry, working men frequently signaled their rejection of both upper class [Anglican] and middle class [Nonconformist] values by Secularism or by simple indifference."[37] That Nonconformity had relatively little appeal in the slums of London is borne out by the testimony of one of the witnesses before the above-mentioned House of

Lords Committee, who was asked if the Dissenters had any appeal in his neighbourhood: "They do among a peculiar class of people; not among the very poor, but among the mechanics, and those who may be made elders, and who consider themselves as part of the establishment of the meeting-house, for that is a great attraction."[38] A Bethnal Green clergyman supported this view when asked a similar question, reasoning that in his neighbourhood, the people were "too poor to be dissenters; they are too poor to support adequately a minister."[39]

The general picture that emerges of popular attitudes among the poor toward religion is one shaped by ignorance, anticlericalism and class resentment. The latter two factors are entirely understandable. The established church had for centuries been the preserve of the middle and upper classes who supported it through their annual rental of family pews and embraced it as a bulwark of the status quo even if they had little interest in its doctrines. It provided important rites of passage: baptism, confirmation and funeral rites, occasions that were at once social and religious. Displays of deference by the poor to their superiors were expected in Anglican churches; in villages with a resident squire, the congregation was expected to rise as he entered to acknowledge his station in the community. It was often complained in the nineteenth century that the poor were made to feel distinctly unwelcome in Anglican churches—often treated condescendingly by the verger who ushered them to the rough benches provided for them at the back of the church where their poverty would not be on display.[40] All of these factors had angered evangelicals such as Wesley who had dared to defy church protocol and preach the gospel in the fields, ignoring ecclesiastical decorum. Responses to the evangelicals' evangelistic efforts displayed a great variety. Undoubtedly there was some hostility, although this seems to have been mitigated by the low social status of the workers themselves. At the same time, there was some positive response, much of which probably did not manifest itself in church attendance. Popular antipathy to church attendance was strong and marked; many who might attend an agent's meeting in his district would have been too embarrassed to ever enter a church.

ASSESSING THEIR IMPACT

What then can be said about the evangelicals' impact on such resistant soil among the poor? Undoubtedly the mission made some contribution to the improvement of social order in the slums, especially in encouraging people to see to the education of their children. Throughout the journal,

Oppenheimer frequently reports efforts to persuade parents to send their children to one of the free Sunday schools so that they might learn to read and write.

In 1849, the Annual Report of the *Scripture Readers' Association* (an evangelical Anglican society that functioned alongside the London City Mission in London) reported that:

> Unanimous evidence is given by readers whose districts have been most notorious for open profligacy and irreligion, that vice has become less bold and obtrusive. The presence of a reader in a court where he had only made one previous round of visits, has been the signal for quiet and decorum. The open drunkenness and rioting which formerly filled the streets on the Sabbath-day has been in some degree suppressed.[41]

This view was strongly supported by the LCM, which asserted that "there is no question that, from the constant visitation of a reader or a missionary, very much that is outwardly evil is prevented, even when not further and more important result follows."[42] Even the popular press acknowledged the omnipresent city missionary as a standard feature of slum life and commended the Christian concern thus evidenced. Reporting on Clerkenwell, the *Illustrated London News* noted that it "is the locality of dirt and ignorance, and vice—the recesses whereof are known but to the disguised policeman, as he gropes his way up rickety [sic] staircases towards the tracked housebreaker's den or the poor, shabby gentell City Missionary, as he kneels at midnight by the foul straw of some convulsed and dying outcast."[43]

At the same time, however, their impact seems to have been much more limited than the evangelicals had hoped. The number of conversions never was great, although this was not the LCM's only indicator of its progress. Each year the mission produced a summary of its accomplishments, a rather dry litany for the hearing of its annual meetings, but one that indicates some of its more specific goals. The following example is taken from the 1855 Annual Report, when the Mission had 328 city missionaries:

> The number of visits paid by the missionaries last year was 1,484,563, which is an increase of 45,245; the number of religious tracts distributed was 2,092,854, which is an increase of 161,149; the number of books lent was 50,458, which is an increase of 13,647; the number of readings of the Scriptures in visitation was 452,851, which is an increase of 21,205; the number of Bibles distributed was 8,155, which is an increase of 1,427; and the number of meetings held for prayer and exposition of the Scriptures was 25,318, which is an increase of 2,283.

Then the report turned to statistics dealing with individuals:

> The number of fallen women persuaded to enter asylums, or to return to their homes, which in 1853, 279, in 1854, was 376, and last year the number of additional cases amounted to 411. The number of drunkards reclaimed last year were 656, or 87 more than in the previous year. 479 persons living improperly together, were persuaded to marry, or 26 more than 1854. 363 families were induced to commence family prayer, which is an increase this year of 56. The number of persons admitted to the Lord's Supper by their respective ministers, as the fruit of the missionaries' labours, was last year exactly 7000, which is an increase of 24. 967 cases of decided reformation of life are also reported by the missionaries this year, or 179 more than in the year preceding. And the number of children sent to school has been 9,561, which shows an increase of 708.[44]

Such bare statistics, however, do not give a feel for what was happening at the local and personal level. Such an appreciation can only be gained by listening to the oral record of those directly involved. This is where Oppenheimer's journal is so helpful, especially because it has not been edited for publication. Rather, it records his daily musings on his work and on what he encountered by knocking on each door in the district.

Oppenheimer functioned then as a sort of cultural broker, mediating between the institutions of the national church and popular evangelicalism, seeking to bridge the chasm between the sober respectability of St. Giles'-in-the-Fields and the devotion of the poor widow freezing in her hovel in the St. Giles' rookery a few hundred yards away, with only her Bible to comfort her, only the Poor Law Relief Board to support her in her extremity and only the City Missionary to visit her in distress. Traditionally, this role in London parishes had been the responsibility of the curate; "the Protestant Poor were by London tradition still often assigned to the Curate, while the Vicar looked after the wealthy."[45] But by the 1850s, the overwhelming scale of urban destitution meant that even curates were inadequate to the task. Now the curate's traditional responsibilities were being taken up by London City Missioners and Scripture Readers. The hard soil of this field was now in the hands of workers who were of more humble social origins; breaking up the soil and sowing the seed had moved down the social scale. It is clear, however, that whatever their religious impact, it was workers like Oppenheimer who by their tending of their fields of labour best knew the daily life of London's desperately poor, playing an invaluable role in drawing the attention of the British public to the social problems of urban destitution.

Notes

[1] Thomas Beames, *The Rookeries of London: Past, Present and Prospective* (London: Thomas Bosworth, 1852), 2nd edition, p. 19.
[2] The twenty-first century "Monmouth Street" that bisects the Seven Dials today is not the same as the 19th century Monmouth Street. In the nineteenth century the northern end of Monmouth Street was Greater St. Andrew Street and the southern end was Little St. Andrew's Street.
[3] Charles Dickens, *Sketches by Boz* (London: Macrone, 1836), "Meditations in Monmouth-street," Chapter 6.
[4] Christopher Clark, *The Iron Kingdom: The Rise and Downfall of Prussia, 1600–1947* (Cambridge, MA: Harvard University Press, 2006), p. 454.
[5] *LCM Second Annual Report*, London, 1837, p. 2.
[6] *LCM Magazine* (Aug. 1841): 129.
[7] *LCM Minutes*, 25 Aug. 1845 and *LCM Magazine* (Aug. 1845): 170–85.
[8] See: Donald M. Lewis, "Evangelism, Social Concern and Social Control," in *Lighten their Darkness* (Westport, CT: Greenwood, 1985), pp. 151–79 and John Wolffe, ed., *Evangelical Faith and Public Zeal* (London: SPCK, 1995).
[9] *LCM Thirteenth Annual Report* in *LCM Magazine* (June 1848): 126.
[10] Sheridan Gilley, "Protestant London, No-Popery and the Irish Poor, 1830–1860," *Recrusant History*, Vol. 10, 1969–70, p. 219.
[11] Norris Pope, *Dickens and Charity* (London: Macmillan, 1978), p. 243–44.
[12] In particular Mayhew acknowledged the assistance of Richard Knight of the City Mission in his work. Henry Mayhew, *London Labour and the London Poor* (London: Woodfall and Son, 1851), p. iv.
[13] Norris Pope, *Dickens and Charity*, p. 70.
[14] Eileen Yeo and E. P. Thompson, *The Unknown Mayhew* (New York: Pantheon Books, 1971), p. 61.
[15] Mayhew, *op. cit.*, Vol, 1, p 318.
[16] Brian Harrison, "The Sunday Trading Riots of 1855," *The Historical Journal* 8, no. 2 (1965): 243.
[17] LCM Minutes, Aug. 26, 1835.
[18] On the LCM's efforts to arouse its middle-class constituency on the matter of common-lodging houses, see my account in *Lighten Their Darkness*, pp. 165–66.
[19] For a discussion of this theme see my *Lighten Their Darkness*, pp. 154–64.
[20] *LCM Mag.* (Dec. 1855): 283 ff.
[21] James Greenwood, *Low-Life Deeps and the Strange Fish to be Found There* (London: Chatto and Windus, 1876), p. 168.
[22] James Greenwood, *Low-Life Deeps*, pp. 169–75.
[23] Jeremy Paxton, *The Victorians: Britain Through the Paintings of the Age* (London: BBC Books, 2010), p. 93.

[24] Paxton, p. 97.
[25] Paxton, p. 98.
[26] Thomas Beames, *The Rookeries of London* 2nd edn. (London: Thomas Bosworth, 1852), p. 43.
[27] David R. Green, "People of the Rookery: A Pauper Community in Victorian London," Occasional Paper No. 26, London, University of London King's College, Department of Geography, June 1986, p. 38.
[28] R. W. Vanderkiste, *Note and Narratives of a Six Years' Mission, principally among the Dens of London* (London: Nisbet, 1852), pp. 36–38.
[29] Vanderkiste, *Narrative of a Six Years' Mission,* pp. 33–34.
[30] Jeffrey Cox, *English Churches in a Secular Society (*New York: Oxford University Press, 1982), p. 97.
[31] Cox, *English Churches,* p. 98.
[32] Vanderkise, *Narrative of a Six Years' Mission,* p. 34.
[33] For versions of this prayer see: W. J. Thoms, "Chaucer's night-spell," *Folk-Lore Record* 1 (1878), and W. D. Macray, "Lancashire & Chesire" 1 (1875–6). Cited by K. Thomas, *Religion and the Decline of Magic* (London: Weidenfeld and Nicholson, 1971), p. 181, n. 2.
[34] R. Tressell, *The Ragged Trousered Philanthropists* (London: Panther Books, 1965), p. 141. Cited by Hugh McLeo1d, "Class, Community and Region," *A sociological Yearbook of Religion in Britain,* vol 6, 1973, p. 61, n. 6.
[35] Testimony of William W. Champneys, *Parliamentary Papers, 1857–8, 9,* Deficiency of the Means of Spiritual Instruction," Select Committee, House of Lords: Report, p. 127.
[36] Hugh McLeod, "Class, Community and Region," pp. 14–19.
[37] Hugh McLeod, "Class, Community and Region," p. 35.
[38] Testimony of William Cadman, *Parliamentary Papers, 1857–8, 9,* Deficiency of the Means of Spiritual Instruction," Select Committee, House of Lords: Report, p. 13.
[39] The Reverend J. Colbourne, *Parliamentary Papers, 1857–8, 9,* Deficiency of the Means of Spiritual Instruction," Select Committee, House of Lords: Report, p. 13.
[40] See: Nigel Scotland, *Squires in the Slums: Squires and Missions in Late Victorian England* (London: Tauris and Co., 2007), p. 4.
[41] *Fifth Annual Report of the SRA,* Quoted in *LCM Magazine* (1850): 25.
[42] *Fifth Annual Report of the SRA,* Quoted in *LCM Magazine* (1850): 25.
[43] *Illustrated London News*, May 22, 1847. Cited by R. W. Vanderkiste, *Notes and Narratives,* p. 5.
[44] *LCM Magazine* (June 1855): 132.
[45] Sheridan Gilley, "Protestant London, No Popery, and the Irish Poor II (1850–1860," *Recrusant History* 11 (1971–72): p. 21.

Part 2

THE SOWER'S WORDS

4

The Journal of Joseph Oppenheimer

This chapter begins by reproducing the three pages at the back of the booklet which appear to be a summary statement drawn up by Oppenheimer in September 1861 for the Rev. Laudon Maud, the curate of St. Giles'-in-the-Fields, and his immediate supervisor. They break off in mid-sentence and the summary never seems to have been completed or the final page has been lost.

According to the London City Mission's hand list, Oppenheimer had been seriously ill the previous year, being granted on the 26th of January 1860 a three-month leave along with 20 pounds from the "Disabled fund" for salary replacement. In the year that Oppenheimer began his rounds, Bishop Robert Bickersteth testified before a House of Lords committee that during the five years (1851–6) he had served St. Giles'-in-the-Fields that nine or ten of his lay agents had suffered complete breakdowns in their health.[1] In 1856 three of the City Mission workers died in a single week; two from typhus and one from smallpox.[2]

Here are the three summary pages:

> Through the mercy of God I am again permitted to give a short statement of my proceeding[s] during another quarter; The quarter opened upon me with fever in my district which thanks be to God did not prove fatal except in 4 cases; I was myself laid aside from labour for 4 or 5 weeks from something like fever which settled in my loins & unfitted me to crofs my own room for 3 weeks but blefsed [sic] be God f[or]ever & I might say all other disees [sic] has vanished from my district & my health has not been so good with me for the Past two years;
>
> My accefs to the people of my district is very good except in a very few cases[.] There seems to be a kind of a thirst among the people for Christian visitation[.] Oh that the waters of life so freely dispenced [sic] though in great weaknefs [sic] may through the Spirit [s]pring up in many souls unto eternal life,
>
> There is much open sin amongst the people who come to sell

or "dolly" their undergarments for drink; these "Dolly shops" as they are called is the bane of my district[.] women of every kind[?] of questionable character come from all parts of London in order to sell or dolly things that Ponbrokers [sic] refuse[.] Much drunkennefs, desparation, & vice of all kinds is witnefsed [sic] every day but the sabbath of the Lord seems to me marked out as a Special season to work work [sic] all iniquity with greedynefs [sic] & madnefs, heastening [sic] them to judgement;

I continue to addrefs the inmates of the Work Woman[']s Home 75 Dudley S[t] though I cannot see that spiritual progrefs this quarter that I have reported in past quarters in this special field of labour yet I trust that a good work is going on in many; The most pleasing attention is given & thank[s] returned[.]

We have those who are Teachers in our Evangelical Church. The Church who bore the brunt of all the sharp arrows of Papacy in the time of its greates[t] power for evil[.] "Lord rise up that power & come amongst us[.] give not thin[e] herritage [sic] over unto the destroyer "who would place thy stately bark [sic] on seas of discord & rebellion, But to return to Mr. T. [?]

The account of his daily visitations

The pages are hand-numbered and indicated in bold italic below. The words in italics are written in the columns and draw attention to something that Oppenheimer considers important. Note that he writes "ss" as "fs."

1

Dudley Street. September 1861

Sunday visitation

Sunday 1
Visited for two hours & a half in my district to day, out of the regular course of my visitation, had some very useful and interesting conversations with working men whom I can't find at home any other day but Sunday, besides distributed tracts at the 5 Dials again, & have been permitted to say a few words to several to whom I offered these tract[s].

A Crowded Room of Irish Catholics

Monday 2

8 Top front-; found 9 persons in this room, men & women, all Irish, & all seem to be at home there, some of them knew my face, especially old M[rs] Sullivan who said "bless you, You Know we are not of your persuasion; we don't reads your tracts & we don't want nothing." After a few minutes conversation however, I was permitted to deliver my message & tell them of Jesus Christ as the only Mediator between God and men; several refused to accept tracts, but we parted good friends.

2

Dudley Street. September 1861

No Scriptures

8 1st back; Another Irish family in a most miserable condition, on account as they said, of having no army work to do, but every thing looked to me as if both were given to drink[.] "No, we have not got no Bible["]; said the woman, ["]we never trouble any church or chapel; we used to send those two girls to St. Patrick's School, but they have not got no cloth[e]s now, so they may as well stay at home &.c." Spoke to them of the one thing needful, but I might have as well spoken to the very stones, they said "Yes" & "No" to every thing I said.

Sunday trading

10 Shop. I had another conversation with M[r] — on the evil of Sunday trading, like all the rest - M[r] — endeavoured to excuse himself by saying "I would be too glad if I could give it up, but I can't, it's no use trying, if I would shut up on Sunday, I would either be obliged to starve, or go into the work house at once." Read several passages of Scripture & left a tract.

3

Dudley St. September 1861

I Know that my Redeemer Liveth

Tuesday 3
13 Top back. Called upon old Cook who said "Thank God I am again able to get out & to go to church, next Sunday if I am

spared, & intend to attend the Lord's Supper;" he is still a great sufferer, but when I alluded to it he said "O my dear Sir, what would have become of me if God had not visited me with this affliction. I would have died like a fool, for I did not know Christ before I was afflicted but I now thank God I can say "I know that my Redeemer lives.'" Read a portion of the word and offered a prayer.

hopeful case

14 Called upon Mr Leighton who told me that since I saw him last he has been reading the New Test[ament] I gave him, almost every evening when he came home from his work, and he has also been twice at St. Giles church at the Sunday evening services, & told me that he would go again next Sunday evening. Read & explained a portion of the word.

4

Dudley St. September 1861.

Domestic quarrel

15 Top back. Old Bonham was not in best possible humor when I entered his room, for he said he has had a quarrel with his old woman, who lost a six pence, but he would not believe that she lost it, but said she had spend [sic] it in a Public house, which is not at all unlikely; whilst I was talking to him, she came in, & they resumed their quarrel & se[e]ing I could not do any good, & left the room.

Visited and Called upon 6 more families in this house, was kindly received by all & permitted to deliver my message in each room, & to leave tracts.

A bigoted Rom[an] Cath[olic].

16 Kitchen; A very bigoted Irish Rom[an] Cath[olic] named Riley, told me to go to the Devil, or he would knock my brains out if I would not leave his room at once, but after a few minutes he got a little calmer, & amidst a great many interruptions, I was nevertheless permitted to warn him to flee from the wrath to come; refused a tract.

5

Dudley St. September 1861

Trust in Christ.

Wednesday 4
18 2nd back. Old M[rs] Carla is still very poorly, spoke to her of death & eternity when she said "I trust in Christ & I prays to him every day of my life; I know if I goes to heaven it's only for what Jesus has done for me. I am very poor you see but am thankful for ever so little, for I know I don't deserve nothing, I have got a bad heart, But I trust & pray to Jesus for I have nobody else to trust in; I read my Bible every day."

Indifference

Kitchen. Called upon Ann Barry, endeavoured to imprefs her with Divine truth but she is so talkative about the things of time, & so indifferent about the one thing needful, that nothing seems to make any impression upon her, read the word & gave her a solemn warning.

19 Top front. An Irish family extremely poor, no Scriptures, attend occasionally St Patrick[']s chapel

6

Dudley Street. September 1861.

A sad case.

their children 5 in number are not going to school at all, for they are all but nacked [sic], two of them were running about the room with nothing about them but an old rags [sic] in a shape of a shirt; "I wish we were all dead["], said the mother, ["]I don't care we could not be worse of[f] than we are now, I don't believe that there is a God at all, if there is He don't care much for us, I know; Maybe we have not tried him, but I don't think it would be any use, I wish he would send us a loaf of Bread now."

Agent rejected

1st back. Another low Irish family, the husband named Lever [?] was apparently the worse for liquor & when his wife opened the door & I went into the room & he used the most filthy language towards the poor woman for letting me in, & told me he did not want any preaching & if I did not go at once, he would be if he did not give me

7

Dudley Street. September 1861.

something I would not like. [I] [e]ndeavoured to pacify him, but he became very ex[c]ited, so that I thought it expedient to leave the room.

A distreſsing case of a poor widow. The Influence of bad company.

Thursday 5.
23 2nd back. M[rs] Baxter a poor widow woman was very much depressed, & upon my asking her what was the matter, she began to cry & said "that her boy, 14 years old, had a situation as a errand boy at a greengrocers in Tottenham Court Rd & used to be a very steady boy much beloved by his employer till of late when he formed a connection with another lad who induced him to frequent play houses &.c. he often did not come home all night & all her talking to him was of no avail, & last week his master found out that he appropriated small sums of money, he was given into custody & got three months imprisonment. "I have brought him up well["], the poor woman continued, & ["]send him to school & did the best I could to make him a good boy, but now

8

Dudley St. September 1861

I am disappointed, it will break my heart;" endeavoured to impress upon her to go to Jesus, to open her heart to him in prayer & ask him to restore to her her child & to make him a child of God &c. Read the word & offered up a prayer.

A bigoted Rom[an] Cath[olic].

Kitchen, M[c]Lerren, a bigoted Rom[an] Cath[olic] told me again that he was not of my persuasion; introduced the virgin Mary & the Holy Mother Church & c. but still I was permitted to deliver my message.

Trust in God's providence

25 Kitchen; poor M[rs] Oldham, was very glad to see me again & I am happy to say that amidst her extreme poverty, & her husband being in a state of consumption, the poor woman retains her trust & confidence in Him who ordered all things according to the counsel of His own will; "It's very hard for me["], she said, ["]but God knows best what is for our good. I pray to him & he gives me strength to bear my trial &c." Read the word & prayed.

9

Dudley Street September 1861.

Indifference

Friday 6
28 2nd back. Called upon M[rs] Terry who is still very indifferent to the things which are made for Peace. "Poor people can't do what they ought, my husband & I work hard, and don't taste a drop of drink from one week[']s end to another & we try to do our best to bring our children up well, they are all going to school; I know that all this won't save us, but there are plenty of people who go to church & all that-; but who are much worse than we are, we don't like to profess what we are not." Read & explained the 3rd chapter to the Rom[ans] & endeavoured to impress upon her the solemn truth "without holiness no man shall see the Lord."

29 Top front. Was kindly received by an Irish Cobbler, whom I saw before in another part of my district some six months ago, but since that he left my district & has now come back again; listened very attentively to the word read & explained & asked me to call again.

10

Dudley Street September 1861.

Saturday 7
Visited the sick & special cases in my district today, to most of these read the word, with some prayed & left tracts with all.

Sunday 8.
Visited for three hours today in my district, out of the regular

course on my visitation, besides distributed tracts at the 5 Dials and corner of Broad St.

The Trinity

Monday 9
34. Shop. Had another very interesting conversation with M[r] Benjamin (a Jew) the chief topic of which was the doctrine of the Trinity, which he said, was contrary to the Old Test[tament] Scriptures "We never read, he said, of three God's [sic] in the Old Test[ament] - a father & a Son & a Holy Ghost, but find it distinctly said, the Lord God is one God." I read to him several passages & proved to him from the very pafsage he quoted, that although it unquesti[on]bly true that it

11

Dudley St. Sept. 1861

The Trinity not confined to the New Test[tament]

afserts the Unity of the Godhead, yet the very term wh[ich] is used to denote that Unity, (אֱלֹהֵינוּ) being a plural noun, denotes a plurality of persons. And from several other O[l]d Test[ament] passages, I proved to him that the doctrine of the Trinity is not confined to the New Test[ament].
M[r] B. knows but very little Hebr[ew] & consequently said he could not argue in that way but as he was taught, so he would believe. We parted good friends & I left him one of Dr M[c]Caul's tracts on the Jewish subject "Can the Jew be saved."

The Christian Conflict

Top front. Called upon poor M[rs] Grove, spoke to her of the power of prayer & the promises of God in answer to believing prayer & c. "O, I do pray, she said, every day in my life, I asks God to pardon my sins & to bless my poor soul but Sir, I sometimes think that I am too bad that God should listen to my prayers & sometimes I can't pray at all." Read & explained an appropriate passage of Scripture & offered up a prayer. 1 John 1 Chapter.

12

Dudley Street. September 1861

35 Top front. Mrs Houghten [Hutton] was very glad to see me again, but am sorry to say is still very indifferent about "the one thing needful" read & explained a portion of Scripture, & left her with the solemn warning "prepare to meet thy God."

A sad case.

Tuesday 10.
40. Top back. A miserable looking old Irishman, in extreme poverty & almost in a state of nudity, said "I don't want no religious talking, don't care a farthing for no religion at all; Laul! never see it don't care no more for heaven or hell as I do for a cat." Endeavoured to impress upon him the certainty of a future judgment & the awful doom of the wicked, but with out success, he used the most filthy language & swore he would one of these days make away with his life, & would not be the least afraid of the consequences. "Need not call again, don't want your tract.[""]

13

Dudley Street September 1861.

Procrastination.

42. 2nd back. Called upon Mrs Macy, an Irish woman, her husband has deserted her some months ago & left her & 4 little children, in a most destressed state; the poor woman seems always to be very glad of my visits & attentive to what I read & speak, but she seems still to be undecided putting off the offer of salvation to a future day. Read & explained a portion of Scripture & offered up a prayer.

Hope in Christ

43. 2nd front. Called upon poor old Mrs Maycock, who is very poorly at present, but am glad to be able to say, she has fixed her hope upon the rock of ages, & is humbly submitting herself to the will of Him who loved her & gave Himself for her. It is encouraging indeed & I have derived many lessons by visiting this poor woman & hearing her (crossed out) express herself, of the hope within her. Read the 23 Psalm and offered up a prayer promising to call upon her again next Saturday.

14

Dudley Street. September 1861

The desecration of the Lord's day.

Wednesday 11
40 Shop. Had another conversation with the Mr Gates, on the sinful practice of Sunday trading, but like on many previous occasions, he perfectly agreed with me, or at least expressed himself to agree with me, but at the same time pleaded necefsity as an excuse to defy the commandment of his God; endeavoured to impress him with the utter fallacy of such an excuse, but seemingly he will persevere [with] his evil practice.

I may here remark that although it is without doubt a great temptation for many poor people in my district, because on the Lord's day they take very often more money than all the week put together, yet still, in the case of Gates, which will apply to many other[s], it is clearly <u>not necessity</u>; but an evil heart of unbelief is the root of the matter; I sincerely wish that that [sic] some means might be found by those in authority, to put a stop to such a desecration to the Lord's day.

15

Dudley Street September 1861.

Missionary encouragement

49. Top front. Young James Lee was very glad to see me again & told me that he regularly attended a place of worship since he saw me last, & read his Bible every day; I am happy to say, the young man, seems now to be very anxious regard[ing] the salvation of his soul & seems to take great delight in reading the word of God, and attending the sanctuary of the Lord; endeavoured to impress upon him the necessity of asking for the Holy Spirit of God, for the right understanding [of] the word of God, as well as for to lead him on in the right path; read the word & offered up a prayer.

Extreme poverty & illness.

back attic; Another Lee, but no relation to the above, has four children ill, the poor little creatures are laying on the floor, there being no bed in the room, they seem more in want of food than aught else, the father having no work they are all but starving. Read the word & explained it; & promised to recommend their case to the proper quarters.

16

Dudley St. September 1861

Poverty

Thursday 12
52. 1st back. Called upon M[rs] I. Lee, who was glad to see me & was permitted to deliver my message; the poor woman is near [?] confinement & being in extreme poverty, I promised to intercede for her to get the loan of a box of Linen from the church; endeavoured to impress upon her the duty & priviledge of prayer.
Visited and called upon 5 more families in this house & was permitted to deliver my message & leave a tract in each room.

Visit in a Hospital.

Went to the Victoria Park Hospital this afternoon to visit Sophia Canon, a poor girl from 81 Dudley St. who is in a decline; she was exceedingly glad to see me & I am happy to say, she is very happy & expressed her entire confidence in her Saviour for the salvation of her soul. - left her a few tracts & promised to see her again if God permit.

17

Dudley Street September 1861.

We take God by His word.

Friday 13
55. Top front. M[r] & M[rs] Woodall were very glad to see me & said that not withstanding their great poverty, they were perfectly content & fully assured that God would provide for their daily wants, the poor old man said "I will tell you Sir what we do, we take God by His word, He says that we should pray & ask Him every day for our daily bread, so we do Sir, we pray every morning & evening, & we get it in some shape or other. We put our trust in Christ & I know he will save us, He died for us & He is a friend of the poor however poor we are, if we believe in him & pray to Him he will save us, won't He? - Read & explained a portion of the word

& offered up a prayer.

1st front. Called upon M[r] Leader was kindly received & permitted to deliver message, both M[r] & M[rs] L. are always very attentive to what I say & read to them, but am sorry to say they are still very indifferent about the one thing needful.

18

Dudley Street. September 1861.

57. Visited in this house & found that 4 families which I saw there the last time have left since, - including the two families Blackaby w[h]o had been living there ever since I came to the district. - Was permitted to deliver my message & leave a tract in each room.

Public house

58 Public house; distributed tracts at the bar of this Public house, to 4 men & 5 women, some of them I knew to be from district; however they they [sic] were very civil & accepted the tracts. The Public Master who was standing at the bar accepted a tract likewise.

59 1st front. Called upon M[rs] Watson who lately confined; endeavoured to impress upon her her duty to give thanks to God for safely delivering her with a healthy Baby &. c. She seemed so very much impressed & was shedding tears; read & explained a portion of the word & prayed.

19

Dudley Street September 1861

Saturday 14.
Visited the sick & special cases on my district today, was kindly received & permitted to deliver my message & read the word in almost every room, besides leaving a tract with each of them.

Sunday 15. Visited for two hours & a half in my district today out of the regular course of my visitation; besides distributing tracts at the 5 Dials & White Lion Street.

Romanist's notion of the Bible reading

Monday 16.
65. Kitchen, a very bigoted Romanist; told him the object of my visitation when he said: "I am one of the old church & not like your Bible christians who are one thing one day & another thing the next; Our church don't deny that the Bible is the Book of God & they try to keep it sacred, it is you protestants which make the Bible a common book; Well I mean to say that you protest[ants] tell everybody to read the Bible & that

20

Dudley Street September 1861.

is the reason that you got so many sects, one makes one thing of it and another something else, but we leave it in better hands, & another thing is "You Protest[tants] have got the Bible from our church you can't deny that" &.c. I have been permitted to quote several passages from Scripture & to explain "Jesus" as the only mediator between God & men; accepted a tract.

The Influence of a religious parent.

66. 2nd front. M^rs^ McKenzie an Irish woman in very distressing circumstances, her husband has deserted her & with 3 little children the poor woman is now in a state of extreme poverty; I urged upon her to go to Jesus & to seek first his Kingdom in the full assurance that all other things will follow with his blessing; read & explained a portion of Scripture & offered up a prayer; the poor woman seemed to be very much impressed & with tears in her eyes said; "Will Jesus listen to such a wretch as I am, I have been brought up by a pious mother who taught me my duty to God, but I have neglected

21

Dudley St. September 1861

Future visit desired

it these many years & I am afraid it's too late now; I have been very unfortunate & very miserable ever since I have left of[f] to follow my poor mother's advice; I have not prayed for more than 6 years, nor have I been at a place of worship all that long time; I have nobody to blame but myself &.c." endeavoured to Impress upon her the exceeding sinfulness of thus neglecting the Lord who bought her, & the necessity of at once fleeing to that Saviour who is able & willing to receive poor penitent sinners. promised to call again[.]

Indifference

Tuesday 17.
68 Kitchen, Called upon M[r] Evans who was again very talkative & approved of every word I said by "Yes" or "no", again I earnestly urged upon him to flee from the wrath of God, read several passages of Scripture &.c. but am sorry to say with seemingly no more success than on many previous occasions.

22

Dudley Street September 1861.

Hopeful case

69 1st front. Called upon Mr[s] M[c]Carthy, an Irish Cath[olic] woman, was kindly received permitted to read and explain a portion of Scripture & to offer up a prayer. M[rs] M[c]C. attends a Rom[an] Cath[olic] place of worship, but am happy to say I have been the instrument of leading her to the word of God, I procured her a copy of Scripture which she very much delights in reading in company with old M[rs] Foxgroft [sic] a true christ[ian] woman.

Agent rejected

70. Top back. Was refused admittance by an elderly woman (Irish) who told me the old story "We don't belong to your persuasion &.c." I was however permitted to deliver message to her whilst standing at the door, refused to accept a tract.
Visited 5 more families in this house & was permitted to deliver my message & leave a tract in each room.

23

Dudley Street. September 1861

Sunday trading.

Wednesday 18.

77 Shop. Had another conversation with Mr Riggs on the evil of Sunday trading & endeavoured to impress him with the exceeding sinfulness of this particular sin, but like on many previous occasion he pleaded "necessity" as an excuse & notwithstanding my convincing him of the fallacy of it, he persisted to say that he was not worse than other people, & was determined to give up Sunday trading altogether, on some future day.

Casting pearls before swine.

top front. A man opened the door whom I at once perceived to be the worse for liquor, his first words were these "What the _____ do you want here; I want to know what _____ business you have here["]; - I did not stay to talk to him, for I found by experience that it does more harm than good to speak about sacred things to one intoxicated, it is actually "casting pearls before swine."

24

Dudley Street September 1861

A very distressing case.

Thursday 19

78 top fr: Mr Heywood was very glad to see me again & told me that his poor wife is getting worse every day, her mind being affected & he has to watch her very closely, lest she does some fatal act, either to herself or some one else. After I had been in the room for some minutes she entered seemingly very pleased to find me there, she spoke in a[n] incoherent manner, saying that her neighbours were all talking about her & telling each other that she was not born in wedlock &.c. she was very unhappy seeing that she was surrounded by enemies, but "God is my friend" & they will all be rewarded &.c. - seing that she is really in a state of mind not fit to be talked to about spiritual things, I endeavoured to impress upon her not to mind what her neighbours say & to keep herself quiet &.c. she took it very calmly & promised to do so.- The poor man has 7 childr[en] I prayed.

25

Dudley Street September 1861

Sunday trading.

78. Shop. Called upon M[rs] Egan, spoke to her again of the evil of Sunday trading when she said "My dear Sir I know it is a great sin, I wish I was not obliged to do it, would much rather do without, but how could I, every body keeps their place open in the street & if I was to shut up I would not do no business at all, it's the only day we do anything, I have not taken more than <u>three shillings</u> & eight pence, since last Monday & how could I live & pay my rent if I was to shut up on Sunday &.c."

A sad case.

79. Kitchen. Called upon Greswood who are in great poverty, her mother is laid up being 82 years of age & in a fearful state of ignorance about ["]the one thing needful;" endeavoured to impress upon her the necessity of preparing "to meet her God", but all the answers I could get was "Yes" or "no" read the word & offered up a prayer. May God have mercy upon that poor old sinner & save her even in the eleventh hour for Christ's sake.

26

Dudley Street. September 1861

Missionary encouragement.

Friday 20.

81. top front; Called upon old M[r] & M[rs] Clark; both are now attending regularly a place of worship; the poor woman expressed herself thus "I am quite happy now, O dear we never went to church before you visited us & my husband did not never read the Bible, but now he reads to me & goes with me to church; O yes we pray to Jesus, I can't say much, but I always says that short prayer you told me, I know it now by heart &.c." When I asked her whether I should read a chapter she said "O yes dear I likes you to read to me & to pray."

Promised a visit in a Hospital.

2nd fr[ont]. Mrs Canon told me that her daughter Sophia, who is in the Victoria Park Hospital, is sinking fast since I saw her last week; endeavoured to impress upon her the necessity of making her peace with God; read the word & promised if possible to visit her daughter again in the Hospital.

27

Dudley St. September 1861.

Where the church was before Luther & An Irish Romanist's question answered.

Kitchen. M[r] Sullivan a bigated [sic] Irish Rom[an] Cath[olic] seemed very averse to my visit & asked me the often repeated story "which was the oldest church? & where was your church before Luther & Henry VIII? I answer[e]d the first question by telling him that that [sic] the Church of Christ at the upper chamber at Jerusalem was the first church in the christian era; & secondly that that church was before Luther exactly where it is now, viz. "the Bible."
M[r] S. introduced a great many different subjects, but I was permitted to read the word & deliver my message; accepted a tract.

Visited and called upon 7 more families in this house, all, with the exception of one are Irish, but I was permitted to deliver my message and leave a tract in each room.

Attended a meeting at St. Giles Vestry.

28

Dudley Street. September 1861

Saturday 21.
Visited the sick & special cases in my district to day, to most of whom I was permitted to read the word, with some prayed and left tracts with all.-

Sunday 22. Was not able to visit my district to day.

Agent rejected.

Monday 23.
86. top back. Was refused admittance by a Rom[an] Cath[olic] Irishman who used very bad language and threatened to push me down the stairs if I was not off at once &.c. but still I have been permitted to deliver my message to him whilst standing at the door.

Sick children

2nd back. Another Irish family named Finey, found two of their children laid up with the whooping cough, the husband is out of work (army tailor) & there is not a particle of furniture in the room, the poor little children are wrapt [sic] up in

29

Dudley Street September 1861

Future visit desired

rags laying on the floor, & are no doubt suffering more from hunger than ought else; No Scripture & don't attend a place of worship; read a portion of Scripture & endeavoured to impress upon them the necessity of seeking first the Kingdom of heaven & it's righteousness &.c. they listened but the only answer I could get was "Yes" or "No", accepted a tract & asked me to call again.

87. top front. Called upon M[rs] Bunt & found that she has been confined with another Baby, is doing well & asked me to speak to her to be churched free of charge as she can't afford to pay & don't like to go out before she has been churched; explained to her the meaning of that rite of the church, & endeavoured to impress upon her to give thanks to God for her safe delivery & to go to Jesus our merciful Saviour & plead his merits for the delivery from the power of sin & Satan. offered up a prayer.

30

Monmouth Court September 1861

Tuesday 24.
2 2nd back; found 3 women & 2 men in this room, all Irish, they did not seem best pleased with my visit, but notwithstanding listened very attentively whilst I spoke to them of Christ's willingness to save & man's responsibility [not] to neglect so great salv[ation];
One of the men seemed to be very much inclined to introduce silly questions about church goverment & the wrongs of the Irish from the English &.c. but I carefully avoided to argue with him, simply confining myself to "the one thing needful"; when I left each accepted a tract.

Agent rejected

front room. An Irish woman who opened the door, refused to let me into the room, saying she was not of my persuasion, & notwithstanding my trying to persuade her to listen to what I had got to say, I could not get her attention, she kept on talking & scolding till she shut the door in my face.

31

Monmouth Court

Dudley St.

A New Test[ament] desired.

3. 2nd back. A young couple lately come over from Ireland received me very kindly & listened attentiv[e]ly whilst I read & explained the 5[th] chapt[er] to the Romans, No Bible & upon my asking him whether he would accept the loan of a New Test[ament] & whether he would read it, he said: "Yes Sir I would like to get one, I can't read much but my missus is a good scholar & we could read it together;"- I promised to procure him a New Test[ament].

No Scriptures

Wednesday 25.
6. Parlour & first floor is kept by a low Irish woman as a lodging house, she repeatedly refused me admittance & I cannot proceed to get into her rooms to see her lodgers, but she gave me permission to day to go upstairs & visit the other inmates who live in the upper part of the house; they are all very low Irish, but was permitted to deliver my message & leave tracts. None of them has a Bible or Test[ament].

32

Monmouth Court. September 1861.

Agent rejected.

Thursday 26.
9. top back. A miserable old Irish woman used the most disgusting language imaginable, so much so that I did not think it prudent to talk to her any longer, but left her after I had given her a solemn warning.

Hopeful case.

2nd back. Another Irish family, Rom[an] Cath[olic] but they received my visit very kindly & the husband, a cobbler, asked me to sit down; found him pretty well versed in Scripture & when I spoke to him of the nature of sin & God's righteousness in saving the sinner through Christ Jesus &.c. he said: ["]I know God is a holy God & he will punish sin, there is a hell I believe it there is not a doubt about it in my mind; Yes we all deserve to go there, I do I know it; Yes I believe Christ has died for me, He is a sufficient

33

Monmouth Court. Sept. 1861.

Saviour; I know He is the way to heaven I trust to no other for salvation; I don't do as I ought but I try to do the best & the rest I leave to Christ, he alone can save me & I pray that he will save me["].
Left a tract & promised to call again.

Unfortunates.

10. 2nd back; found three young women apparently bad women (prostitutes) in this room, they behaved very well & listened attentively whilst I talk[ed] to them about the exceeding sinfulness of sin & the awful doom of the sinner. One especially a girl about 20 years old seemed very much affected. Each accepted a tract.

Visited & called upon 7 more families in this house, was permitted to deliver my message in each room except the back parlour, where I was refused admittance, but permitted to leave a tract.

34

Broad St. September 1861

A Jews Opinion of the Person and Work of the Redeemer.

Friday 27.
23 Had another conversation with M[r] Angel (a Jew) was permitted to read to him again several old Test[ament] prophecies relating to the Messiah & explained to him how each and all of them have had their litteral [sic] fulfilment in the person & work

of Jesus of Nazareth & that "He" was the Light of the Gentiles & the glory of His People Israel. Mr. A. listened very attentively to all I read & said, but am sorry to say notwithstanding he calls himself a reformed Jew & entirely ignores the authority of the traditions of the Rabbies [sic], yet he is as far from the Kingdom of heaven as any of his more bigoted Jewish brethren. "I admire, he said, the precepts & doctrines of the New Test[ament] Jesus has been a great benefactor to the human race, he was no doubt a great man, but he was no more than other great men; if he had been God as well as man he would have been able to convince the whole of the Jews that he was the Messiah &c." We parted good friends & I left him a tract on the Jewish subject.

35

Broad St. September 1861.

24 Public house. Distributed tracts at the bar to 7 men & 5 women, two refuse to accept them, the rest did accept each a tract & so did the Public master himself.

Sunday trading.

26 shop. Had another conversation with Mr Sullivan, an Irishman on the evil of Sunday trading, read a portion of Scripture, and endeavoured to impress upon him the exceeding sinfulness of sin & the reallity [sic] of that place where the worm never dieth & fire is never quenched; list[en]ed attentively but brought forward the usual miserable excuse "that because others do it["] he is compelled to do the same. After my urgent pleading with him to flee from the wrath to come, I left him with that solemn warning "Be not deceived God is not mocked for what a man soweth that also shall he reap."

36

Dudley St. September 1861.

Saturday 28.
My Division day, attended at the Mission house.

Sunday 29
Visited for two hours today out of the regular course of my visitation; Had some interesting & I hope useful visits.

Distributed tracts at the 5 Dials & corner of Broad & Dudley St.

Monday 30.
27 Broad Street. 1st. fl[oor] front
Called upon M[rs] Herring who received me kindly & told me that her husband wanted to see me & would be obliged if I would call upon him any day after 5 ° clock p.m. or on Sunday wh[ich] I promised to do. Read and explained a portion of Scripture and offered up a prayer. Mr & Mrs H. attend St. Giles church & their children the Ragged school George St.

37

Broad Street. September 1861.

An interesting & hopeful case.

top back. found a young couple who received me very kindly, found them very teachable & willing to listen to the glad tidings of salvat[ion] when I read & explained to them the 3rd chapt[er] of St. John & dwelt more especially upon the necessity & nature of the New birth, the husband remarked "Yes I know that if we would think more about it & remember what a[n] awful thing it is to die unprepared, & to go to hell afterwards for ever, I am sure there would be more people living a better life as they now do, but most of them don't know their danger, it's as you say their heart is so bad & wicked that they live in sin & don't know the end of it; it's quite true that I know I have [not] thought quite as much as I ought about it myself, but I shall try to do so now &.c." Promised to call again.

Visited 5 more families in this house & was permitted to deliver my message in each room.

38

Dudley Street. October 1861.

Tuesday 1.
8 top front. Called upon M[r] Sullivan an Irish Rom[an] Cath[olic] & found 3 other Irishmen besides M[r] S. in the room, most of whom I knew: M[r] S. told me to call some other day as he was busy just now, but knowing that this was a mere excuse to get rid of my company & not inclined to let the opportunity go to speak to these poor Irishmen about their immortal souls, I offered

each a tract "Repentance without fruits" & made some remark upon "Repentance" & from that I quoted several verses of Scripture & was thus permitted to deliver my message notwithstanding Mr S's grumbling all the while.
2nd back. Old Mrs Wilson was glad to see me, she said everybody had forsaken her in the world, she had no one who cared for her but she knew God would never forsake, Christ was her only hope & trust & having

39

Dudley Street. October 1861.

Hope in Christ.

Him she could bear all her troubles, & trials, knowing that she shall soon be in that land "where the wicked cease from troubling & the weary are at rest;" Read & explained a portion of Scripture and offered up a prayer. M[rs] W. has seen better days but her husband[']s drinking habits, which by the way were the cause of his dead [sic], & sickness have reduced the poor woman to poverty; she is a member of the Wesleyan body and attends Queen St. chapel regularly.

10. 2nd back. Was refused admittance by an elderly woman, but permitted to deliver my message whilst standing at the door; refused to accept a tract.
1st fr[ont]. Was kindly received by a poor widow named Nickol & permitted to read & explain the word; besides induced her to send to childr[en] a boy & a girl to St. Giles school.

40

Dudley Street October 1861.

A Communicant.

Wednesday 2.
13. top back. Read the word & offered up prayer with poor old Cook, who, I am happy to say, is growing in grace & the the [sic] knowledge of Christ his Saviour.

Hopeful case.

front room. Called upon M[r] Haig, who is now thank God quite another man, not that he is converted to God, he is but an earnest inquirer after truth, and I have a fair hope that with God's blessing upon the reading of his blessed book M[r] H. will soon find peace & joy for his guilty conscience.

1st front. Old M[rs] Barnet, a Jewess, was very glad to see me again & I have once more been permitted to speak to her of Jesus of Nazareth as the only name given under heaven whereby we can be saved; & that Jew or Gentile are all alike in the sight of Him who is no respector of persons.

41

Dudley Street. October 1861.

15 Visited 7 families in this house & was permitted to deliver my message & leave a tract in each room. 2nd floor back induced a woman to send her boy 10 years old to George St. Ragged school.

Hopeful case.

Thursday 3.
17 top back. Called upon old M[rs] Nelms who was very glad to see me; has regularly attended St. Giles church since I saw her last twice on Sunday & once in the week; Can't read but prays to God for Christ's sake to pardon her sins & to give her His Holy Spirit & make her meet for the Kingdom of heaven. Read & explained part of the 3 chapt[er] to the Rom[ans] & offered up a prayer.

2nd back. An old woman, named Collins complained very much of poverty, so much so, that I found it extremely difficult to avert the subject from things temporal to things spiritual; read the word.

42

Dudley Street. October 1861

A sad state of things.

19 top back. An Irish family. the husband I found was the worst for liquor & as the natural consequence was quarreling with his wife, whom he called very disgusting names, in my presence; the woman in return was determined to have the last word & so they went on for about 5 minutes. I endeavored to persuade both

to leave off, but seeing I could not succeed I left the room.
It is really heart rending to see these poor creatures in extreme poverty, without clothes & no doubt oft times without a morsel of bread, yet not withstanding they manage somehow to get money for drink.

Visited 8 more families in this house, they are all with the exception of one Irish, but I was permitted to deliver my message to seven of them in their rooms.
1st back. Was refused admittance but permitted to deliver my message at the door.

43

Dudley Street October 1861.

hopeful case.

Friday 4.
24. 2nd front. M[r] Lizzard whom I found at dinner was very glad to see me & I found that he has been reading the New Test[ament] I gave him some time ago; he knew several passages by heart & seemed much pleased for my commending his boy whom I got into a place; endeavored to impress upon him the necessity of prayerful reading of the word of God.

25 Called upon M[r] Johnson in the shop & endeavored again to persuade him to leave off Sunday trading, but seemingly without success.
Kitchen. Mr. Oldham was glad to see me, he came home last week from Walton on Thames where he was sent to recover his health, he is very much improved and likely to get on again. Read the word & prayed.

44

Dudley Street October 1861.

Saturday 5.
Visited and called upon the sick & special cases in my district to day to most of whom read the word with some prayed and left tracts with all.

Sunday 6. Visited for two hours to day out of the regular course of my visitation & distributed tracts at the 5 Dials & corner of Broad & Dudley Street.

Monday 7.
28 top back. Called upon M[rs] Terry; was glad to see me; has been in great trouble since I saw her last her husband being out of work; has not been to a place of worship for a very long time, don't know why but would be almost ashamed to go now & in fact she could not now because she has pledged all her clothes. has got a

45

Dudley Street. October 1861.

Bible & does read it occasionally; her children attend St. Giles school.- read & explained a portion of the word & left a tract.

Promised a copy of Scripture.

2nd back. A young couple named, Tanner, received me kindly; found them very teachable, the husband, a cobbler can read a little, has not Scriptures but would like to get a copy would read it. Read & explained a portion of the word & promised to procure a New Testament.

A bad husband.

30. 1st front. M[rs] Blackaby was glad to see me & listened attentively whilst I delivered my message and read the word to her; attends St. Giles church & [sends] her children [to] the [N]ational [S]chool. her husband I am sorry to say is given to drink & ill using the poor woman.

46

Dudley Street. October 1861.

A sad case.

Tuesday 8.
Went with a young girl named McCarthy, to several institution[s] to get her in, but am sorry to say did not succeed in either. The poor girl is only 16 years old, has no parents or friends in England

& unfortunately fell in with a girl of bad character who induced her to walk the streets with her, which she has done for the last three months & now as far as I can see she seems truly penitent & anxious to amend her life. I got her into the lodging house No. 75 Dudley St[reet] for the present & hope by next week to get her into a Reformatory.

A Jew desires future visits.

34 Called upon M[r] Benjamin (a Jew) was kindly received and had another conversation with him on the claims of Jesus of Nazareth as the Messiah promised to Abraham & his seed; Read several passages from the old Test[ament] relating to the Messiah; listened attentively to what I read &

47

Dudley St. October 1861.

said & when I left him he accepted a tract & asked me to call again.

top front. Poor old M[rs] Groves is very much in trouble not having any work, she complained a great deal & I had some difficulty to avert the subject from things temporal to things spiritual; read the word and endeavoured to impress upon her to seek first the Kingdom of heaven &.c. M[rs] G. is a regular attendant at church but is still far from the Kingdom of heaven.

Roman Catholic

Wednesday 9.
38 2nd back. Was refused admission by an Irishwoman who told me she was not of my persuasion &.c. endeavoured to speak to her concerning her soul but she was so talketive [sic] about her her [sic] church & her country (Ireland) that I could not get any hearing; refused to accept a tract.

48

Dudley Street October 1861.

Future visit desired.

38 1st back. Another Irish family received me very kindly,

they introduced the Virgin Mary into our conversation, but still I was permitted to declare to them repentance toward God & faith towards Our Lord Jesus Christ as the only Mediator between God & men; accepted a tract & asked me to call again.

Visited & called upon 5 more families, all very low Irish, but I was permitted to deliver my message & leave a tract in each room.

Missionary desired to speak to a backsliding husband.

40. top front; Poor M[rs] South was anxiously waiting to see me & said "I want you to speak to my husband Sir, he goes on very bad lately he has got into bad company & won't listen to me at all, I don't know what I shall do; I know he will take advice from you sooner than from any body. O do speak to him &.c.["] Promised to call next Sunday & meantime endeavoured

49

Dudley Street. October 1861.

to impress upon her to pray to Him who is able & willing to heal the broken hearted & to comfort his People in all their trials & make all things work together for their good.

43 Thursday 10. 2nd front. Called upon old M[rs] Maycock, who is rather poorly at present, she was glad to see me & expressed once more her entire confidence in her God & her Lord; read the 23[[rd]] Psalm & offered up a prayer.

Visited and called upon 7 more families in this house was kindly received by all & permitted to deliver my message in each room.

Sunday desecration

44 shop. Had another conversation with M[r] Saunders, on the evil & sin of desecrating the Lord's day in keeping his shop open; read several passages of Scripture bearing on the subject, but he brought forward the wretched excuse which they all make "compulsion."

50

Dudley Street. October 1861.

Rejoicing in Christ.

Visited Sophia Cannon in the Victoria Park Hospital this afternoon, found her but very little improving, there is hardly any hope of recovery for she is to all appearance in a consumption, but am happy to say her mind is fixed upon Christ, she said to me to day, "I wish to get well again if it is God's will but if not I shall be the sooner with my Saviour" & when I asked her whether she felt any comfort now in believing in Jesus, she said "All is comfort to me now, Jesus is my all & I am happy in Him &.c." Promised if possible to visit her again.

Friday 11.
48 Called upon M[r] Gates[?] & endeavoured again to impress upon him the exceeding sinfulness of sin & the awful consequences of the sinner; read portion [of] the word bearing upon God's renunciation against Sabbath breakers,

51

he listened attentively & although he agreed with all I said against it, yet I am sorry to say he don't seem to make any effort to give up Sunday trading.

Agent rejected.

top back. A miserable looking old man refused to let me into his room, saying I had no business there & he would not be preached to & did not a care a pin about anything I had to say, yet I was permitted to deliver my message to him whilst standing at the door; refused to accept a tract.

A sad case.

49 Kitchen. A woman whose husband has deserted & left her with 5 little children in the most distressing circumstances, she expecting shortly to be confined & there is not a particle of furniture & anything else in the place; After I had spoken to her of the merciful & sympathising Saviour & endeavoured to impress upon her to go to him &.c. I advised her to go into the Union wh[ich] she promised to do so.

52

Dudley Street. October 1861

Saturday 12.

Visited & called upon the sick and special cases in my district to day, to most of whom read the word with some prayed & left tracts with all.

Sunday 13. Visited for two hours & a half today out of the regular course of my visitation. Called according to promise upon Mr South N° 40 Dudley St[reet] found him at home but just about to go out, was apparently glad to see me; his wife according to arrangement with her went out of the room & left us by ourselves, after a few preliminary remarks I told him the object of my visiting him to day & had a good plain talk to him about his irregular habits to the neglect of his wife & family; he took it very quietly & acknowledged that he had acted foolishly, & in the presence of his wife afterwards promised to amend.—

53

Dudley Street. October 1861.

I made them shake hands in my presence & promise to forgive each other; read a portion of Scripture & offered up a prayer.

Monday 14.
52. 1st back. Called upon Mrs Lee who has lately been confined, received me kindly & was permitted to read the word to her & impress upon her duty to her heavenly Father for her save [sic] delivery from nature's trouble; she seemed to be impressed & I offered up a prayer & left a tract.

A deceptive character.

1st front. Mrs Leader complained again [of] a great deal of poverty, so much so that I found it exceeding[ly] difficult to avert the subject from temporal to spiritual things, & there I am sorry to say she seemed not all interested in; she is one of those who attends every Mother's & other Meeting in the Parish for the sake of what she can get.

54

Dudley Street October 1861.

An Irish spirit

53 Kitchen. A Rom[an] Catholic family did not seem best pleased with my visit; I have not visited them before as they only are there about a fourthnight [sic]; seem to be very bigoted, the husband a Cobbler, said in a true Irish spirit "You are Protestants & a fine set you are look at your Protestant government they are a set of rogues who want to oppress us Catholics & are our old holy religion; it's very well to say [sic] to make good christians but you are one of those who goes about to make turncoats["] &.c. Refused to accept a tract.

2nd back. Called upon M[rs] Ellis, was permitted to deliver my message & induced her to send her boy 9 years old, to St. Giles Ragged school, she is a Catholic, but don't attend a place of worship & can't read; listened attentively to the word read but is very indifferent about her soul.

55

Dudley Street October 1861

Missionaries [sic] encouragement

Tuesday 15.
59 top back. Called upon poor blind Miss Tyler who was very glad to see me; read the word & offered up a prayer. Miss T. is one of those who know in whom they have believed, is it [sic] really very comforting for the Missionary to have such bright jewels in a district full of sin & misery, where he can go for a short space of time to hear from the lips of one surrounded by all the evil influence, what the Lord can & does do for those who receive the Lord Jesus Chr[ist] & love him as their Saviour & their all.

Sick case.

1st front; found M[rs] Watts very poorly & her husband out of work; endeavoured to impress upon them the necessity of seeking the Kingdom of heaven, read & explained part of the 3rd ch[apter] of St. John and left a tract, both seem to be impressed & desired me to offer up a prayer.

56

Dudley Street October 1861.

Public house.

60 Public house, distributed tracts at the bar to several men & women, the Public master likewise accepted one & I had a short conversation with him in which I was permitted to warn him to flee from the wrath to come, although he is a notorious character for using bad language, yet he has been pretty civil to me & shook hands when I left him.

Agent rejected.

61 top front. Was refused to enter the room, but permitted to deliver my message to an Irishman whilst standing at the door; accepted a tract.
Visited & called upon 7 more families in this house, was kindly received and permitted to deliver my message and leave a tract in each room.

57

Dudley Street October 1861.

A sad case of indifference.

Wednesday 16.
63 2nd back, An old couple named Dawkins very indifferent concerning "the one thing needful" the old man 72 years of age said when I spoke to him of the uncertainty of life & the reallity [sic] of a Judgement day "I hope God will have mercy on me, he knows I have been trying to do the best I could, I have never been a drunken fellow, I worked hard & tryed [sic] to keep a little home together; it's true I have not been what is called a religious sort of chap, but you see I had no time to spare to attend to it & I am not a scholar." endeavoured to awake him from his awful delusion by describing the the [sic] terrors of the Lord &.c. read a portion of Scripture, but am sorry to say he did not seem the least concerned about all I said & read.

Visited 7 more families in this house & delivered my message in each room.

58

Dudley Street October 1861.

Self righteousness.

Thursday 17.
68 Kitchen. Called upon Mr Evans; was again very talketive [sic] complaining about the wickedness and evil propensities of his neighbours, which he said were all hating him because he would not speak to them; Read & explained to him the parable of the Publican & sinner endeavouring to impress him with its moral and religious bearing.

Missionary encouragement.

1st front. Read the word & offered up a prayer with poor Mrs Foxgroft who was very glad to see me. I am happy to say that Mrs McDonald a bigoted Catholic woman with whom Mrs Foxgroft lives & who was at first very averse to my visits, at times when I came into the room & began to talk to her she was sure to leave til I was gone, but now she listens very attentive whilst I read the word and kneels down with us in prayer.

59

Dudley Street October 1861.

Skepticism.

71 shop. Mr Viney was glad to see me & I was again permitted to warn him to flee from the wrath to come; when I spoke of the fearful doom of those who neglect so great salvation &.c. he said "now do you think that God punish[es] all who don't believe what you call the gospel & if there is a hell do you think they will all go to hell; well you tell me you are sure of that because your Bible tells you so, but i tell you then that God must be very cruel & would act like a tyrant to send to hell more than half the human race, what did he send them in the world for if it [is] only for to damn them." Explained to him that God willeth not that any should perish in proof of wh[ich] he gave his son to redeem them, so that like the fall was universal, redemption is universal, but men will not accept that provision freely made, hence they are under the curse of the law, entirely of their own choice.

60

Friday 18

72 2nd back. Called upon poor M[rs] Thompson whose little child 11 months old is lying dead, the poor woman seems to grief [sic] very much; endeavoured to impress upon her to prepare to meet her child in glory; read & explained a portion of the word & offered up a prayer. She seemed to be much impressed & I promised to call again.

top back, An Irish woman refused me admittance, telling me the old story, she was not of my persuasion &.c. but was permitted to deliver my message to her whilst standing at the door, refused a tract.

61

Saturday 19.

Visited and called upon the sick and special cases in my district to day to most of whom I read the word with some prayed & left tracts with all.
Sunday 20. Have not been able to leave my home to day having a very bad cold wh[ich] settled on my chest, my Medical attendant advised me to keep in doors for a couple of days.

Monday 21. ill as above.

Tuesday 22.

75. Visited the inmates of the Lodging house & addressed them for a few minutes on the necessity of the New birth from the 3[[rd]] chapter of St. John's gospel, they listened very attentively & each accepted a tract.

77 top back. M[rs] Deneman did not seem best pleased with my visit to day for which I

62

Dudley Street. October 1861.

A sad case of a drunken woman & Mother.

could easily account by se[e]ing that she had a drop of liquor too much; I talked to her very severely but she was too much confused although she was not so bad as not to know what she was about; she was just about going out again, no doubt for getting more drink & her children which in school if they come home will find her out & will have to run the streets hungry & perhaps stay away from school for the remainder of the school.
Visited & called upon six more families in this house & was permitted to deliver my message & leave a tract in each room.

78 top front. Read the word & offered up a prayer with M[r] & M[rs] Heywood.

No Scriptures

back kitchen. An Irish woman received me kindly, No Bible & can't read; read the word & delivered my message.

63

Dudley Street October 1861

Missionary encouragement

Wednesday 23.
81 top front. Called upon poor old M[r] Clark, was glad to see me; "is very poorly & lost the sight of one eye entirely, but can still read his Bible; don't expect to live much longer for I feel I am sinking fast; thank God I am now more prepared to die than I was this time a year [ago]; Yes I am truly thankful that God did not take me away unprepared, if I think of it now I see what a fool I was not to think of it before; if God had[n]'t sent you I would have gone on & never would have thought what was to become of my soul, but now thank God I am thinking of it all day & I read my Bible & I prays that God would pardon all my life long sins & I goes to St. Giles church twice upon Sunday, with Missus [sic] she always goes with me,["] &.c: read the word & offered up prayer.

64

Dudley Street. October 1861.

Temporal & spiritual destitution.

83 2nd back. An elderly man refused me admittance at first, but after a few minutes conversation I succeeded to enter his room where I was astonished to find 4 children in a perfect state of nudity, the eldest 7 & the youngest not quite 2 years old; not a particle of furniture or bedding is in the room & the windows being shut the smell is most offensive; after inquiry I learned that the children don't belong to him but to another family with whom the old man is living, both parents go out in the morning & come home at night what they do, he said he did not know. I spoke to the old man about his soul but I might just as well have spoken to the very wall, I could not get a single sentence out of him, besides "Yes" or "no". Left a tract.

65

Dudley Street. October 1861.

Thursday 24.

87 top front. Called upon M[rs] Bunt who was very glad to see me; she attends now a regular place of worship & promises very fairly indeed, she desired me to day to speak for her to get her child of which she has been lately delivered, free christened wh[ich] I promised to do; read the word & offered up a prayer.
Visited & called upon six more families in this house, was well received by all & permitted to deliver my message & leave a tract in each room.

Visits in hospital.

Visited 2 persons from my district in Hospitals this afternoon, one in the Middlesex & the other Victoria Park Hospital, both were very thankful for my visit & I have been permitted to speak to them of [the] malady of sin & the Royal Physician Jesus Christ.

66

Dudley Street October 1861.

Saturday 26.
Attended at the Mission house being my Division day & not visited [sic] my district.
Sunday 27. Visited for three hours in my district to day out of the

regular course of my visitation & distributed tracts at the 5 Dials & corner of Broad & Dudley streets.

Two unfortunates.

Monday 28.
1 Monmouth Court. 2nd back. two young girl[s] (unfortunates) did at first seem not to be very favourable to my visit, but still were pretty civil, endeavoured to impress them with the terrors of the Lord &.c. both listened attentively & one the eldest seemed to be much affected & with tears in her eyes said, "I know, sir, I am ruining body & soul, but what

67

Monmouth Court. October 1861.

Future visit promised

shall I do, I have been seduced whilst in service by decrees [sic] I have become what you see me now, I could not now get any place, my character & all is gone & I must put up with it there is no chance left &.c." The poor girl seemed to feel what she said & I could not but feel with her; promised to see her again.

top back; Found an elderly woman named Jones in a state of intoxication, utterly helpless laying on the floor, and two younger women apparently friends, were the worse for liquor too but not so bad; the sight of the poor old sinner & the state of the room were sickening, without adding to it the awful bad language the two others made use of; they were not in a fit condition to be told about the love of God, but I spoke to them of the terribl[e]ness of the Lord's anger.

68

Monmouth Court. October 1861.

An Irish Politician

Tuesday 29.
5 top front. An Irish family named Davy late of 19 Dudley St. the husband a red hot Irishman began to talk about Politics at such a rate that I found it extremely difficult to get him to listen to what I had got to say, at last succeeded to call his attention to

the 26th verse of the 16th chapt[er] of Matth[ew] "What shall it profit a man &c." & here too he began to be as talketive [sic] as he has [sic] been before, but have been permitted to tell him of the vast importance to seek first the Kingdom of heaven &c. read the word & left a tract.

2nd back. Was refused admittance by a young man who told me to go to the -- & not preach to him or he would let me know what his creed was, he went on thus whilst I endeavoured to speak to him & at last shut the door in my face, & I could hear him swear & curse whilst going down the stairs.

69

Monmouth Court. October 1861.

Influence of a Catholic Priest.

6 2nd back, An old woman named Collyer said "You always come here & I told you the last time I was not of your persuasion; I am not one of your people & I never goes to any of your people for nothing at all & don't want to be visited; I know all you can tell me. Father Kelly bless his soul, is my priest & I knows him & he knows me, he is as good a soul as ever breathed & I will never listen to nobody else; Yes he told me of Jesus blessed be His name & his blessed mother & here,["] taking a Crucifix out of her pocket, ["] he gave me that & told me never to part with it, which I never shall &.c.["] Have been permitted to speak to her of Jesus as the only Mediator between God and men.

No Scriptures.

top front; induced a poor woman to send her girl 11 years old to St. Giles Ragged school, the poor girl has never been to school & is as ignorant of the name of Jesus as if brought up amongst heathen.

70

Monmouth Court. October 1861.

Migration.

Wednesday 30.

9 Did not find a single person of those I visited last time, they all have left & the house is let out to new Tenants, the change I am sorry to say is not much for the better, I called at 6 rooms in the upper part of the house, but three refused me admittance, all Irish, 1st floor back, I found a sick woman in most deplorable circumstances, spoke to her of Jesus & her immortal soul, she listened but with little interest; promised to procure her a letter for the Bloomsbury Dispensary.

Bad characters.

10 This house is inhabited by all sorts of bad characters; prostitutes thiefs [sic] &c. but still I have been permitted to deliver my message in 3 rooms, the rest refused me admittance to day; There is not a Copy of Scripture amongst any of the 7 families; most are Irish.

71

Monmouth Court October 1861.

Thus I have once more with the help of the Almighty, visited through that Court of wh[ich] it can be truly said, "full of the habitation of cruelty, a dark place without even a spark of the light of the glorious gospel;" O may the Lord Jesus Christ bless my humble efforts; & may the blessed spirit bring home upon the hearts & consciences of these poor benighted people, the words of Life & Truth, for the salvation of their immortal souls & the glory of His holy name, for Christ's sake; Amen.

Thursday 31.

24 Broad Street. Public house; Distributed tracts at the bar of this Public house, to 5 men & 4 woman [sic]. they accepted them & I was permitted to say to them a few words on the importance of its contents. The Public master also & a young woman behind the bar accepted tracts.

72

Broad Street. October 1861.

Future visit desired.

26 top fl[oor] back. An Irish cobbler did not seem best pleased with my visit, telling me the old story, "was not of my persuasion, has his own church &.c." however after a few observation[s] I succeeded to get into better graces & he offered me a chair to sit down, and notwithstanding his introducing the Virgin Mary, I was permitted to read the word and endeavour to impress upon him "repentance towards God & faith towards our Lord Jesus Christ;" accepted a tract & asked me to call again.

A christian poor woman.

1st. back. Mrs Page an elderly woman, was glad to see me; "is always glad to see the Missionary or any other christian man; Yes I do love the Lord Jesus Christ; I know it well that if He had not loveth me first, I would never have loveth Him; I have my troubles & trials but I take everything God sends me is for my good, sometimes I murmur but I know it's my evil heart &.c." Read the word & prayed.

73

Broad St. October 1861.

27 Visited 7 families in this, all of them received me kindly & was permitted to deliver my message & leave a tract in each room.

74

Dudley Street. January 1862.

Wednesday 1.
Attended our annual meeting at Exeter Hall.

Thursday 2.
72 1st front. Called upon Mrs Watson who was again inclined to be talketive [sic] about her Superior qualities, but when I read & explained to her the story of the "Publican & sinner" she was shut up & I was permitted to deliver my message; & when I left she asked me to call again.
top back; An Irish family two children ill & the mother confined with another poor little creature; "I can't say that I feel well, she said, I got everything to knock me down, I could wish I was dead if it was not for this little baby & he would be much better off if he was dead too; don't know as I would be better off but I could

75

Dudley Street.

not be much worse; well I heard a great deal about heaven & hell, but I am sure I have got my hell here I need not have another I am sure if anybody ought to go to heaven I ought; No I can't say I have never done no wrong, I know I have not done as I ought always & I hope God will have mercy on me; Yes I have heard of Jesus who was crucified & died to save poor sinners; No I have not gone to Him yet; Yes I believe he is willing to save me as well [as] anybody else & I hope He will &.c."
Read & explained a portion of Scripture to which the poor woman listened attentively & seemed to be impressed, when I left she asked me to call again.

76. 2nd back. Old M[r] Bell a bigoted Rom[an] Catholic refused me admittance; but I was permitted to deliver my message to him whilst standing at the door.

76

Dudley Street January 1862.

Communicant.

Friday 3.
78 top front. Called upon M[r] Haywood, who was glad to see me again; he has been very poorly lately, but am happy to say he seems to grow in grace & the knowledge of Christ his Saviour. Attends regularly St. Giles church & is a Communicant.

2nd back; persuaded a young man to read the Bible, he is very fond of reading & is as he expressed it a first rate scholar; He came there only a few weeks ago & I found that he has several books (novels) but no Bible & upon his promising that he would read it I gave him a nice copy which I had in my pocket. His name is Baker & I promised to call again next Saturday.

81 top front. Old Mr. & Mrs

77

Clark received my kindly; I am happy to say both are now very regular in their attendance upon the means of grace; he reads his Bible everyday & has entirely given up to work on the Lord's day. I examined him to day on the most important doctrine of the gospel "the Atonement" & was very much pleased with his answers.— Read the word & offered up a prayer.

2nd back. Sophia Canon is still confined to her bed, but is happy in her Saviour. ["]My father is out of work["], she said, & ["]we are very bad off now, but I must do the best I can, I am not afraid I know my Saviour won't let me starve; I love Him more now than ever did before, I am happy in spite of all my pains & troubles["]. Read the word & prayed.

78

Dudley Street January 1862.

Saturday 4.

Visited & called upon the sick & special cases in my district to day, was well received and permitted to read & explain the word to most of them, and with some offered up prayer, leaving a tract with each.

Sunday 5.
Was again engaged at St. Martin's Hall in the afternoon, at the Special service.

Monday 6.
85 top back. Called at M[r] Neal, an Irishman & found him in a state of helpless drunkeness & when I spoke to him he made use of very bad language; se[e]ing that my visit would not be any good, I left, but intend to call in the course of the week & speak to him when sober.

79

Dudley Street. January 1862.

A dutch Jew

85 Shop. A dutch Jew, did not seem best pleased with my visit at first, but after a few preliminary remarks he entered into conversation & I was permitted to speak to him of Jesus of Nazareth, as He who was promised to be the light of the Gentiles

& the glory of his people Israel; I was listened to very attentively but found both Mr & Mrs Emanual very indifferent to their own, as well as to any other religion. left a tract.

86 1st back; persuaded Mrs Kenny to send her girl 10 years old to the Irish free school, she assented to do so if I would take her there myself, which I promised. Mrs K. is a Rom[an] Cath[olic] but don't attend a place of worship; her husband is at present in prison for theft; No Scriptures. Read the word.

80

Monmouth Court.

There is no heaven nor hell.

Tuesday 7.
1 2nd back; An old woman told me to leave her room "don't want to be bothered with preaching I don't hold with it; don't care for nobody & you need not trouble yourself about me I am old enough to know all about it; it's nothing to nobody else as I have a soul or not; What of that, I am not such a fool that I don't know I will have to die, of course I must die & so must you; O, I never bother myself with heaven or hell, my old man when he was alive he always said it was all parson's [sic] tricks & no more & I believe so too."—endeavoured to impress upon her the reallity [sic] of both heaven & hell, but made little or no impression upon her, she refused to accept a tract, because she can't read.

81

January 1862.

Future visit desired

2 1st front; A young couple received me very kindly & I found the husband to be an interesting & teachable man, he told me that a few years ago he was very well to do & did not think he should ever come into such a state as he is at the Present; & when I asked him what effect that change produced upon his mind & whether it did lead nearer to God &c. he answered "it certainly made me think more of God than I did before, but I came to the conclusion that God don't interfere in our little matter, for if he did how is that sometimes the drunkards & worst men are better to do than an industrious, sober man if he try ever so hard &c." I read to him several passages of Scripture bearing on that subject,

especially the Conclusion the Psalmist came to on this matter. he asked me to call again.

82
Monmouth Court

Agent rejected

Wednesday 8.
6 2nd back; Was refused admittance by an Irish man who said "he was not of my persuasion"; ["]I am a Catholic & a good one too & don't want to have nothing to do with you Bible christians you are no good." I endeavoured to speak to him but did not succeed for he shut the door in my face.

Poor unfortunate girls.

second front; found two young girl[s] in the room (unfortunates) they did not seem best pleased with my visit but after a few minutes they seemed to be more inclined to listen & I was permitted to warn them to flee from the wrath to come; both are Country girls & neither can read; they told me that both their parents were dead & have no friends or relations in London.

83

January 1862

A sad case.

7 2nd back; An old man, named Evans; found him ill in bed & in a most deplorable condition "I am laying here these three weeks I am tired of my life, if it was not for the poor people next room, I would have been starving on this here bed; God has not sent me nothing, I have not got much to thank him for, He don't seem to care much about me; could be no worse off as I am; A fellow can't think much about his soul if he lays here ill & hungry & nobody does anything for him &c."—read the word & endeavoured to impress upon him "the one thing needful" but he seemed unconcerned & remained unmoved.

Visited & called upon five more families in this house, was well received & permitted to deliver my message & leave a tract in each room.

84

Broad Street January 1862.

Tracts distributed at a Public house.

Thursday 9.
24 Public house, distributed tracts at the bar to five men & three women; one rough looking man, who seemed to have had a little too much to drink, said to me on my offering him a tract "Yes governor I shall take it, if it won't do for nothing else it will do to light my pipe." but when I told him that I should feel very much obliged to him if he would first read & after that he might do with it what he liked; "O I did not mean it governor he said, it was only a joke I mean to read it."

26. top back. An Irish family named Nelly; did not seem best pleased with my visit, on several former occasions I was refused admittance altogether, but I have been permitted to day to deliver my message & for the first

85

Broad Street. January 1862.

time did they allow me to leave a tract. No Scriptures.

Visited & called upon six more families in this house, was kindly received & permitted to deliver my message & leave a tract in each room.

27 2nd back; An elderly woman her daughter & three children of the latter in a most wretched & miserable condition, not a particle of furniture in the room & the poor children in a state of nudity; the old woman told me that they had not broken their fast to day & that she did not know where they should get the next bit to eat; but accidentally one of the children opened the covert where I saw a loaf of bread & some pieces too, so that it was clear she told me a lie. Their spiritual condition is quite as bad, for both women are most ignorant, & what is worse still they are indifferent about it.

86

Dudley Street. January 1862.

Future visit desired.

Friday 10.

7 2nd front. Called upon M[r] Kenley; is still very indifferent [to] "the one thing needful" but more willing to listen to the message & I was permitted to read & explain to him part of the 1st chapter to the Romans & when I left him he asked me to call again, which he never did before.

Temporal & spiritual poverty.

8 2nd back. An old woman in a most distressing state of poverty, she complained a great deal & I had some difficulty to avert her mind from things temporal to things spiritual, she is a Rom[an] Cath[olic] but has not been to a place of worship for six years; "I knows I have a soul; Yes I believe there is a heaven & a hell; because every body says so; it would be very hard

87

Dudley Street.

if poor creatures like me would go to hell I am sure we has got our hell here; I can't do no more I says my prayers sometimes["] &c. endeavoured to explain to her that "without holiness no man shall see the Lord"; read the word & left a tract.

A bigoted Rom[an] Cath[olic]

1st front. M[r] Ancle, an Irish bigoted Rom[an]Cath[olic] received me kindly & I had a long & interesting conversation with him again; he introduced as usual the Virgin Mary & the Holy Church but I was permitted to explain to him once more "Jesus" as the Way, the Truth & the Life; accepted a tract

Saturday 11. Visited and called upon the sick & special cases in my district & was permitted to read the word to most of them & with some prayed.
[signed in pencil: H. Laudon Maud]

88

Dudley Street. January 1862.

Sunday 12. Have not been able to visit my district to day.

Monday 13.

13 top back; found poor old Cook in bed ill, but very happy & content in fact he never complained, although I know him to be very bad off, he told me to day that he is sure God will care for him "I like to keep out of the Workhouse as long as I can["], he said, ["]but if it is God's will that I should go in, I am willing; I can truly say that it was good for me to be afflicted, it has brought me to Jesus & I should be happy now even in the workhouse; I know he loves me & I never knew before as I do now what it is to have a Saviour, there is not anything like it I would not change with a Lord for I am as happy as if I was a King." Read the word and offered up prayer.

89

Dudley Street Jan. 1862.

Hopeful case.

13 top front. M[r] Haig was glad to see me, & I can see a great change in him for the better; he seems now to be anxious for my visits & is very attentive to the word read & explained to him, whilst sometime ago he would not even look at me, much less listen to the message. He told me to day that he reads his Bible everyday & from the questions he put & the answers he gave me I have every reason to look upon him as a sincere & anxious inquirer after truth. May the Lord by His Spirit lead him into all truth, for his dear Son Jesus Christ's sake.

2nd front. Called upon M[rs] Barnet, an old Jewess, who is always very glad when I call, I urged upon her once more to accept Jesus of Nazareth as the Messiah & explained to her several passages from the old as well as the New Test[ament] she listened attentively but said "Nobody

90

Dudley Street. January 1862.

What is truth?

knows who is right, we think we are & you think you are, so nobody knows who is & I am no scholar so I shall die as I was born, a Jewess." I endeavoured to impress upon her that the Bible is the only rule to be guided by & that God has promised His

Spirit, in answer to prayer, for to lead us into all Truth. left a tract.

Where the Prot[estamt] religion is & was.

Tuesday 14
19 top back; an Irishman did not seem best pleased with my visit at first, but after a few remarks entered into conversation when I found that he had read the Bible but only for the sake of argument. I endeavoured as much as possible to avoid Controversy, but he insisted upon my answering him where the Protestant religion was before Luther and Henry VIII & when I told him that the religion of Jesus Christ was to be found in the Bible & that it was there before Luther as well as now, he said,

91

Promised future visit

Dudley Street. Jan. 1862.

["]Well how is it then that you Bible christians all differ from one another but we don't profess to read the Bible & we have one church & one faith." I told him that there were differences of opinion in the Rom[an] Church as well, but that all Protestants agreed upon the Cardinal doctrines of the Bible, as an instance I read & explained to him part of the 3rd chapter to the Romans upon which all true Protest[ants] agree; left a tract & promised to call again.

1st back, Was refused admittance by an elderly Irishman, but permitted to deliver my message to him whilst standing at the door. tract refused.

22 2nd back; found a poor woman whose husband has deserted her in a most distressing condition, two of her children are ill & she has not been able to get any work for some time; more Complete destitution I hardly ever saw, the poor children were crying for bread, the want of which I believe to be

92

Dudley Street. January 1862.

the cause of their illness; for they look half starved. I endeavoured to impress upon the poor woman "the one thing needful" above all others, she listened attentively & cried very much when I offered up a prayer. I urged upon her to go with her poor children in the workhouse & I think I shall succeed.

24. Wednesday 15. 2nd front; Called upon M[r] Linnard, an Irishman who was in the Middlesex Hospital sometime ago where I visited him twice; he was very glad to see me to day & expressed his thanks for my coming to see him in the Hospital; is a Rom[an] Cath[olic] & can read but very little, but I gave him a New Test[ament] which he is trying to read, he seems to value it very much, although he is still very indifferent about "the things which belong to his peace" listened attentively to the word read & explained & desired me to call again.

93

Dudley Street. Jan[uary] 1862.

A sad case of a dying girl.

Was called to see a young woman who I was told was dying fast, went to N° 7 Monmouth Court top front room & found a girl, 18 years old, in most dreadful agony, crying & tearing everything to pieces; two other young women were with her & tried to keep her quiet in bed, the lat[t]er two I know to be bad girls who walk the streets & from which fact I judge that the sick girl is of the same unfortunate class. I endeavoured to speak to her, but she did not, or could not, answer me, for I could not get a word out of her, although she cried repeatedly to one of the young women "O Mary Ann I die, O I die Mary Ann." I was quite overcome with the sight I beheld, but used the opportunity and endeavoured to impress upon the living, the awful condition of the dying & I promised to call again.

25 2nd back; found a young couple recently come there, both husband & wife seemed pleased with my

94

Dudley Street. January 1862.

visit; the former I found to be a nice, teachable young man, who told me [sic] that he reads his Bible & attends Queen's Street chapel, being a Wesleyan, read & explained a portion of the word

& offered up a prayer.

Visited six more families in this house was kindly received & permitted to deliver my message & leave a tract in each room.

Thursday 16.

28 Kitchen; found in this dark & wretched place two families living together, the one a husband, wife & one child & the other a blind man, his wife & three children; it was 11 o clock when I came in and found the blind man & his wife still in bed whilst the others were at their breakfast. The blind man whose name is Gorman is a bigoted Rom. Cath: he is pretty well versed in Scripture & rather an intelligent man of his class, and told one that he had conversed with the greatest

95

A Rom. Cath: mode of interpreting Scripture

men in England & Ireland & when I asked him whether he ever Converses with a great & more exalted still "the King of Kings & Lord of Lords" he said "Yes I do I pray every day, I do as my church teaches one for I believe her to be the best judge in matters of faith; Yes I believe the Bible is the word & the will of God but you will read there ~~that~~ "Spiritual things must be Compare with Spiritual"; well it means that spiritual men aught to compare or to interpret spiritual things." I never heard such an interpretation before, but I endeavoured to show him that it was inconsistent with the text to explain it thus, And even if he was right each individual Christian who is born again from above is a new man, a spiritual man & as such would become a competent judge of spiritual things; he listened attentively & was rather perplexed for he could not answer me. I left him a tract & promised to call again.

96

Dudley Street. January 1862.

28 2nd back, Called upon Mrs Terry, a respectable poor woman, endeavoured to persuade her to send her girl 11 years old to St. Giles school again, the poor girl used to go there some time ago but of late is kept at home to help her mother; she promised me to comply with my request as soon as her Baby is a few weeks older. Read the word & left a tract.

30 top back, Was refused admittance by an old Irish woman who said she was not of my persuasion, & when I endeavoured to say a few words to her whilst at the door she told me to go to the & shut the door in my face.

Visited all the other people in this house, was kindly received & permitted to deliver my message & leave a tract in each room.

Friday 17.

34 shop. Had another conversation with M[r] Benjamin, a Jew, on the claims of Jesus of Nazareth

97

as the Messiah; read several old Test[ament] prophecies relating to the Messiah & explained to him their fulfillment in Jesus &c. he listened attentively & when I left him accepted a tract on the Jewish subject.

top front; Called upon old M[rs] Graves who complained a great deal about poverty & having no work & I had some difficulty to avert the subject from things temporal to things spiritual, although very talkative as regards the former I could not get anything out of her, when I urged the lat[t]er; read the word & left her with a solemn warning.
Visited a young man in the Brompton Hospital, this afternoon, he formerly used to live in my district, but left some sixteen months ago & went to live near Victoria Park where I saw him since several times; he was admitted into the above hospital being in a rapid consumption; he wrote me a letter from the hospital & requested

98

Dudley Street. January 1862.

me to come & see him; he was very much pleased with my visit & seemed to be impressed with what I read & said to him. he has hope in Christ & is happy & content. I left him a couple of tracts written by the Rev. J. C. Ryle, one "Do you pray" & the other "Are you an heir;" he was much pleased with them & requested me to send him a few more, or if possible to come & see him again.

Saturday 18.

Visited & called upon the sick & special cases in my district to day, was kindly received & permitted to deliver my message to all of them, to some read the word & with a few prayed.

Sunday 19. Visited for three hours to day out of the regular course of my visitation, besides

99

distributing tracts & handbills for the St. Martin's Hall special services. Attended at the evening service at the Hall.

Brought nearer to God.

39 Monday 20. top back; Called upon poor M[rs] Sullivan, found her girl is much recovered since I called last; read & explained a portion of Scripture to both mother & child, both of whom listened attentively & seemed to be much impressed; when I spoke to her of God's merciful design in sickness & affliction, the poor woman said; "I know you are right God don't willingly afflict any of his creatures without some good purpose; & I know my afflictions have brought me nearer to God but sometimes I think that God deals very hard with me; Yes it is very wrong to think so; I do pray & ask God to give me a new heart["] &c. offered up a prayer & left a tract.

100

Dudley Street. January 1862.

40 2nd front. Called upon M[rs] Stevens, was well received and permitted to deliver my message & succeeded to induce her to send her eldest girl 10 years old to St. Giles school.

2nd back, A poor old man, named Carey was not best pleased to see me, but after a few preliminininary [sic] remarks I was permitted to read and explain to him a portion of the word "don't attend a place of worship; can do without it & plenty people go there are not a bit better for it" has no Bible & ["]is not much of a scholar"; left a tract.

41 top front. M[rs] Whittenton was glad to see me & thanked

me for visiting her daughter in the Middlesex Hospital, who is now quite well & at home again; both Mother & daughter attend the Bloomsbury Mission Hall & read their Bible.

101

Dudley Street. January 1862.

A happy christian.

Tuesday 21.
43 2nd front. Called upon poor old M[rs] Maycock, who was glad to see me; found her as usual very happy & content, the only regret she expressed was, that she can't get out to go to a place of worship, which she always did as long [as] she possibly could manage to walk; "My daughter reads the Bible to me every day & we keep all the tracts & read them over & over again; Yes I pray & my daughter prays too; I shall soon be gone I know[,] but I am not afraid[.] Jesus is my Saviour & I shall soon be with him & be happy." read the word & offered up prayer.

No Scriptures.

1st back; An old woman & her daughter, both widows, in very great poverty; when I spoke to them of the "one thing needful" they had nothing to say for themselves but "Yes" or "No" although both were very talkative as regards their temporal condition. No Bible & don't attend a place of worship.

102

Dudley Street. January 1862.

An interesting case.

44. top front. An old man, named Frost seemed to be very much affected whilst I read & explained to him part of the 53[[rd] chapter] of Isaiah; "Yes there was love["], he said, ["]God giving His Son to die for us poor creatures who are so wicked; I believe that he died for me, I pray to him & try to love him He knows; if he did not love me first I would never know anything of Him; I know I do a great many things I ought not to do, but I pray to Him & he pardons my sin &c" left a tract & offered up prayer.

Sunday trading.

Wednesday 22.
48 shop. Had another conversation with M[r] Gates, on the subject of Sunday trading, but like on many former occasions he pleads necessity as as [sic] excuse; endeavoured to impress upon him god's denunciations against this particular sin, as recorded in the prophecy of Ezekiel; read the word & left a tract.

103

Dudley Street. January 1862.

Sad indifference.

1st. front. Called upon old blind M[r] Law, whom I found ill in bed; he is very well versed in Scripture, but am sorry to say very indifferent about "the things which belong to his peace" "I know all about it, you can't tell me anything which I do not know, but I think we shall be all right at last; do to others as you would be done by; if we do that we need not fear; God made us what we are & he won't require what we can't do;" I endeavoured to explain to him that God did not make us what we are, but that sin has entered &c; but all I said did not seem to have the least impression upon him.

50. Visited & called upon 8 families in this house & was permitted to deliver my message in each room & leave a tract.

Visited a person in the German Hospital this afternoon.

104

Dudley Street. January 1862.

Thursday 23.
52. 2nd front; called upon M[r] Leader who is still very indifferent, although he attends regular[ly] at Bloomsbury Mission Hall; endeavoured to impress upon [him] the awful end of those who know the will of God & don't do it; left him with the solemn warning "be not deceived God is not mocked."

1st back; found a woman in a state of intoxication quite helpless laying on the floor, and two little children were playing in the room; I made inquiry in the next room & was told that such was not an unfrequent [sic] occurance; the name of the wretched woman is Miller & I was told that her husband was a sober & hard working man.

55 shop; Called upon Mrs Joseph a Jewess & was permitted to speak to her of Jesus of Nazareth the crucified & glorified Redeemer of Jews & Gentiles.

105

Dudley Street. January 1862.

55 top front. Mr & Mrs Woodall were very glad to see me & listened very attentively to the word read & explained; attend a place of worship regularly & read their Bible; offered up a prayer & left a tract.

Future visit desired.

56 2nd back; An Irish family, very bigoted, but still receive my visits very kindly & I was again permitted to explain to them Jesus as the only Mediator between God & men; when I left the husband accepted a tract & asked me to call again.

Friday 24.
Was not able to visit my district to day, as I had to write a quarterly Report to take in tomorrow.

Saturday 25. My Division day; attended at the Mission house.

106

Dudley Street. January 1862.

Sunday 26.
Visited for two hours & a half to day out of the regular course of my visitation & distributed tracts at the 7 Dials & 5 Dials, besides Hand-bills for the St. Martin's Hall special services for the working people.

Monday 27.

58 Public house; distributed tracts at the bar to five men & three women, they accepted them kindly & I was permitted to say a few words.

A happy christian.

59 top back; Called upon poor blind Miss Tyler, who was very glad to see me; read & explained the 23rd Psalm & offered up a prayer. The poor blind woman is one of the happiest christians I ever saw & each time I visit her, I really feel that it does me good. front room. M[rs] Day, likewise a blind woman, is still in an indifferent state of mind, through the influence of Miss Tyler, her

107

Dudley Street. January 1862.

friend, she has been induced to attend to the outward forms of religion, but is still, as far as ever, from the Kingdom of heaven.

60 2nd back; An Irishman, did not seem best pleased with my visit; "Am not of your religion, don't care what you are I don't want to be bothered you better go to your own people; I am a Catholic, if you want to know & never will have nothing to do with you protestants." I endeavoured to speak to him, but he became very much excited & very abusive in his language, he would not let me say a word but kept on swearing & cursing so that I thought it best to leave the room; refused a tract.

Irish Rom[an] Catholics.

top back; Another Irish Rom[an] Cath[olic] named Collinger; was permitted to deliver my message, although he constantly interrupted me & introduced the Virgin Mary; accepted a tract.

108

Dudley Street. January 1862.

A sad case of Indifference.

Tuesday 28.
65 top front. A. Dale, an Irishman, has been poorly for a long

time; ["]don't attend a place of worship["] & has not done so for more than 10 years; ["]don't see the use of it, can be as good as other[s] who attend regular; has no Bible & would not read it; has to work hard if he can get it & has no time to read the Bible; Yes, of course must take time to die, but hopes to be all right; because God won't be so hard with poor people." Endeavoured to persu[a]de him to flee from the wrath to come.

Visited 7 more families in this house, was kindly received, and permitted to deliver my message & leave a tract in each room.

67 2nd fr[ont] called upon M[r] Warton who was glad to see me again, & I was permitted to read & explain to him a portion of the word & to offer up a prayer.

109

Dudley Street. January 1862.

Wednesday 29.
72. top front. Called upon M[r] Paine, found him poorly & not able to work; "can't say that his trials & difficulties have brought him nearer to God; knows the importance of religion, but has been very careless indeed, about it; has not attended a place of worship for a long time; has a Bible & reads it sometimes. Read & explained a portion of the word & offered up a prayer.

1st front. Called upon M[rs] Watson who was again very talkative, but was permitted once more to warn her to flee from the wrath to come. Read the word & left a tract.

74 2nd back; was refused admittance but permitted [to] deliver my message whilst standing at the door; tract being refused.

Visited 7 more families in this house, was kindly received & permitted to deliver my message in each room.

110

Dudley Street. January 1862.

Thursday 30.

future visit desired.

77 1st back; Called upon Mrs German, a respectable poor woman who seemed to be impressed with what I read & said to her;--has a Bible but can't read, does not attend a regular place of worship, but promised me to attend the Cottage Lecture at St. Giles old school this evening.

80 2nd back; Poor old Mrs Piggons, who lately came there from some other part of the Parish; found her in a most distressed state, the poor old woman is very ill indeed & her two daughters, both widows, are without work. Endeavoured to impress upon them the privilege & the power of prayer to which they listened very attentively; when questioning the old woman of the hope within her she said: "Jesus, in Him I trust; He is my Saviour; He loves me in my poverty just as much as when I was better off; I pray to him & I know I shall soon be with Him["] &c. Is a communicant at St. Giles Church.

111

Dudley Street. January 1862.

81 2nd back; Poor Sophia Canon is still very poorly, & has been obliged to keep her bed again for the last two or three days; expressed again her hope & confidence in her Lord & Saviour Jesus Christ, in whom she enjoys peace & happiness; read & explained the 23rd Psalm & offered up a prayer.

82 2nd back; Was again refused admittance, by Mr. Daley, an Irish Rom[an] Cath[olic] & when endeavouring to speak to him whilst at the door he got very much excited told me to go to the & shut the door in my face.

Friday 31.
84 1st front; found a young man very willing to listen to the message; used to attend a Sunday school when he was a boy; has still got a Bible which he had given to him as a price [sic] for regular attendance; has not been to a place of worship since last Christmas twelf [sic] month. has not got tidy

112

Dudley Street. January 1862.

Future visit desired.

clothes now which are fit to go in; knows God looks into the heart & not at the cloth[e]s; reads his Bible occasionally. I had a long talk with the young man, whose name is Tennet, & found him very teachable, he seemed to be impressed when I read & explained a portion of the word; & when I left him asked me to call again.

87 Visited 7 families in this house was kindly received & permitted to deliver my message & leave a tract in each room.

Visited a poor man, in the Brampton Consumption Hospital, this afternoon.

[signed in pencil "H. Laudon Maud"]

113

Dudley Street & Monmouth Court.

February. Saturday 1.

Visited the sick & special cases in my district to day; was well received & permitted to deliver my message with each, to most was able to read the word, with some prayed & left tracts with all.

Sunday 2. Visited for two hours to day out of the regular course of my visitation; had some very interesting conversations with working men in my district to whom I was permitted to explain "repentance towards God & faith in our Lord Jesus Christ."

What is it about?

Distributed tracts and handbills for the St. Martin's Hall special services, at the 7 Dials & the 5 Dials. One Irishman accepted a tract, but said to me, "what it is I don't know, tell me what it is about?" I told him what it is about when he said "I can't read myself, but I'll get it read."

114

Monmouth Court. February 1862.

A poor unfortunate girl.

Monday 3.
1 2nd back; found Jane King by herself, her companion being out, she seemed to be very much in trouble & told me she wished she was dead; "I know I would be worse off if I died as I am now but I am tired of my life;--it's all very well to look at us poor creatures & tell us that's our own fault, but I know better[.] I must suffer now for that wretch who seduced me; I got in it now & can't get out again; I owe ever so much to my companion & sometimes she will take my clothes off my back & tells me she would turn me out naked in the street;" I endeavoured again to persuade her to come away from her companion & give up her wicked life &c. but again without success. She told me not to call when her companion is at home for she told her that she would pay me outright well, but I told her I was not afraid of it.

top back; Old M[rs] Jones complained

115

Monmouth Court. February 1862.

A deceptive woman.

a great deal of poverty & want. "I never drinks a drop of anything, have not done so for more than six month[s]; I could swear to it I never tells a lie in my life, you may ask my landlord." But when I told her that about a month ago when I called she was laying on the floor beastly drunk; she said, ["]O bless you sir, that must be a mistake it was not me, If it was me I don't know how it happened, it must have been when my sister was here she persuaded me to go with her & we had only a drop between us."
front room; was refused admittance but was enabled to deliver my message to an Irishman whilst standing at the door; refused to accept a tract.

2 1st back; A woman of apparently bad character, was very abusive in her language when I told her the object of my visitation, but was permitted to give her a Solemn warning to flee from the wrath to come.

116

Monmouth Court. February 1862.

Tuesday 4. ill.

Wednesday 5
6 2nd back; Old M[rs] Collyer, did not best pleased to see me again, "it's of no use telling you not to come[,] I wish you would go to your own people & leave us alone;" Was permitted to deliver my message, not withstanding she introduced the Virgin Mary & father Kelley; refused to accept a tract.

A child send to school.

top front; Called upon M[rs] Jones & found that her girl is still going to school, to which I brought her a month ago (Irish free school) & the mother expressed her thanks to me for getting her there; read a portion of the word & endeavoured to express [sic] upon her "the one thing needful;" left a tract.

Visited 4 more families in this house & was permitted to deliver my message to each of them & leave tracts.

8 shop. was refused admittance & told that if I come again

117

Monmouth Court. February 1862

Agent insulted.

I would repent it; the man who spoke thus seemed to be intoxicated; when I left he threw a piece of wood after me which just passed my face.

2nd front; found an old couple in great distress, they expected temporal relief, but when I told them the object of my visitation they seemed not to care very much, but was nevertheless permitted to deliver my message & leave a tract. No Scriptures.

Thursday 6.
Finished to day the visitation in Monmouth Court; once more have I visited from house to house and room to room in that Court, where poverty & misery, sin & profligacy are predominant; there is not one christian family to be found; and more than half the population change every month, so that I very seldom meet the same people again.

118

Broad Street. February 1862.

Friday 7

25 Public house; distributed tracts at the bar to several men and woman, who accepted them kindly & to two I was permitted to say a few words concerning their immortal souls.

24. Shop. Had another conversation with M[r] Angel, a Jew, concerning "Jesus of Nazareth" was permitted to read several passages of Scripture from the New as well as the old Test[ament] to which he listened attentively & when I left him accepted a tract.

27 1st front; Called upon M[r] Herring who received me kindly & told me that he reads now his Bible regularly & attends St. Giles church every Sunday evening. [He] can't go in the morning for his clothes are so bad; would be very glad to attend the Thursday evening lecture, but he don't leave off work & he has got it, before 11 and sometimes 12 ° clock at

119

Broad St. February 1862.

night; read & explained a portion of the word & offered up a prayer.

Visited & called upon 6 more families in this house, was kindly received by five of them & permitted to deliver my message, the sixth an Irishman refused to let me into his room, but accepted a tract a the door.

Saturday 8.
Visited and called upon the sick and special cases in my district to day; read the word to twelve & offered up prayer with seven, leaving tracts with all.
[signed "H. Laudon Maud"]

Sunday 9.
Visited for two hours & a half out of the regular course of my visitation, had some very interesting & profitable conversations with working men to whom I was permitted to deliver my message.

120

Dudley St. February

A bigoted Rom[an] Cath[olic].

Monday 10.
30 top back; found a very bigoted Rom[an] Cath[olic] in this room, who told me the old story viz: "I am not of your persuasion" but still after a few minutes conversation I was permitted to read the word to him & to explain Jesus as "the way, the truth & the life"; when I left he accepted a tract.

Visited 7 more families in this house, was kindly received & permitted to deliver my message & leave tracts.

Temporal & Spiritual poverty.

32 1st front; found M[r] Blackaby in great distress on account of having lost all his little furniture for 22 shillings of rent which he owed to his Landlord; endeavoured to impress upon him that this world is not our home, & that trials & troubles are sent for the purpose of bringing us to our senses & leading us nearer to God &c. read & explained a portion of Scripture, but am sorry

121

1862 Dudley St.

to say M[r] B. remained unmoved to all I said & read, although he listened attentively.
Visited this afternoon in company with the Rev. L. Maud Senior[?] Curate of St. Giles.

Tuesday 11.
35 Had another interesting Conversation with M[r] Benjamin, a Jew, on the Claims of Jesus of Nazareth as the Messiah promised to be "the light of the Gentiles & the glory of his people Israel["]; he listened pretty attentively to all I said & read to him, but still persists, that if these things were so the Jews as a nation would not have rejected him; explained to him that it was for[e]told that the Jews would crucify the Lord of life & glory & that as a nation that they would reject him &c. left a tract on the Jewish subject &

promised to call again.

2nd back. poor old M[rs] Hart was very glad to see me again &

122

Dudley St. February

told me that since I saw her last & spoke to her of the power & privilege of prayer, she began to pray more that ever she had done before "it's true["], she said, ["]you told me that saying prayers was not to pray; I know now that it is not, I said my prayers for a great many years but now I know I never prayed before, but I began to pray now & I can't tell you what a comfort it is to me, I feel as happy as a queen; I read my Bible & I pray & don't have half the troubles I had before, for I know that Jesus my Saviour will take care of me &c.&c."; read a portion of the word & offered up a prayer.

Hopeful case.

36. top front. poor old David Sauter[?] was glad to see me & I was again permitted to deliver my message to him, to which he listened attentively; promised me to attend the special services at St. Martin's Hall; reads the Bible I gave to him some time ago; accepted a tract.

123

future visit desired.

Wednesday 12.
40. 2nd back; An Irish family in great distress; the husband, a cobbler, told me he had not broken his fast all day; (being 12 ° clock) his children are out seeing where they can get something to eat;--the poor fellow seemed really to be half starved; whether or no it is a genuine case I cannot say, for it is the first time I saw them, but certain it is that there is extreme poverty.
I promised to apply for him to the relieving officer of the Parish & at the same endeavoured to impress upon the poor man the urgent necessity of going to Jesus, the friend & Saviour of the poor; read and explained a portion of the word, left a tract & promised to call again.

top front; An elderly woman, named Smith, received me remarkably well, although the last time I called she refused me admittance altogether; I thought at once that the change was too sudden to be true & soon found it out too;--for

124

Dudley Street. February

the wretched old woman began to complain of her poverty & distress in such a manner that I was obliged to tell her "the real & only object of my visitation["], which I had no sooner done, than she began to swear at me & to curse most awfully & told me she would be_____if she did not pay me out if I came again into her room.

41 top front. Mrs Wittonten received my visit kindly & listened attentively to the word read & explained; the poor woman seems in [sic] to be earnest & sincere in her christian profession, reads her Bible & attends a place of worship. Offered up a prayer.
back room; found that poor Mr Leary has left this room, I endeavoured to find out where they went to but nobody could tell me; I had good hope concerning them.
Visited 5 more families in this house, was kindly received & permitted to deliver my message in each room.

125

1862. Dudley St. district.

Hope in Christ

Thursday 13.
43. Top front. Called again upon Mr Fidoe who was glad to see me; his son John Fidoe is still alive but fast sinking & can't possibly last much longer; the poor young man is a great sufferer, apparently he has not had any sleep for months & months & is not able to keep anything on his stomach;--when I spoke to him of Christ & his hope concerning his immortal soul he said; "I trust I am all right, my hope is in Christ, I love him; I pray to him & I hope soon to be with him; I know he is the only Saviour & I think I can say that his blood was shed for me to wash away my sin & make me fit for heaven." -- read the word and offered up a prayer.

1st back. Was glad to find poor old Mrs Taylor reading her Bible, in the words [of] St. Phillipp [sic] of old[.] I addressed her by asking her "un[der]standet[h] thou what thou reads["]?

126

Dudley Street. February

when I took up her Bible, and explained to her part of the 5th chapter of St. Mark's gospel wh[ich] she has been reading.

A communicant.

43 2nd front; found poor old Mrs Maycock very ill; but am happy to say she knows & loves her Saviour Christ & is longing for the time when she shall see Him in heaven; read & explained the word & offered up a prayer.

Friday 14.
48 2nd back; Was again refused admittance but permitted to deliver my message whilst standing at the door.

1st front; found that poor old blind Mr Law, has gone into the work-house, where I intend to visit him.

49 top front; young Mr Lee was glad to see me again & I am happy to say that he reads now his Bible & attends St. Giles

127

1862. Dudley St. district.

church very regularly. Read & explained a portion of Scripture & endeavoured to impress upon him the necessity & privilege of prayer.

Living without God in the world.

1st back; a poor widow woman with three children in great distress, they have no furniture whatever in the room, besides a few rags on which they sleep. When I spoke to her of "the one thing needful" she said, "I have not served God as I ought to have done; have been brought up in school & my mother was a very pious poor woman; Yes I know it's wrong of me to neglect my soul & to live without God, but I have done so for a great many years; it's too late now &

I am too poor I will have to go in the workhouse before long; Yes I know God is everywhere &c".

I read the word and endeavoured to impress upon her to make her peace with God.
Attended a Meeting this afternoon at the Vestry of St. Giles.

128

Dudley Street. February

Saturday 15.
Visited & called upon the sick & special cases in my district to day, was kindly received & permitted to deliver my message to all of them; with some read the word with others offered a prayer & left a tract with each.

Sunday 16. Visited for three hours to day out of the regular course of my visitation. Besides distributed tracts & notices for the St. Martin's Hall special services, at the 7 Dials & 5 Dials.

54 Monday 17. top front; found poor M[rs] Dinham in great distress on account of having no work; averted the subject from things temporal to things spiritual when she said "I am very wicked I know my troubles ought to lead me to God but I got a very bad heart; I tried to pray but I can't I am too bad God won't have no mercy on me; Know my poverty won't save me but it's

129

1862. Dudley St. District.

a very hard thing & nobody knows better than me; hope to get on a little better when I get work again & then I shall serve God better than I have done I hope &c." read the word & endeavoured to impress her with the uncertainty of life & the reallity [sic] of a judgment to come.

2nd front; poor M[r] Shean died last Friday in the Middlesex Hospital after a long illness; I visited him there several times & have reason to believe that my visits have been attended with the blessing of the Almighty; read & explained a portion of the word to the poor widow & endeavoured to impress upon her to "prepare to meet her God" she shed tears when I offered up a prayer & expressed her thanks before I left for the interest I took in her poor husband.

55. Visited 8 families in this house & was permitted to deliver my message & leave tracts with each of them.

130

Dudley Street. February

false interpretation of Scripture.

Tuesday 18.
55. Had another conversation with M[r] Joseph, a Jew, who told me when I explained to him that "without shedding of blood there is & can be no remission of sin" that this passage had reference to the circumcision. I endeavoured to convince him of the fal[l]acy of this interpretation by reading & explaining to him several passages from the old Test[ament] we parted good friends & he asked me to call again.
top front; poor old M[r] Woodall received me kindly & listened again attentively to the word read and explained. Attend[s] a place of worship & reads his Bible.

Hopeful case.

57 2nd back. Called upon M[r] Riley, an Irishman to whom I gave a Bible some time ago; told me to day that he reads it very frequently; attended twice St. Martin's Hall on Sunday evening since I saw him last & I think his case to be a hopeful one.

131 [A]

1862. Dudley St. District.

58 Public house. Distributed tracts at the bar of this Public House to several men & women & also to the barmaid & the Public master.

59. top front & back; Called again upon M[rs] Day & Ann Tyler, both blind; read and explained the word to them & endeavoured to impress upon M[rs] D. the Duty & privilege of prayer. Miss Tyler is a sincere & faithful christian woman who though blind, yet sees with the eye of faith Him who has loved her & given Himself for her.

Agent rejected.

1st back; Was again refused admittance by M[r] Kenney, an Irish Rom[an] Cath[olic] but permitted to deliver my message whilst standing at the door; refused to accept a tract.

60. Was sorry to find M[r] Terry to have left the shop, a young couple who occupy it now did not seem best pleased with my visit; but still I delivered my message.

131 [B] **[Oppenheimer mistakenly numbered two consecutive pages 131.]**

Dudley Street district. February

Wednesday 19.
61 Visited & called upon 8 families in this house, was kindly received and permitted to deliver my message in each room & to leave tracts.

No Scriptures.

63 2nd back; An Irishman, named Sullivan, seemed better inclined to listen to me to day than he did on any former occasion "is a Catholic; don't go to any place of worship; but should not like to change his religion; well my Catholic religion of course, don't think that them who goes to church or chapel are the better people for it; may be that them who stays at home are not better neither["]; has got no Bible & can't read.

child sent to school.

1st back; prevailed upon M[rs] Dunn to sent [sic] her girl 10 years old to St. Giles school; M[rs] D. attends a Roman Cath:[olic] chapel, but her husband is a protestant although he don't attend any place of worship; has a Bible; read & explained the word to her & left a tract.

132

1862. Dudley St. district

65 top front; Called upon M[r] Dale & was again permitted to deliver my message to him, is still very indifferent, but listened

more attentively to the word than he did the last time.

Visited 7 more families in this house & was permitted to deliver my message & leave a tract in each room.

Missionary encouragement.

Thursday 20.
67 top front; Mr Warton was glad to see me & listened attentively to the word read & explained; attends still regularly St. Giles church & is a Communicant there "under God you are the only person in the world, he said, to whom I have to be thankful for what I am now; Well I can't help to look upon you as the only one who has brought me to my senses, if it has [sic] not been for you I would have died in my sins, God knows that there is not a day now in all my life that I don't pray for you &c." offered up a prayer.

133

Dudley St. February 1862.

A christian's temptation.

67 shop; Called upon blind old Westhall & found him very poorly, but thanks be to God, he knows his Saviour & hopes presently to be with him in glory. — said to me to day "I believe & trust in Jesus God knows, but I am always troubled with such wicked thoughts, my heart is so bad I sometimes don't know what to do; Yes I pray & prayer is the only comfort I have; I know it is Satan who puts these wicked thoughts is my heart but I can't always very soon get rit [sic] of it & that troubles me so &c.—". Read the word and offered up prayer.

Self righteousness.

68 top back; Called upon Mrs Evans[,] a sick woman, received me kindly but am sorry to say my visits from time to time have made but very little impression upon her, she told me again to day that she hopes to go to heaven, because she thinks she has done what she could &c. Read the word and endeavoured to impress upon her

134

Dudley St. February 1862.

that nothing but the blood of Jesus can wash away her sins & that nothing but His merits can save her from everlasting destruction. offered up a prayer & left a tract.

Friday 21.
72 top front; M[r] Paine received my visit very kindly & listened attentively to the word read & explained; attends occasionally a place of worship & reads his Bible.
1st front; M[rs] Watson was again very talketive [sic], but I was nevertheless permitted to deliver my message to her.

Visited & called upon 5 more families in this house, was kindly received & permitted to deliver my message in each room.

Visited 2 sick people this afternoon, one in the St. Giles Union & the other in the Middlesex Hospital, both were glad to [see] me & listened attentively to the message.

135

Dudley Street. February 1862.

Saturday 22. My Division day; attended Devotional Meeting at the Mission house.
Sunday 23. Visited for two hours to day out of the regular course of my visitation; Besides distributed tracts & notices for the St. Martin's Hall special services, at the 7 Dials & 5 Dials.

75 Monday 24. Model Lodging house for single women; distributed tracts among them & in the Kitchen was permitted to speak to eight young women collectively of "Jesus as the Way, the Truth & the Life["].

Drunken husband.

77 1st back; Called upon M[rs] German who received me kindly, but complained very much of her drunken husband who abuses her very shamefully when under the influence of liquor; he can earn between 30 shillings & 2 a week, the whole of that sum he spends in drink & the poor woman must provide for her

136

Dudley Street. February 1862.

future visit desired

self & two children. Read & explained a portion of the word endeavouring to impress upon the poor woman the duty & priviledge of prayer &c. offered up a prayer & promised to call again.

Visited & called upon 7 more families in this house, was kindly received & permitted to deliver my message & leave a tract in each room.

Sunday trading

78 Shop; Had another conversation with M^{r} & Mrs Egan on the evil & the sin of Sunday trading; both listened attentively whilst I read & explained several passages of Scripture bearing on that subject; but am sorry to state that like on many former occasions they pleaded again "poverty & necessity" as an excuse, notwithstanding that they were constrained to confess that they were continually breaking God's holy law; left a tract.
Kitchen; Called upon Mrs Griswood read & explained to her part of the 3rd [chapter] of St. John & offered a prayer.

137

Dudley St. February 1862.

Tuesday 25. Visited for five hours to day out of the regular course of my visitation, in company with Lord Burghley.

Wednesday 26 Thursday 27 Friday 28
Have been writing my Annual Report & brought it to the Mission house this afternoon.

138

Dudley Street. [February crossed out] May 1862.

Thursday 1st of May to Wednesday the 7th have been under treatment of Dr Burrows who advised me not to visit my district.

Visitation & kind Reception after more than a month absence from my district on account of ill health.

Friday 9. Began to visit again to day but Dr Burrows told me to visit not more than three hours a day to begin with, until I get a little stronger.

Visited only a few special cases to day was kindly received & the poor people were very much pleased to see me again; poor blind Ann Tyler of 59 Dudley Street told me that she had prayed for me twice every day ever since she heard I was ill & sent to the church several times to enquire after my health. I read & explained to her & Mrs Day who was present the 23rd Psalm after which we knelt down in prayer to the throne of heavenly grace.

Saturday 10. finined [sic] to day the visitation of the sick & special cases & those put down in the Vestry room for visitation was again kindly received & permitted to deliver my message.

139

Dudley Street May 1862.

Sunday 11. Attended St. Giles church twice to day & partook of the Lord's supper; was in the district a short time in the afternoon & distributed tracts at the 5 Dials & corner of White Lion Street.

Indifference

Monday 12. Began full work to day at 24 Broad Street; Mr Angel received my visit kindly; he was in the shop when I called but asked me in the parlour where I was permitted to speak to both him & his wife of "Jesus of Nazareth as the Saviour of both Jews & Gentiles &c."

Mr A. is called & rather calls himself a liberal Jew, which is plainly speaking no Jew at all, for [it] is equally as far from real Judaism than it is from Christianity; endeavoured to impress upon him the individual responsibility of man & his lost condition without a Saviour; he listened pretty attentively & may the Lord have mercy upon his soul & bring him to a more serious state of mind for Christ's sake.

25 Distributed tracts at the bar of this

140

Dudley Street District. May 1862.

A Publican.

Public house to several men & women & also to the Publican & his wife, the former seemed inclined to abuse me and asked to know whether I would take the trouble to go about with tracts & talk about religion if I was not paid to do so; I answered him his question when his wife began to remonstrate with him upon which he got in a passion & made use of bad language when I thought best to leave the house, for he seemed to have had a little too much to drink.

Future visit desired.

27 Visited all the people in this house was kindly received by all & permitted to deliver my message in each room.
Poor Mr & Mrs Haywood 1st front were particularly glad to see me, the lat[t]er has only come home from the workhouse last week w[h]ere she had been confined for more than a month in the insane ward, but she seems to have quite recovered again; read & explained a portion of Scripture & offered up a prayer.

29 Tuesday 13. Visited Mrs Younen [?] who desired me to get her child in St. Giles school which I promised to do. delivered my message.

141

Dudley Street. May 1862.

An interesting young girl; future visit desired.

7 I visited Smith & had an interesting conversation with both him & his wife and their daughter. I very seldom find anyone at home except Mrs S. but to day I found them all there; they received me kindly & listened attentively to the word explained. I liked very much the appearance of their daughter, a girl 15 years old who goes out to work at the book folding; she seems to delight in reading her Bible of which she is very proud as having received it as a present for regularity at the school; they attend a Baptist chapel & speak very highly of the Minister there, of the name of Wilkins; left a tract & promised to call again.

Refused admittance.

9 3rd back; Was refused admittance in this room, but permitted

to deliver my message to a rough Irishwomen whilst standing at the door; put a tract into her hand which she did not want to accept but it dropt [sic] on the floor inside the room & I left it & went away. Have repeatedly been refused admittance in this room.

142

Dudley Street May 1862.

Bigoted Romanist.

Wednesday 14.
12 Visited old Mr Sullivan 2nd front[,] received my visit kindly as usual & was permitted to speak to him once more of Jesus as the only Mediator between God & men. Mr S. is a Rom[an] Cath[olic] & attends a catholic chapel he used to be very averse to my visit and for a long time never permitted me to enter his room, but now I am always a welcome visitor & he converses with me freely about the one thing needful; is still very bigoted & believes there is no salvation out of the holy mother church. No Scriptures but accepted a tract.

A brutal husband

3rd back found an Irish family in this room in very distressing circumstances, the husband is a labourer and has constant employment as his wife told me, but all his earnings he spends in the Public house & gin shop & the poor woman with 4 little children are almost starving, the lat[t]er in a state of nudity; the poor creature cried very much whilst she told me her troubles for not only

143

Dudley Street May 1862.

does he spent [sic] all his money in drink but alfo [sic] ill uses the poor woman most shamefully according to her statement;- read the word & endeavoured to impress upon her the nature & consequences of sin & the remedy provided for it &c. &c. but found her extremely ignorant and very indifferent as regards the welfare of her immortal soul.

A drunken woman.

15 1st front; Called upon M[rs] Jones who was seemingly the worse for liquor, I taxed her with it when she first denied it but afterwards confessed that a friend of her visited her whom she has not seen for some time & she had to send for a drop of drink but she took very little of it herself, she said, she hardly wet[t]ed her lips; - spoke to her seriously on the subject for which she seemed rather inclined to abuse me; left her with a solemn warning.
Visited all the other people in the house.

144

Dudley Street May 1862.

Thursday 22. I have not been able to go into my district to day as it has been raining fast all the day long & I was afraid to go into the wet lest I should be laid by again.

Future visit desired

Friday 23.
19 2nd b[ack]. An Irishman did not seem very pleased with my visit, but after a few preliminary remarks I was permitted to speak to him of Jesus as the only Mediator between God & man; accepted a tract & asked me to call again.
Visited 6 more families in this house, most Rom[an] Cath[olic] was kindly received & permitted to deliver my message in each room.

23 An Irishman named Leary, seemed to be much better inclined to listen to me to day than he did on former occasions; Read a portion of the word to which he listened attentively & accepted a tract asking me to call again.

145

Dudley St. May 1862.

Saturday 24.
Visited & called upon the sick & special cases in my district to day; was kindly received & permitted to deliver my message to each of them & to leave tracts.

Sunday 25. Visited for two hours to day out of the regular course of my visitation had some very interesting conversations with working men.

besides distributed tracts at the 5 Dials & corners of White Lion & Dudley Streets.

146 [Unnumbered in original.]

[Handwriting erratic from this point on]

Sickness in my family
When I survey this little city of a District &c
Many of whom I reported last year are gon[e]
Ast [sic] to the general state of my district I can repo[r]t progrefs
Those houses on either side of Monmouth Ct as yet I have not been able to make any headway agains[t] that soul degraiding [sic] & destroying evil, ie, Sunday Trading.
My labours are entirely confined to visitation. Widows Thomas & B- attended my meeting & Mr -

23 Dudley St 1st front is [an] example of the above. The above facts illusterated [sic] by the case of Mrs Morgan

Visitation among the Jews

13 Dud[ley] St[reet] The aged woman & her daughter; Mr Hagen, 82 Shop Mrs Josephs. 75 Mrs Lee sceptics. 85 - 2nd front

147

24 top back gowing [sic] to the church to repo[r]t me. Handcock seems confirmed in the faith

Repulsive Romanists

26 Shop - 44 1st front

54 Dudley St When reading to Mr Foley Neal, McCart[h]y, F [?] Cronin, 2 who are gon[e] out of my district.

21 card table & [?].
19 The drunken tailors & the women &c-
54 Sullaven [sic]. Brother Thornburg requesting Rev M Maud to visit a case gon[e] out of my district (ie) Mr Craley 72 top back - Joyce dying[?] case Sumners & Gutrage, Plant 26 Dud[l]ey St

[end of diary entries]

Notes

[1] *Parliamentary Papers, 1857–8,* 9, Deficiency of the Means of Spiritual Instruction, Select Committee, House of Lords: Report, p. 187.
[2] *LCM Minutes*, July 28, 1856. See also *LCM Magazine* (Nov. 1847): 242 for the death of the first St. Giles missionary from fever.

Part 3

THE SOWER'S SOIL

5

The Irish Catholic Soil In Darkest London

> Rookeries are bad, but what are they to Irish Rookeries?[1]
>
> Thomas Beames, *Rookeries of London*

> The Protestant mission to the Irish in London, was a distinctly evangelical mission as High Churchmen were generally happy to leave the Irish poor to Rome.[2]
>
> Sheridan Gilley

Few outsiders knew the Irish rookeries as well as Joseph Oppenheimer, who encountered their inhabitants on a daily basis. The high concentration of Irish Roman Catholics in St. Giles' had long been an important distinctive of the parish; its Irish settlement began during the reign of Elizabeth I.[3] In the "Dudley Street district" where Oppenheimer visited, some 303 of 697 families were Catholics, a remarkably high proportion. Roman Catholics constituted about 44 per cent of the inhabitants of Dudley Street, compared to a national average of about 4 per cent. St. Giles was in fact one of five specific areas in London where the Irish poor congregated. As a centrally located parish, it was often the first place of settlement in London for new migrants.

From Elizabethan times sporadic immigration had sustained the Irish community, but after 1790 the migration became continuous. It reached new heights in the 1820s with the advent of inexpensive sea-travel between England and Ireland, which facilitated the traffic of manual labourers at harvest.[4] The Roman Church in England found itself overwhelmed by this Irish influx well before it reached flood levels in the 1840s with the Irish Potato famine. Yet the Irish poor rarely found the English Catholic Church very welcoming; they often experienced it as both remote and foreign. As Sheridan Gilley has observed, historically—from the time of the Reformation—the English Catholic church had been composed primarily of devout landed gentry, but by the mid-nineteenth century its priests were being called upon to labour among a rough Celtic proletariat. Previously, small Catholic congregations had met mostly in the chapels of manor estates; the Irish multitudes needed large cathedrals, which required vast amounts of money and sympathetic clergy.

In the 1830s and 1840s, however, the Vicar Apostolic in London built only one new church. By 1840, Irish leakage from the faith as measured by religious practice "was, through sheer want of chapels, hopelessly beyond control."[5] The influx of some 46,000 new Catholics into London in the decade between 1841 and 1851 increased the city's Catholic population by almost 50 percent to about 150,000, mainly Cockney Irish and Irish-born.[6] Catholic practise, however, fell far short of what the Church desired from this population. The Religious Census of 1851 revealed that less than 40,000 of the faithful attended morning mass in London chapels, just over a quarter of those whom the Church claimed.[7]

Aiding the Roman Church in its mission was the compact nature of Irish settlement. The pauper migration of the 1840s had been to the historic heart of the old city, rather than to its periphery. Concentrated in three bands, the Irish formed "more than a tenth of the population in the census district of St. James's, east through the Strand, St. Giles and Holborn"; the two other concentrations were in waterfront areas north and south of the Thames.[8] At mid-century it was often observed that Irish immigrants rarely stayed in an area long enough to set down deep roots, but appearances were deceptive. The poor often moved around out of economic necessity, but they only moved short distances within a small area. It was crucial that they not leave their parish of residence; otherwise, under the Poor Law they would forfeit their right to relief.

The Irish Catholics constituted a relatively closed ethic community, somewhat isolated from the rest of society, even from their working-class English neighbours.[9] Immigrant Irish households—following rural Irish practices—incorporated lodgers, visitors, friends and sometimes extended relatives, creating a structure of obligation and kinship beyond the nuclear family, whereas unmarried "working-class Englishmen were much less likely to live in nuclear families."[10] The experience of migration heightened the importance of the family as an identity marker in a new and sometimes hostile environment. The Irish, however, attracted relatively little attention from writers of the day and were generally "ignored rather than scorned, and scorned rather than feared."[11] Surprisingly, "the Irish in England do not significantly figure in the enormously specifically religious literature of

Victorian anti-Catholicism."[12]

The single most important factor in the resurgence of English anti-Catholicism was the sustained growth of Protestant evangelicalism, which appears to have grown rapidly from the 1820s through the 1850s. English evangelical "No Popery" agitation was in part theological, but it was certainly fuelled by a fear of Roman Catholicism in Ireland as a potentially disruptive force. The avid defence of a collapsing confessional state, whose death throes were traced to the passing of Catholic Emancipation in 1829, sharpened anti-Catholic feelings among many evangelical Anglicans. Distrust of Ireland, however, was only one element in a complex set of materials. Catholics were suspect because of a dual allegiance to a Protestant monarch and a Roman Pope, considered politically unreliable because of past Catholic attempts to undermine the British state (reinforced each 5th of November on Guy Fawkes Day), and socially regressive in their association with "continental peasant poverty symbolized by wooden shoes, and the national stereotypes of Spanish cruelty, French immorality and Italian guile." As Sheridan Gilley has observed: "The Roman Catholic Church was a complex of such associations, all of them unpleasant. It was the living embodiment of every un-English vice, the national anti-type which defined all manner of native virtue, and as such was loathed before 1830 by Englishmen of all shades of theological opinion and of none at all."[13] The British government's decision to give an annual grant to fund the Irish Catholic seminary in Maynooth aroused the anger of the No Popery movement in 1845, as did the re-establishment of the Catholic hierarchy in England in 1850 that was widely seen as an act of "Papal Aggression." For a time these events spurred Protestant interests in the evangelization of the Irish poor, both in Ireland and England, but by the late 1850s, the furore had subsided and the attention of the religious public became focused elsewhere.[14]

It is helpful to understand that the background of the evangelical-Catholic conflict was, as Gilley observes: "on the plane of ideas and institutions, between two religious traditions in the process of becoming more exclusive, and therefore ever more hot in competition for Irish souls."[15] English Catholicism had for centuries operated on the fringes of English society, almost apologetic for its existence, circumspect in dress and seeking to maintain a low profile. Things began to change in the wake of the French Revolution, with the arrival of large numbers of French émigré clergy fleeing the anti-clerical and anti-Catholic storm. Young clergy enraptured by the Romantic appeal of the resurgence of Ultramontane

Catholicism on the continent began to challenge the traditionalism and the caution of their elders; by the late 1840s, the English "Church threw off the threadbare rags of outlawry and became fully Roman. Thus catholic devotional life aped the religious fashions of France and Italy as a means to reclaim Irishmen, convert England, and as an all-desirable end in itself."[16] English evangelicalism also became more strident and shrill, especially as the sons and daughters of some of the movement's leaders changed their churchmanship—moving toward Tractarianism, or on to Rome itself. As it has been observed, many who made their way from Oxford to Rome began their pilgrimage in Clapham, the home of the famous Clapham Sect—that coterie of leading evangelicals who gathered around William Wilberforce. It is important to recall that some of the most famous English Catholic converts of the nineteenth century began as evangelicals: most notably Cardinal John Henry Newman, but also Cardinal Henry Manning and three of Wilberforce's four sons.

However, the clash was not simply one of organizations. It was also a clash of mentalities and of social theories. Gilley identifies these differences not in their cures, founded upon the proper exercise of class obligation and self-help, but in their "notably dissimilar notions of almsgiving and a notably dissimilar charitable idea."[17] Gilley further observes that "the Catholic recognised in Our Lady Poverty a prime source of holiness, and though deploring its corruption in the brutish nastiness of St. Giles's, was forced by polemic into a pietistic appreciation of the Irishry, which he found reflected in a celtic proletarian sanctity enshrining the virtues of ultramontane hagiography, and the highest idea of an ideal good with which the Church strove to nourish the life of the poor."

English Catholics were divided in their responses to Irish poverty. Some "felt that Irish poverty held a special evangelical virtue, affording a challenge which men seeking sanctity must face; others ignored the poor as a distraction from the task of converting England, or worse, deplored their celtic folkways, their brawling, drinking, their rags and revolting smell."[18] The Catholic radical, however, was receptive "to contemporary continental social Catholicism ... [which] gave him a wider perspective than England alone could provide, and continental ultramontanism brought a demand for the recatholicisation of catholic social methods in a better personal witness to that idea of 'poverty of the spirit', which was reborn in the flowering of monastic and neo-feudal and pseudo-medieval romance, and was also of a piece with loyalty to Rome."[19]

In some ways, these differences can be seen in the differing attitudes

Oppenheimer evidences toward poverty. One striking difference from the Catholic approach is that in Oppenheimer there is no admiration or sanctifying of poverty: He regarded it as a "trial," an "affliction," as "troubles" or a time of "distress." John Wesley, influenced as he was by High Church Anglican writers who highly valued the patristic tradition of the early church, was closer to the Catholic view. Wesley "gained a romantic view of the primitive Church as a kind of extended family, bonded together by love, sharing its resources and prizing its poor as the 'treasure of the Church.'"[20] None of the spirituality (common to both Wesley and Roman Catholics) that envisioned "the poor as the embodiment of the suffering Christ-figure" is evident in Oppenheimer.[21] On the other hand, his observations are generally free both of censoriousness and condescension. Neither does he castigate the poor for indiscipline or idleness. In many ways, he tends to see the poor as exemplars of piety who could appreciate grace as God's free gift, rather than as a reward for merit. Yet poverty is not seen as something to be acquiesced in; rather, as an opportunity to cast oneself on the mercies of God:

> Dudley St. September 1861
>
> 25 Kitchen; poor Mrs Oldham, was very glad to see me again & I am happy to say that amidst her extreme poverty, & her husband being in a state of consumption, the poor woman retains her trust & confidence in Him who ordered all things according to the counsel of His own will; "It's very hard for me,["] she said, ["]but God knows best what is for our good. I pray to him & he gives me strength to bear my trial &c." Read the word & prayed.
>
> Dudley Street. October 1861.
>
> Tuesday 1.
> 8 2nd back. Old Mrs Wilson was glad to see me, she said everybody had forsaken her in the world, she had no one who cared for her but she knew God would never forsake, Christ was her only hope & trust & having Him she could bear all her troubles, & trials, knowing that she shall soon be in that land "where the wicked cease from troubling & the weary are at rest;" Read & explained a portion of Scripture and offered up a prayer. Mrs W. has seen better days but her husband[']s drinking habits, which by the way were the cause of his dead [sic], & sickness have reduced the poor woman to poverty; she is a member of the Wesleyan body and attends Queen St. chapel regularly.

Dudley St. February 1862

Monday 10.

Temporal & Spiritual poverty.

32 1st front; found Mr Blackaby in great distress on account of having lost all his little furniture for 22 shillings of rent which he owed to his Landlord; endeavoured to impress upon him that this world is not our home, & that trials & troubles are sent for the purpose of bringing us to our senses & leading us nearer to God &c. read & explained a portion of Scripture, but am sorry to say Mr B. remained unmoved to all I said & read, although he listened attentively.

THE SCHOOL BATTLEGROUND

Oppenheimer was undoubtedly aware that the parish of St. Giles had a special place in the history of evangelical efforts to woo Irish Catholics: The Irish Society of London, an Anglican foundation, was formed in 1822 as a sister organization to the Irish Society of Dublin (founded 1818), with the aim of evangelizing the Irish poor resident in London by means of circulating the Scriptures and the Anglican *Book of Common Prayer* in the Irish language and—perhaps more importantly—by establishing schools for the children of Irish immigrants.[22] Charlotte Elizabeth, the prominent evangelical novelist by the 1830s, was an important promoter of the Irish Society. In 1831, she moved to London so that she could personally visit and relieve the Irish poor of St. Giles' and help found the Irish Free Schools in St. Giles'. Although Charlotte Elizabeth was born into an English clerical family, she experienced an evangelical conversion as an adult while living in Dublin and was nurtured by Irish Anglican evangelicals before moving back to England. She was therefore closely associated with the "Celtic Fringe" of British evangelicalism; Hugh McNeile, the Irish Anglican who dominated Liverpool evangelicalism and a leading figure in the No Popery Movement, was her on-going mentor.

A major figure in evangelical circles from 1830, she embraced pre-millennialism through the influence of Hugh McNeile, whose articles often appeared in her *Christian Lady's Magazine*. The magazine was a huge publishing success, and she used it to serialize fictional accounts of human distress, working closely with Lord Shaftesbury and others to alert middle- and upper-class women to social evils—particularly those associated with the factory reform acts, and with the treatment of women and children. She used her remarkable writing talents to produce a steady stream of anti-Catholic rhetoric (supplemented by the mid-1830s by strongly anti-Tractarian sentiments). In her view, a staunchly Protestant England needed continually to resist Catholic oppression. This bears out Sheridan Gilley's observation that "the Protestant witness to the Irish in England was less English than Irish and Scottish in its inspiration and personnel, and if it owed little to continental Protestantism, it prayed for the conversion of Spain and China, and all the lands in between—even Rome."[23]

The Irish Free School was a forerunner of the ragged schools, a popular movement that developed in the early 1840s and sought to offer a rudimentary education to the poorest of the poor. These soon were patronized by Irish Catholic children, and the ragged schools became a key instrument of evangelicals seeking to proselytize among the poor, particularly the Irish poor. In his journal Oppenheimer mentions encouraging parents to send their children to the "George Street Ragged School" and the "St. Giles's ragged school", which appear to be names for the same school—the St. Giles's Ragged School in George Street. One of the earliest of the ragged schools in London had been the St. Giles's Ragged School in Streatham Street, formed in 1843 and begun in a cow-shed. It was in the loft of this building where the founding meeting of the Ragged School Union was held in 1844. In 1848 Streatham Street made way for New Oxford Street, and school moved to Neale's Yard Ragged School (located in the triangle on the northeast side of the Seven Dials bounded by Great St Andrew Street, Queen Street and King Street). Two other ragged schools operated in the immediate area—one in Little Coram Street just north of the British Museum (founded by a City Missionary in 1847)—but this was some distance from Dudley Street. The Neale's Yard School was replaced by the St. Giles's Ragged School at the corner of George Street and Broad Street (opposite Endell Street) in 1852, which meant that the Ragged School was now within the small district visited by Oppenheimer.

The success of the ragged schools in attracting Roman Catholic children was demonstrated in July of 1851, when the Italian Father Faa di Bruno forcefully entered a ragged school and took down the names of any Irish Catholic student with a view to pressuring their parents into withdrawing them. *The Times* of London reported the event, and a war of words erupted between *The Tablet*, the Roman Catholic periodical that welcomed the intervention, and the *London City Mission Magazine,* which objected. As Sheridan Gilley has observed, the "visit was followed by the predictable assault of an Irish mob throwing mud and manure."[24]

The confrontation coincided with a Catholic mission to the area, in which Archbishop Wiseman preached at an evening service. Gilley describes it as follows:

> There were three thousand spectators; the rooftops and parapets were crowded with men and women holding candles; the windows and walls were lit with lamps in the Italian fashion—"it had the appearance of a street Madonna festival in Rome," [Wiseman wrote to Monsignor Talbot]. Wiseman's train included children rescued from the Evangelicals, now singing hymns to the Virgin; and the Cardinal exacted from the excited crowd a promise to drink in moderation and to shun the Protestant schools. Well might he rejoice in so Latin an expression of popular faith: a Roman means to a Catholic end.[25]

Such enthusiasm, however, soon ebbed away. The hard work of reclaiming the Irish poor from religious disinterest, let alone Protestantism, remained to be done.

Oppenheimer encountered the impact of the Roman Catholic revival that had begun in the 1840s in his visits. It was "old Mrs. Collyer" at 6 Monmouth Court who twice mentioned "Father Kelly"—the first time on the 29th of October, 1861:

> You always come here & I told you the last time I was not of your persuasion; I am not one of your people & I never goes to any of your people for nothing at all & don't want to be visited; I know all you can tell me.
>
> Father Kelly bless his soul, is my priest & I knows him & he knows me, he is as good a soul as ever breathed & I will never listen to nobody else; Yes he told me of Jesus blessed be His name & his blessed mother & here, taking a Crucifix out of her pocket, he gave me that & told me never to part with it, which I never shall &.c.

Oppenheimer apparently got the spelling of "Old Mrs. Collyer's" name wrong, for the census record indicates that the name was spelt Collopy; she may have been Mary Collopy, 57-year-old wife of William Collopy. Her husband of the same age was Irish-born, but Mary was born in Hertfordshire. The census records that their three children lived with them: a 28-year-old daughter (also Mary); a 22-year-old son (also William); and a 15-year-old son, Richard. All three children were born in Middlesex, which would indicate that the family had lived in England for at least about 30 years. But as Oppenheimer elsewhere in the journal seems to use the term "old" to describe people in their 70s, it would seem more likely that he writes above of William Collopy's elderly Irish mother, who may have lived with the family but is not listed on the census form.

His second encounter with "Old Mrs Collyer" was on 5 February, 1862:

> 6 2nd back; Old M[rs] Collyer, did not best pleased to see me again, "it's of no use telling you not to come[,] I wish you would go to your own people & leave us alone;" Was permitted to deliver my message, not withstanding she introduced the Virgin Mary & father Kelley; refused to accept a tract.

Father William Kelly was known well beyond his East End church. He was a master publicist; in the twenty-year period between 1840 and 1860, his letters appeared regularly in the Catholic press. He well represented the younger radical Catholic clergy, who were supported by Cardinal Wiseman in the struggle with the older English Catholic clergy. The older clergy were hostile to innovation, particularly to the attempts to make the small, wealthy Catholic chapels into churches for the poor. The radicals wanted large and splendid buildings with ample accommodation for the poor, who were by and large excluded from Catholic worship by pew rents and areas effectively segregated by class—in order to keep the traditionally wealthy and aristocratic English Catholics a good distance from the poor, with their stench and their fleas. Kelly's new church, Saints Mary and Michael on Lukin Street off Commercial Road, was built in 1857, some four miles east of Dudley Street. Saints Mary and Michael represented the efflorescence spirit of the "Second Spring" of English Catholicism, as the Continental Catholic spirit of revival that had begun flowering in the 1840s had been called. The Second Spring "aroused a wholly new kind of religious enthusiasm through the ordinary forms of post-Reformation continental worship that England had never known: the *Quarant' Ore*,[26] certain cults of the Virgin, the renewal of baptismal vows, frequent communion, processions with lights and banners and bearing the host."[27] In the year of its opening, Kelly boasted in *The Tablet* that "This splendid new church has doubled my congregation ... it beats hollow in beauty the finest of the [gin] palaces," outshines its sulking heretical rivals, and "has in the eyes of our protestant neighbours, raised this poor congregation at least fifty years in social position and consideration."[28] A more recent observer has described it as "a defiant act of communal assertion and self-display."[29] Still, Kelly's approach—that of building large and ostentatious churches to serve the poor—was an approach that had been opposed by Wiseman's predecessor, Bishop Thomas Griffiths, Vicar Apostolic of the London District who died in 1847.

Father William O'Connor represented the conservative Catholics who, exasperated with the antics of his subordinates Fathers John Kyne, di Bruno and Dr. Melia, complained to an unsympathetic Archbishop Wiseman: "I esteem missions because I believe this to be the means of bringing back the poor ... but they must be conducted with utility—with propriety and *order*; and it is a matter of notoriety that in these missions these three requisites are eminently wanting. My principle is obedience ... we want *cool* and *sound* heads ... otherwise your Lordship's whole district will be in confusion, and your chapels deserted by the stranger, by the sober and calm."[30] Ironically, O'Connor's sentiments were similar to those of the members of the governing body of the London City Mission.

If Oppenheimer found a great deal wanting in the popular religious sentiments of the Irish poor whom he encountered, he might have been surprised to learn, as Sheridan Gilley has observed, that "even to the more sympathetic English Catholic, Irish religion seemed both more and less than the official creed of the Church, a compound of ignorance, tribal hate, perversion of orthodox Catholicity and idolatrous trust in the Mother of God." It was the case, he concedes, that "Many London Irish knew their Pater and Ave, and little besides; while the articulate who argued so pointedly with Protestant proselytizers retained a lively belief in the picturesque embellishments of the folk religion of the Irish west and south."[31]

OVERT WITH THREATS OF PERSONAL HARM

This backdrop of religious rivalry helps us to make sense of the fact that the Irish Catholic community offered Oppenheimer his strongest resistance. Threats of personal harm were not the norm, but were often made upon the first contact of Roman Catholics with the missionary, as is demonstrated in the three following entries:

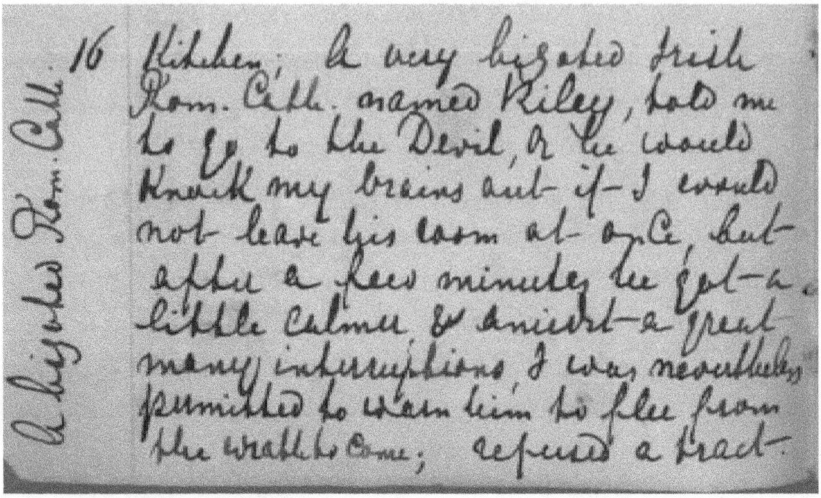

Tuesday 3 September 1861
Dudley Street

A bigoted Rom[an] Cath[olic].

16 Kitchen; A very bigoted Irish Rom[an] Cath[olic] named Riley, told me to go to the Devil, or he would knock my brains out if I would not leave his room at once, but after a few minutes he got a little calmer, & amidst a great many interruptions, I was nevertheless permitted to warn him to flee from the wrath to come; refused a tract.

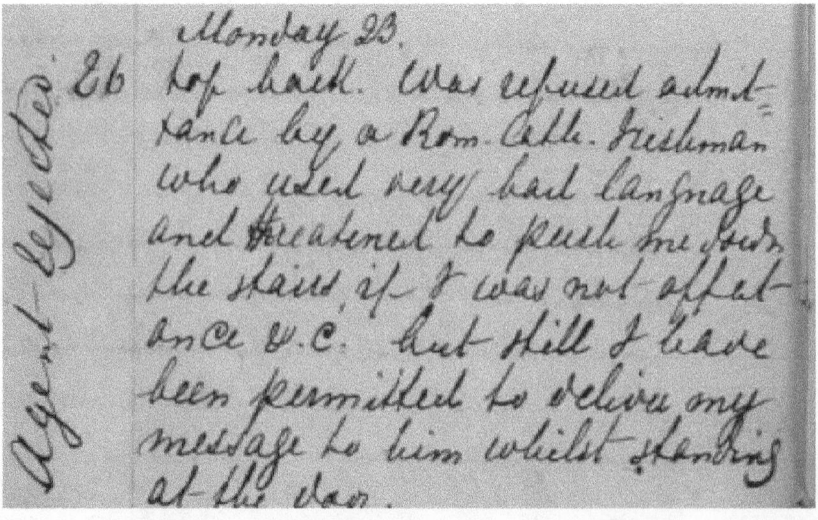

September 23, 1861
Dudley Street

Agent rejected.
#86. top back. Was refused admittance by a Rom[an] Cath[olic] Irishman who used very bad language and threatened to push me down the stairs if I was not off at once &.c. but still I have been permitted to deliver my message to him whilst standing at the door.

Agent-rejected.

1st back. Another low Irish
family, the husband named
Lever was apparently the worse
for liquor & when his wife opened the door & I went into the
room he used the most filthy
language towards the poor woman
for letting me in & told me he
did not want any preaching &
if I did not go at once he would
be — if he did not give me

7

Dudley Street — September 1861
something I would not like. Endeavoured to pacify him, but he
became very excited, so that I
thought it expedient to leave the
room.

September 4, 1861
Dudley Street

Agent rejected

[#19] 1st back. Another low Irish family, the husband named

Lever [?] was apparently the worse for liquor & when his wife opened the door & I went into the room & he used the most filthy language towards the poor woman for letting me in, & told me he did not want any preaching & if I did not go at once, he would be_____if he did not give me something I would not like. [I] endeavoured to pacify him, but he became very ex[c]ited, so that I thought it expedient to leave the room.

VERBAL HOSTILITY

Threats of personal violence seem to have been made more often in the early years of the mission's work. Over the years such opposition seems to have died down, although verbal hostility continued to be encountered, especially from Irish Catholics. Open hostility was generally most intense from Irish Roman Catholics. Here are two entries (in addition to the second and third cited above) from a single week in September, 1861:

September 24, 1861
Monmouth Court

Agent rejected

[#2] front room. An Irish woman who opened the door, refused to let me into the room, saying she was not of my persuasion, & notwithstanding my trying to persuade her to listen to what I had got to say, I could not get her attention, she kept on talking & scolding till she shut the door in my face.

September 26, 1861

Monmouth Court

Agent rejected.

Thursday 26.
#9. top back. A miserable old Irish woman used the most disgusting language imaginable, so much so that I did not think it prudent to talk to her any longer, but left her after I had given her a solemn warning.

Given the high proportion of Roman Catholics in the district, and the fact that many had just arrived from Ireland, more principled and non-threatening opposition was encountered among Catholics, some of whom were quite devout. Others, while not devout, apparently found their Catholic identity threatened by the presence of a Protestant missionary and were especially defensive about his reading of the Bible. Ever since the London City Mission had begun campaigning in the late 1830s to place free copies of the New Testament and the full Bible in the hands of the poor, some of the strongest resistance came from Catholics who viewed the offer with suspicion. The Roman Church taught, of course, that the Christian Scriptures were authoritative, but repeatedly cautioned that they were only properly interpreted by the Catholic clergy. In the nineteenth century, the popular understanding among many Catholics was that the laity should not be encouraged to read the Scriptures on their own, for fear of falling into Protestant error. The view that Bible reading was a peculiarly Protestant activity was repeatedly advanced by Catholic lay people. The following report from an early issue of *The London City Mission Magazine* in 1839 is typical:

> On the New Testament being presented to one woman, who is a Roman Catholic, she sternly refused to have it, saying, that she would rather be drawn to pieces by horses than she would have it and deny her religion. She said, that if she received it she must make confession of it to the priest, and she was sure that he would not grant her absolution for such a sin. Two other women were also present, and they all appeared highly offended with me for bringing them a book which was intended to draw them from the religion in which they had been baptized and also to deny the blessed Virgin Mary, which they would never do for any body.[32]

Oppenheimer often encountered a similar reaction from devout Irish Catholics:

> Monday, 16 September 1861
> 65 Dudley Street
>
> *Romanist's notion of the Bible reading*
>
> Monday 16.
> 65. Kitchen, a very bigoted Romanist; told him the object of my visitation when he said: "I am one of the old church & not like your Bible christians who are one thing one day & another thing the next; Our church don't deny that the Bible is the Book of God & they try to keep it sacred, it is you protestants which make the Bible a common book; Well I mean to say that you protest[ants] tell everybody to read the Bible & that is the reason that you got

so many sects, one makes one thing of it and another something else, but we leave it in better hands, & another thing is "You Protest[tants] have got the Bible from our church you can't deny that" &.c. I have been permitted to quote several passages from Scripture & to explain "Jesus" as the only mediator between God & men; accepted a tract.

It is significant that Oppenheimer is called a "Bible Christian," a term evangelicals often used of themselves. In this instance Oppenheimer seems to have avoided arguing with the man, trying to keep the discussion focused on the person of Christ and Christ's atonement for sin, beliefs that were common ground between Protestants and Catholics.

Another antagonistic conversation occurred between him and a Mr. Sullivan, and again Oppenheimer sought to bring the conversation back to Scripture, demonstrating the appropriateness of the label of being a "Bible Christian":

Friday, 20 September 1861

81 Dudley Street

Where the church was before Luther & An Irish Romanist's question answered.

Kitchen. Mr Sullivan a bigated [sic] Irish Rom[an] Cath[olic] seemed very averse to my visit & asked me the often repeated story "which was the oldest church? & where was your church before Luther & Henry VIII? I answer[e]d the first question by telling him that that [sic] the Church of Christ at the upper chamber at Jerusalem was the first church in the christian era; & secondly that that church was before Luther exactly where it is now, viz. "the Bible."
Mr S. introduced a great many different subjects, but I was permitted to read the word & deliver my message; accepted a tract.

A very similar line of argument was put forward by another Irishman at 19 Dudley Street a few months later:

14 January 1862
Dudley Street

Where the Prot[estamt] religion is & was.

Tuesday 14
19 top back; an Irishman did not seem best pleased with my

visit at first, but after a few remarks entered into conversation when I found that he had read the Bible but only for the sake of argument. I endeavoured as much as possible to avoid Controversy, but he insisted upon my answering him where the Protestant religion was before Luther and Henry VIII & when I told him that the religion of Jesus Christ was to be found in the Bible & that it was there before Luther as well as now, he said, ["]Well how is it then that you Bible christians all differ from one another but we don't profess to read the Bible & we have one church & one faith." I told him that there were differences of opinion in the Rom[an] Church as well, but that all Protestants agreed upon the Cardinal doctrines of the Bible, as an instance I read & explained to him part of the 3rd chapter to the Romans upon which all true Protest[ants] agree; left a tract & promised to call again.

IRISH INDIFFERENCE

Both Oppenheimer and the Catholic clergy were aware that many of the Irish poor were not at all devout. Many had fallen through the cracks when it came to Catholic pastoral care. Oppenheimer often encountered Irish who were seemingly indifferent to his approach, more annoyed by his preaching than angered by what he said, although they "parted good friends":

2 September, 1861

A Crowded Room of Irish Catholics

Monday 2
8 Top front—; found 9 persons in this room, men & women, all Irish, & all seem to be at home there, some of them knew my face, especially old Mrs Sullivan who said "bless you, You Know we are not of your persuasion; we don't reads your tracts & we don't want nothing." After a few minutes conversation however, I was permitted to deliver my message & tell them of Jesus Christ as the only Mediator between God and men; several refused to accept tracts, but we parted good friends.

A month later when Oppenheimer returned for a follow-up visit, he encountered Mr. Sullivan who gave him a less sympathetic reception:

Dudley Street. October 1861.

Tuesday 1.

8 top front. Called upon Mr Sullivan an Irish Rom[an] Cath[olic] & found 3 other Irishmen besides Mr S. in the room, most of whom I knew: Mr S. told me to call some other day as he was busy just now, but knowing that this was a mere excuse to get rid of my company & not inclined to let the opportunity go to speak to these poor Irishmen about their immortal souls, I offered each a tract "Repentance without fruits" & made some remark upon "Repentance" & from that I quoted several verses of Scripture & was thus permitted to deliver my message notwithstanding Mr S's grumbling all the while.

Oppenheimer made even less headway with another Irish Catholic, as is shown in the following exchange:

27 January 1862
60 Dudley Street

60 2nd back; An Irishman, did not seem best pleased with my visit; "Am not of your religion, don't care what you are I don't want to be bothered you better go to your own people; I am a Catholic, if you want to know & never will have nothing to do with you protestants." I endeavoured to speak to him, but he became very much excited & very abusive in his language, he would not let me say a word but kept on swearing & cursing so that I thought it best to leave the room; refused a tract.

POLITICAL OPPOSITION

Not surprisingly, the issue of politics surfaced with some frequency, complaints generally related to the historic Irish grievances toward the English, a line of argument that Oppenheimer sought to avoid. He tried instead to steer the conversation to specifically theological questions upon whose theological significance both Catholics and Protestants could agree:

Monmouth Court September 1861
24 September 1861

Tuesday 24.
2 2nd back; found 3 women & 2 men in this room, all Irish, they did not seem best pleased with my visit, but notwithstanding listened very attentively whilst I spoke to them of Christ's willingness to save & man's responsibility [not] to neglect so great salv[ation]; One of the men seemed to be very much inclined to introduce

> silly questions about church government & the wrongs of the Irish from the English &.c. but I carefully avoided to argue with him, simply confining myself to "the one thing needful"; when I left each accepted a tract.

About three weeks later Oppenheimer encountered a similar response from another Catholic family, who interpreted his work as an attempt to make Catholics become "turncoats," inducing them to betray their community with his Protestant propaganda:

> Monday, 14 October 1861
>
> 53 Dudley Street
>
> *An Irish spirit*
>
> 53 Kitchen. A Rom[an] Catholic family did not seem best pleased with my visit; I have not visited them before as they only are there about a fourthnight [sic]; seem to be very bigoted, the husband a Cobbler, said in a true Irish spirit "You are Protestants & a fine set you are look at your Protestant government they are a set of rogues who want to oppress us Catholics & our old holy religion; it's very well to try to make good christians but you are one of those who goes about to make turncoats["] &.c. Refused to accept a tract.

Again a few weeks later, the politics card was played by a "red hot" Irish cobbler by the name of Davy:

> Tuesday, 29 October 1861
>
> 5 Monmouth Court.
> 5 top front. An Irish family named Davy late of 19 Dudley St. the husband a red hot Irishman began to talk about Politics at such a rate that I found it extremely difficult to get him to listen to what I had got to say, at last succeeded to call his attention to the 26th verse of the 16th chapt[er] of Matth[ew] "What shall it profit a man &c." & here too he began to be as talketive [sic] as he has [sic] been before, but have been permitted to tell him of the vast importance to seek first the Kingdom of heaven &c. read the word & left a tract.

PERSISTENCE SLOWLY WINS ACCESS

Oppenheimer's remarkable tenacity and persistence did enable him to make some headway amongst his Irish Catholic listeners. His first aim was to win a hearing so that he could read a portion of Scripture; his second goal was to engage in meaningful conversation about what he had read. If his listeners were willing, he would leave them a tract. His great hope, however, was that they would be willing to accept a copy of the New Testament or a complete Bible, with a view to their reading of the same. His ultimate goal was their personal conversion and participation in a local church. He was careful to record whether he established a cordial relationship with those he visited, and he indicated whether or not they expressed a desire for him to visit again. The following is a typical entry:

> Wednesday, 25 September 1861
>
> *No Scriptures*
>
> Wednesday 25.
> 6. Parlour & first floor is kept by a low Irish woman as a lodging house, she repeatedly refused me admittance & I cannot proceed to get into her rooms to see her lodgers, but she gave me permission to day to go upstairs & visit the other inmates who live in the upper part of the house; they are all very low Irish, but was permitted to deliver my message & leave tracts. None of them has a Bible or Test[ament].

In the case of Mr. Sullivan at 63 Dudley Street, his repeated visits seem to have resulted in making some headway:

> 19 February 1862
> Dudley Street
>
> *No Scriptures.*
>
> 63 2nd back; An Irishman, named Sullivan, seemed better inclined to listen to me to day than he did on any former occasion "is a Catholic; don't go to any place of worship; but should not like to change his religion; well my Catholic religion of course, don't think that them who goes to church or chapel are the better people for it; may be that them who stays at home are not better neither["]; has got no Bible & can't read.

Another example of Oppenheimer's persistence paying off is seen in his visit to another Mr. Sullivan, who lived at 12 Dudley Street:

> 14 May 1862

Dudley Street

Bigoted Romanist.

Wednesday 14.
12 Visited old Mr Sullivan 2nd front[,] received my visit kindly as usual & was permitted to speak to him once more of Jesus as the only Mediator between God & men. Mr S. is a Rom[an] Cath[olic] & attends a catholic chapel he used to be very averse to my visit and for a long time never permitted me to enter his room, but now I am always a welcome visitor & he converses with me freely about the one thing needful; is still very bigoted & believes there is no salvation out of the holy mother church. No Scriptures but accepted a tract.

PROGRESS WITH CATHOLICS

Clearly a number of Irish Catholics were receptive of his reading of Scripture and his attempts to engage them in conversation, such as the following Irish cobbler:

September 1861
Friday 6 Dudley Street

29 Top front. Was kindly received by an Irish Cobbler, whom I saw before in another part of my district some six months ago, but since that he left my district & has now come back again; listened very attentively to the word read & explained & asked me to call again.

Another Irish cobbler and his wife surprised Oppenheimer with their knowledge of Scripture, and his theology was close enough to Oppenheimer's for them to talk cordially and for Oppenheimer to leave a tract:

Monmouth Court. September 1861.
Thursday 26.

Hopeful case.

2nd back. Another Irish family, Rom[an] Cath[olic] but they received my visit very kindly & the husband, a cobbler, asked me to sit down; found him pretty well versed in Scripture & when I spoke to him of the nature of sin & God's righteousness in saving the sinner through Christ Jesus &.c. he said: ["]I know God is a holy God & he will punish sin, there is a hell I believe it there is not a doubt about it in my mind; Yes we all deserve to go there, I do I know it; Yes I believe Christ has died for me, He is a sufficient Saviour; I know He is the way to heaven I trust to no other for salvation; I don't do as I ought but I try to do the best & the rest I leave to Christ, he alone can save me & I pray that he will save me["]. Left a tract & promised to call again.

Two other Irish Catholic families were receptive to Oppenheimer's visits:

Wednesday 9.

Dudley Street October 1861.

Future visit desired.

38 1st back. Another Irish family received me very kindly, they introduced the Virgin Mary into our conversation, but still I was permitted to declare to them repentance toward God & faith towards Our Lord Jesus Christ as the only Mediator between God & men; accepted a tract & asked me to call again.

Tuesday 24. September 1861
Monmouth Court
Dudley St.
A New Test[ament] desired.

3. 2nd back. A young couple lately come over from Ireland received me very kindly & listened attentiv[e]ly whilst I read & explained the 5[th] chapt[er] to the Romans, No Bible & upon my asking him whether he would accept the loan of a New Test[ament] & whether he would read it, he said: "Yes Sir I would like to get one, I can't read much but my missus is a good scholar & we could read it together;"— I promised to procure him a New Test[ament].

Oppenheimer often found that the elderly were responsive to his visits. This was the case with the 78-year-old Sarah Foxcroft from Scotland, who lodged at 68 Dudley Street with 50-year-old charwoman Anne MacDonald from Ireland, and two other boarders in their 30s. Her neighbor, Mrs. McCarthy at 69 Dudley Street, was Sarah Foxcroft's friend and a devout Bible-reading Roman Catholic:

Dudley Street

Tuesday, 16 September 1861

Hopeful case

69 1st front. Called upon Mr[s] McCarthy, an Irish Cath[olic] woman, was kindly received & permitted to read and explain a portion of Scripture & to offer up a prayer. Mrs McC. attends a Rom[an] Cath[olic] place of worship, but am happy to say I have been the instrument of leading her to the word of God, I procured her a copy of Scripture which she very much delights in reading in company with old Mrs Foxgroft [sic] a true christ[ian] woman.

Oppenheimer describes Mrs. Foxcroft as both old and poor and a "true christian woman" when we next encounter her. Like Mrs. McCarthy, her flatmate Mrs. MacDonald is a Roman Catholic; it is clear from the entry that Oppenheimer was able to make progress in winning her respect and trust, as he had Mrs. McCarthy's:

Dudley Street October 1861.
Thursday 17.

Missionary encouragement.

[68] 1st front. Read the word & offered up a prayer with poor Mrs Foxgroft who was very glad to see me. I am happy to say that Mrs McDonald a bigoted Catholic woman with whom Mrs Foxgroft lives & who was at first very averse to my visits, at times when I came into the room & began to talk to her she was sure to leave til I was gone, but now she listens very attentive whilst I read the word and kneels down with us in prayer.

Another Catholic who responded positively to Oppenheimer was Dennis Fitzgerald, a 43-year-old Irish-born bootmaker. His wife, Catherine, was 27. The census report indicates that two boys, both named Patrick Fitzgerald (ages 3 and 14) lived with them, but they are not listed as their children, but rather as lodgers.

Broad Street. October 1861.

Future visit desired.

26 top fl[oor] back. An Irish cobbler did not seem best pleased with my visit, telling me the old story, "was not of my persuasion, has his own church &.c." however after a few observation[s] I

> succeeded to get into better graces & he offered me a chair to sit down, and notwithstanding his introducing the Virgin Mary, I was permitted to read the word and endeavour to impress upon him "repentance towards God & faith towards our Lord Jesus Christ;" accepted a tract & asked me to call again.

The challenge of providing pastoral care to the Catholic faithful is seen in the following encounter with an elderly Catholic woman:

> *Temporal & spiritual poverty.*
>
> 8 2nd back. An old woman in a most distressing state of poverty, she complained a great deal & I had some difficulty to avert her mind from things temporal to things spiritual, she is a Rom[an] Cath[olic] but has not been to a place of worship for six years; "I knows I have a soul; Yes I believe there is a heaven & a hell; because every body says so; it would be very hard if poor creatures like me would go to hell I am sure we has got our hell here; I can't do no more I says my prayers sometimes["] &c. endeavoured to explain to her that "without holiness no man shall see the Lord"; read the word & left a tract.

Another person who can be identified from the census record is William Leonard, a 30-year-old Irish-born labourer, married to 28-year-old Catherine Leonard (also Irish-born). Their three children, 5-year-old William, 3-year-old Johanna, and one-year-old Patrick, had all been born in London. Norah Condon, a 50-year-old Irish nurse, lived with the family as a lodger. The first recorded visit was on the 4th of October:

> Dudley Street October 1861.
>
> *hopeful case.*
>
> Friday 4.
> 24. 2nd front. Mr Leonard whom I found at dinner was very glad to see me & I found that he has been reading the New Test[ament] I gave him some time ago; he knew several passages by heart & seemed much pleased for my commending his boy whom I got into a place; endeavored to impress upon him the necessity of prayerful reading of the word of God.

Oppenheimer had visited him twice while in hospital, and followed up with more visits in his lodging:

> Dudley Street. January 1862.

> 24. Wednesday 15. 2nd front; Called upon M[r] Leonard, an Irishman who was in the Middlesex Hospital sometime ago where I visited him twice; he was very glad to see me to day & expressed his thanks for my coming to see him in the Hospital; is a Rom[an] Cath[olic] & can read but very little, but I gave him a New Test[ament] which he is trying to read, he seems to value it very much, although he is still very indifferent about "the things which belong to his peace" listened attentively to the word read & explained & desired me to call again.

Two final entries illustrate how Oppenheimer was able to deal with difficult and argumentative Catholics, avoid points of controversy, and keep his message focused on central truths of the faith:

> 10 January 1861
> Dudley Street
>
> *A bigoted Rom[an] Cath[olic]*
>
> 8. 1st front. M[r] Ancle, an Irish bigoted Rom[an] Cath[olic] received me kindly & I had a long & interesting conversation with him again; he introduced as usual the Virgin Mary & the Holy Church but I was permitted to explain to him once more "Jesus" as the Way, the Truth & the Life; accepted a tract
>
> Dudley Street
> 23 January 1862
>
> *Future visit desired.*
>
> 56 2nd back; An Irish family, very bigoted, but still receive my visits very kindly & I was again permitted to explain to them Jesus as the only Mediator between God & men; when I left the husband accepted a tract & asked me to call again.

In the face of the Roman church's inability to meet the pastoral needs of the Irish poor, those Roman Catholic clergy who adopted the attitude of St. Paul in Colossians 1:18 surely would have been able to rejoice in Oppenheimer's work among Irish Catholics, even if they didn't agree with all of Oppenheimer's doctrine. In that verse the Apostle wrote, "The important thing is that in every way, whether from false motives or true, Christ is preached. And because of this I rejoice."

Notes

[1] Thomas Beames, *Rookeries of London,* p. 58.
[2] Sheridan Gilley, "Protestant London, No Popery and the Irish Poor: II (1850–1860)," *Recrusant History*, II (1971–72), p. 21.
[3] Sheridan Gilley, "Papists, Protestants and the Irish in London, 1835–70," in *Studies in Church History: Popular Practice and Belief*, eds. G. J. Cuming and David Baker (Cambridge, 1972), p. 263.
[4] Ibid.
[5] Gilley,"Papists, Protestants and the Irish in London," p. 263.
[6] Gilley, "Papists, Protestants and the Irish in London," p. 264.
[7] The census returns revealed an attendance of 35,584. Sheridan Gilley has estimated that up to 4,000 worshippers attended chapels that did not submit returns. Gilley, "Papists, Protestants and the Irish in London," p. 264, n. 2.
[8] Gilley,"Papists, Protestants and the Irish in London," p. 264. The two waterfront areas included on the north: Poplar, Stepney and St. George's-in-the-East; and on the south St. Olave's, Southwark and adjacent areas of St. Saviour's, Bermondsey, Lambeth and Rotherhithe.
[9] Sheridan Gilley, "Protestant London, No Popery and the Irish Poor, 1830–1860," *Recusant History,* vol. 10, p. 211.
[10] Lynn H. Lees, "Patterns of Lower-Class Life: Irish Slum Communities in Nineteenth-Century London," in *Nineteenth Century Cities*, eds., Stephan Thernstrom and Richard Sennett (New Haven: Yale University Press, 1969), p. 377. Lees comments: "Far from destroying the Irish family, migration into London made family life all the more important as a source of an identity in a new and hostile world."
[11] The novels of Charles Dickens were brilliant at bringing the world of the poor to the attention of the middle classes. However, the Catholic poor of an area like St. Giles were virtually ignored by Dickens although he often explored its rookeries. Sheridan Gilley, "Protestant London, No-Popery and the Irish Poor, 1830–1860," *Recusant History*, vol. 10, p. 210–11.
[12] Ibid., p. 212.
[13] Sheridan Gilley, "Protestant London, No Popery and the Irish Poor," p. 213.
[14] For a full discussion of these events and the reason for the falling off of Protestant efforts, see Lewis, *Lighten Their Darkness*, pp. 200–02.
[15] Gilley, "Papists, Protestants and the Irish in London," p. 259.
[16] Gilley, "Papists, Protestants and the Irish in London, 1835–70," p. 259.
[17] Sheridan Gilley, "Papists, Protestants and the Irish in London, 1835–70," in *Studies in Church History: Popular Practice and Belief*, eds. G. J. Cuming and David Baker (Cambridge, 1972): p. 260.
[18] Sheridan Gilley, "Papists, Protestants and the Irish in London, 1835–70," in *Studies in Church History: Popular Practice and Belief*, eds. G. J. Cuming and David Baker

(Cambridge, 1972): p. 262.

[19] Sheridan Gilley, "Papists, Protestants and the Irish in London, 1835–70," in *Studies in Church History: Popular Practice and Belief*, eds. G. J. Cuming and David Baker (Cambridge, 1972): p. 261.

[20] John Walsh, "John Wesley and the Urban Poor," *Revue Française de Civilisation Britannique* 6, No. 3, p. 19.

[21] Walsh, "Wesley," p. 20.

[22] In 1830 it opened the Irish Episcopal Chapel (a proprietary chapel later known as West Street Episcopal Chapel) in St. Giles' under the pastoral care of Henry H. Beamish, an Irish-born clergyman and the clerical secretary of the Irish Society. *Record*, 17 Jan. 1833. Beamish left the chapel in 1832 to become Perpetual Curate of Trinity Chapel, Conduit Street, a fashionable congregation. On Beamish, see Sheridan Gilley, "Beamish, H.H." in Lewis, *Dictionary of Evangelical Biography* (Oxford, 1995).

[23] Sheridan Gilley, "Papists, Protestants and the Irish in London," p. 261.

[24] Sheridan Gilley, "Catholic Faith of the Irish Slums, London, 1840–70," in *Studies in Church History: Popular Practice and Belief*, ed. G. J. Cuming and David Baker (Cambridge: Ecclesiastical History Society, 1972), p. 845.

[25] Catholic Faith of the Irish Slums, p. 845.

[26] In this devotional practice, forty hours of continuous prayer in one church is followed the exposing of the sacrament. Often it is succeeded by another church starting the round of prayer again.

[27] Sheridan Gilley, "The Roman Catholic Mission to the Irish in London, 1840–1860," *Recusant History*, vol 10, 1969–1970, p. 132–33.

[28] Kelly quoted in Gilley, "The Roman Catholic Mission to the Irish in London, 1840–1860," *Recusant History*, vol 10, 1969–1970, p. 129.

[29] Gilley, "The Roman Catholic Mission to the Irish in London, 1840–1860," *Recusant History*, vol 10, 1969–1970, p. 129.

[30] O'Connor to Wiseman, A.A.W., 4/9/1849 quoted in Gilley, "The Roman Catholic Mission to the Irish in London, 1840–1860," *Recusant History*, vol 10, 1969–1970, p. 135.

[31] Gilley, "The Roman Catholic Mission to the Irish of London," p. 139

[32] *LCM Magazine* (Jan. 1839): 26.

6

The Jewish Soil
In Darkest London

Joseph Oppenheimer's interactions with the Jews of his district raise a host of questions that require a good deal of background if they are to be understood in the larger context of Jewish-Christian relations in general, and in particular with regard to the relationship of Victorian evangelicals to the Jews. In the nineteenth century significant shifts occurred in evangelicals' attitudes towards the Jews. They did much to shape popular understanding, particularly in the matter of support for the idea of Jews being "restored" to their ancient homeland in Palestine. This chapter seeks to explain some of the complex relations between evangelicals and Jews, to show how these were at work in Joseph Oppenheimer's life, and how they affected his relationships with fellow Jews in his district.

Jewish converts such as Oppenheimer were of special interest to Victorian evangelicals, for in these conversions to Christianity they saw a vindication of evangelicalism. The 1830s and 1840s were a time of sharp conflict between evangelicals and the rising Tractarian movement within the Church of England, as well as with Roman Catholicism. Each of these three traditions laid claim to the term "apostolic," which referenced the earliest days of the Christian church. For the Tractarians and the Catholics, this claim to "apostolicity" was vindicated by the unbroken tradition of bishops consecrated in historical succession traceable back to the original apostles of Christ. For the evangelicals, "apostolicity" was centered in the doctrine received from the apostles rather than the rule of bishops in historical succession. All three traditions thus claimed to be authentically "apostolic," but the authenticity of the evangelicals' claims came to be visually validated by the conversion of Jews to evangelical forms of Christianity rather than to Tractarianism or Roman Catholicism.[1] Thus Oppenheimer's Jewishness was of special interest to Victorian evangelicals.

Evangelicals for their part sought to establish a new view of Jews that was in marked contrast to the long-prevailing position adopted by the Roman Catholic Church, which can be traced back to St. Augustine in the fourth and fifth centuries and has often been termed a "teaching of contempt toward the Jews."[2] In the early nineteenth century, English evangelicals—in particular Calvinist evangelicals associated with the LSJ—promoted a view of Jews that broke with Augustine and might properly be called a Christian "teaching of esteem" toward the Jews.

GERMAN AND JEWISH: THE LINKS WITH OPPENHEIMER'S ADOPTED WORLD

Oppenheimer's identity as a German Jew requires a somewhat lengthy historical exegesis, since during the first half of the nineteenth century, one of the strongest links between the German territories—particularly Brandenberg-Prussia—and Britain was their shared Protestantism, which was closely related to this new mutual interest in the Jews. The most visible expression of this concern was the combined action of the British and Prussian governments in 1841 that created a joint Anglican-Lutheran bishopric in Jerusalem. The arrangement was highly unusual, but was intended as a concrete expression of Protestant unity and a visible demonstration of concern for "God's ancient people." The first bishop appointed was Moses Solomon Alexander, who was—like Oppenheimer—a German Jew who had converted to Christianity after moving to England.

To understand these developments, one needs to appreciate the religious movement known as "German Pietism" that emerged in the last quarter of the seventeenth century. Pietism was a major movement of renewal within German Lutheranism, emphasizing a strong Christ-centered devotion, the study and promotion of the Bible, a new interest in cross-cultural mission, a revolution in popular education, a profound concern for the poor and the marginalized, and a passionate concern to bring a non-coercive Christian witness to the Jews. The founding of the London Jews' Society, and the conversion of German Jews such as Oppenheimer, were direct outcomes of the growing influence of German Pietism in the English-speaking world.[3]

The implications of this movement for Jewish-Christian relations are little understood. It is crucial to appreciate that both Philipp Jakob Spener (1635–1705), the founder of the Pietist movement, and his successor, August Hermann Francke (1663–1727), conceived of their mission as a world mission, and the Jews were a central aspect of that mission. In

Pia Desideria [Pious Longings], Spener in 1675 had outlined the Pietists' program for the renewal of the Lutheran Church from within.[4] The book is built around the theme of an anticipated mass conversion of Jews to Christianity.[5] The imperative work of Jewish conversion would require highly skilled workers with specialized knowledge and appropriate financial and communal support. In Spener's view, the Pietist mission to the Jews was at the very heart of Protestant identity. As Christopher Clark puts it: "The mission was urgent because God's honour was at stake. It was a question of making amends for the history of human ingratitude in the face of God's grace and favour. In this way, Spener made the conversion of the Jews the keystone in the arch of revealed Christian truth."[6]

Significantly, Spener called for Jews to be proselytized by voluntary agency, not by state initiative. He developed his ideas on Jewish conversion further in his 1702 *Theologische Bedencken,* making the case for the duty of noncoercive Christian missions to the Jews. His anointed successor, August Hermann Francke, set to work putting Spener's program into effect by establishing in 1702 the Collegium Orientale Theologicum. It was one of this college's students, Johann Heinrich Callenberg (1694–1760), who gave concrete expression to Francke's concern for the Jews in 1728 by establishing the Institutum Judaicum in Halle, where students could study Yiddish as well as Hebrew and devote themselves to Talmudic studies. Highly innovative in their "attention to proselyte care, occupational rehabilitation and broader questions of identity and assimilation" the Pietists created "a uniquely energetic missionary programme whose legacy can be discerned in the missionary revivals of London, Basel and Berlin after the turn of the nineteenth century."[7]

One of the most striking evidences of German Pietist influence in England in the eighteenth century was in the matter of missionary recruitment, and this concern proved to be the bridge for Jewish evangelism between Germany and Britain. The majority of missionaries working in the mid-eighteenth century for the [Anglican] Society for the Propagation of Christian Knowledge (SPCK) were German-speaking Lutherans in the Pietist tradition,[8] and when the SPCK's mission to India was disrupted by the Napoleonic Wars in the 1790s, a new but similar pattern emerged: German-speaking Lutheran Pietists were sent abroad by the new English evangelical societies, because they too were unable to find an adequate supply of English-speaking candidates. This connection was crucial to the growth of British interest in the evangelization of Jews. In the early 1800s, the critical link between the German Pietist and the English evangelical worlds was Karl Steinkopf (1773–1859), whose German-speaking Lutheran Church in London Oppenheimer probably attended.[9]

The German Pietist example was equally important in establishing the first British evangelical mission to the Jews, which was responsible for Oppenheimer's conversion. In the same year (1801) that Steinkopf arrived in London, so too did a German Jewish convert, Joseph Frey (1771–1850).[10] Frey's significance cannot be overestimated; he established the LSJ, and whatever his shortcomings, he was crucial in bringing the German Pietist concern for the evangelization of Jews to the English-speaking world. Frey was one of three German Pietist students at Johannes Jänicke's *Berliner Missionsschule* who were chosen to go to London, responding to an appeal from the London Missionary Society for ary recruits to serve in the Cape of Good Hope.[11] In London he received further missionary training, and here he came to know Steinkopf. Frey eventually decided that his mission was to London's Jews rather than to South Africa. Ever the religious entrepreneur, in 1808 Frey began his own society independent of the London Missionary Society that had brought him to London; this was superseded in 1809 with the founding of the LSJ,[12] the first of twenty-three such societies in England and Scotland alone, many of which continue to the present day.

The early years of the LSJ were marked by great ambitions, exalted claims, and little success despite the support of prominent evangelicals. Relations between Frey and the LMS were deeply strained, and in 1810, the LMS closed its Jewish mission. In 1815 the LSJ underwent a major reorganization and was refounded on a strictly Anglican basis but without Frey.[13] Undoubtedly, the establishment of the LSJ owed much to its Pietist origins and to the personalities recruited from Germany. Now, the long-held Pietist concern for the evangelization of Jews was being transplanted into the English-speaking world by a Jewish convert.[14] Just as the inspiration for Jewish evangelism had come in large part from the German Pietist world, so too did the missionaries to carry out the task. Furthermore, many of the German missionaries who worked for both the CMS and the LSJ received their training at the same institution: Jänicke's *Berliner Missionsschule,* which was to become the model for the LSJ's school in London, where Oppenheimer studied.

OPPENHEIMER AND LONDON'S JEWS

Joseph Oppenheimer was in many ways uniquely qualified to converse with the Jews in his district. Given his German Jewish background, and particularly his knowledge of German and Hebrew, he was able to overcome the isolation in which English Jews had long been accustomed to living. His own cultural, ethnic and religious background enabled him to navigate a divide that few Gentiles were able to understand. This isolation from the mainstream of British society was particularly true of recently immigrated English Jews. The majority of English Jews—even well into the nineteenth century—were heavily concentrated in a few areas of London. Even by 1850, the number of British Jews was quite small—between 30,000 and 35,000, with between 20,000 and 25,000 resident in London.[15] The major sources of employment among English Jews were, as they had been since the Middle Ages, "finance and its offshoots, such as commodity dealing and the sale of pawns."[16] In the eighteenth century few Englishmen ever encountered a Jew, and "some of those who had were probably acquainted only with the poor Ashkenazi hawker who peddled his wares from time to time in their district."[17]

The Anglo-Jewish community, like other Jewish communities in Europe, was made up of two broad groupings, Sephardim and Ashkenazim. The Sephardic Jews, while a minority of the English Jewish population, constituted the majority of the wealthy and prominent Jews in England. It was members of the Sephardic community who found conversion to Christianity convenient. As R. M. Smith has observed, "a large number of Sephardim [in England] converted during this period, [yet] few, (if any) did so out of religious conviction, and they made no pretense of having done so."[18] However, in 1800 only about a quarter of English Jews were Sephardim. Sephardic immigration into Britain decreased in the period from the late eighteenth century through to mid-century, while Ashkenazi immigration increased rapidly as poor Jews from Eastern Europe moved to Britain, where they could enjoy a greater degree of toleration than elsewhere in Europe. The very fact that Oppenheimer was able to overcome the social isolation of primarily Ashkenazi London Jews, and engage with them in dialogue, is remarkable.

TRACKING OPPENHEIMER'S INTERACTIONS WITH THE JEWS IN HIS DISTRICT

The *LCM Magazine* study of the Dudley Street district in 1855 reported that there were 17 Jewish families out of the 697 families in the district, and twelve references to encounters with Jews occur in Oppenheimer's journal. Four Jewish families and a sole Jewish widow appear to have been willing to engage Oppenheimer in religious discussions, and he seems to have been able to establish friendly, even cordial and repeated contacts with them—better, it seems, than with many of the Roman Catholics on his district—in spite of his persistent efforts to persuade them that Christianity was the fulfillment of Judaism. He records no incidents in which he met open hostility from Jews, but rather had friendly interactions with them.

The Angel family

Oppenheimer records three conversations with Mr. Angel, whom he describes as a "liberal Jew" who received him "kindly" and with whom he parted as "good friends." In the last entry, Mr. Angel's wife was drawn into the conversation. We can glean more about the Angel family from the census records. The family lived at 67 High Street, which was immediately adjacent to the family clothing shop at 24 Broad Street. The Angels were both London-born Jews: Edward Angel, aged 38 (in April 1861), was a clothier; his wife Julia was 34, and they were parents to five children: Philip, 8 years; Bloomer, a 6-year-old son; Elizabeth, 4 years; Edward, 2 years; and Rachel, 6 months old. Ann MacArty, a 24-year-old servant, lived with the family.

Broad St.

27 September 1861

A Jews Opinion of the Person and Work of the Redeemer.

Friday 27.
23 Had another conversation with M[r] Angel (a Jew) was permitted to read to him again several old Test[ament] prophecies relating to the Messiah & explained to him how each and all of them have had their litteral [sic] fulfilment in the person & work of Jesus of Nazareth & that "He" was the Light of the Gentiles & the glory of His People Israel. Mr. A. listened very attentively to all I read & said, but am sorry to say notwithstanding he calls himself a reformed Jew & entirely ignores the authority of the traditions of the Rabbies [sic], yet he is as far from the Kingdom of heaven as any of his more bigoted Jewish brethren. "I admire,["] he said, ["] the precepts & doctrines of the New Test[ament]. Jesus has been a great benefactor to the human race, he was no doubt a great man, but he was no more than other great men; if he had been God as

well as man he would have been able to convince the whole of the Jews that he was the Messiah &c." We parted good friends & I left him a tract on the Jewish subject.

7 February 1862

24 [sic] Dudley Street
24. Shop. Had another conversation with M[r] Angel, a Jew, concerning "Jesus of Nazareth" was permitted to read several passages of Scripture from the New as well as the old Test[ament] to which he listened attentively & when I left him accepted a tract.

12 May 1862

24 Broad Street

Indifference

Monday 12. Began full work to day at 24 Broad Street; M[r] Angel received my visit kindly; he was in the shop when I called but asked me in the parlour where I was permitted to speak to both him & his wife of "Jesus of Nazareth as the Saviour of both Jews & Gentiles &c."
M[r] A. is called & rather calls himself a liberal Jew, which is plainly speaking no Jew at all, for [it] is equally as far from real Judaism than it is from Christianity; endeavoured to impress upon him the individual responsibility of man & his lost condition without a Saviour; he listened pretty attentively & may the Lord have mercy upon his soul & bring him to a more serious state of mind for Christ's sake.

The Benjamins

Oppenheimer gives us four accounts of his conversations with Mr. Benjamin, another Jewish shopkeeper. Again the census record is most helpful. John Benjamin was 58 years old and his wife Mary was 59—both were London-born Jews; a 24-year-old servant, Margaret Downing, lived with the couple. Their clothing shop was at 34 Dudley Street and their home next door at number 35. A similar friendly relationship developed between Oppenheimer and John Benjamin.

9 September 1861
34 Dudley Street

The Trinity
The Trinity not confined to the New Test[tament]

Monday 9
34. Shop. Had another very interesting conversation with M[r] Benjamin (a Jew) the chief topic of which was the doctrine of the Trinity, which he said, was contrary to the Old Test[tament] Scriptures "We never read, he said, of three God's [sic] in the Old Test[ament] - a father & a Son & a Holy Ghost, but find it distinctly said, the Lord God is one God." I read to him several passages & proved to him from the very pafsage he quoted, that although it unquesti[ona]bly true that it afserts the Unity of the Godhead, yet the very term wh[ich] is used to denote that Unity, ( ) being אֱלֹהֵינוּ·al noun, denotes a plurality of persons. And from several other O[l]d Test[ament] passages, I proved to him that the doctrine of the Trinity is not confined to the New Test[ament]. M[r] B. knows but very little Hebr[ew] & consequently said he could not argue in that way but as he was taught, so he would believe. We parted good friends & I left him one of Dr M[c]Caul's tracts on the Jewish subject "Can the Jew be saved."

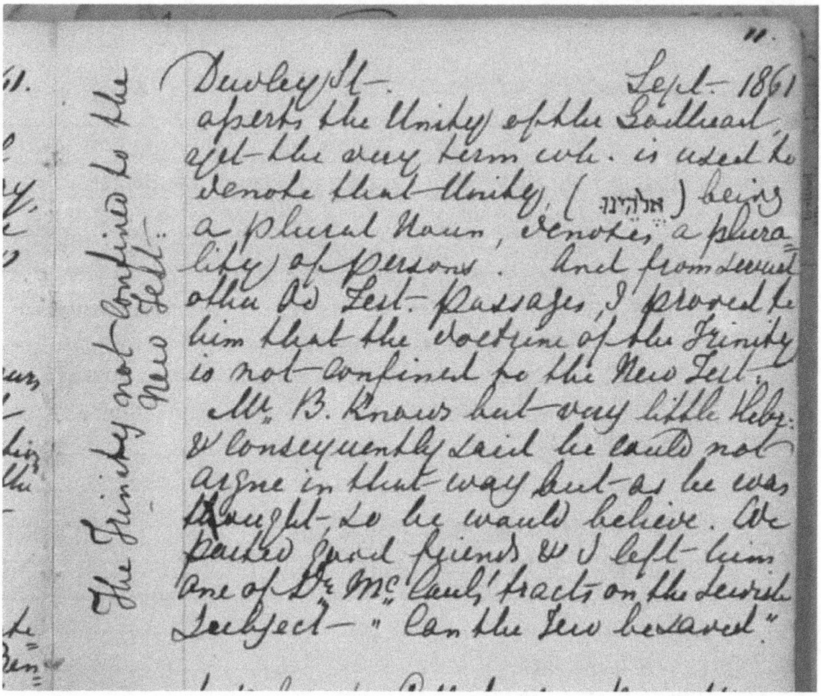
11.
Dudley St. Sept. 1861
The Trinity not confined to the New Test:
asserts the Unity of the Godhead yet the very term wh. is used to denote that Unity, (אלהינו) being a plural Noun, denotes a plurality of persons. And from several other Od Test. passages, I proved to him that the doctrine of the Trinity is not confined to the New Test. Mr. B. knows but very little Hebr: & consequently said he could not argue in that way but as he was taught so he would believe. We parted good friends & I left him one of Dr. Mc Caul's tracts on the Jewish subject — "Can the Jew be saved."

8 October 1861
34 Dudley Street

A Jew desires future visits.

34 Called upon M[r] Benjamin (a Jew) was kindly received and had another conversation with him on the claims of Jesus of Nazareth as the Messiah promised to Abraham & his seed; Read several passages from the old Test[ament] relating to the Messiah; listened attentively to what I read & said & when I left him he accepted a tract & asked me to call again.

17 January 1862
34 Dudley Street

Friday 17.
34 shop. Had another conversation with M[r] Benjamin, a Jew, on the claims of Jesus of Nazareth as the Messiah; read several old Test[ament] prophecies relating to the Messiah & explained to him their fulfillment in Jesus &c. he listened attentively & when I left him accepted a tract on the Jewish subject.

11 February 1862
35 Dudley Street

Tuesday 11.
35 Had another interesting Conversation with M[r] Benjamin, a Jew, on the Claims of Jesus of Nazareth as the Messiah promised to be "the light of the Gentiles & the glory of his people Israel["]; he listened pretty attentively to all I said & read to him, but still persists, that if these things were so the Jews as a nation would not have rejected him; explained to him that it was for[e]told that the Jews would crucify the Lord of life & glory & that as a nation that they would reject him &c. left a tract on the Jewish subject & promised to call again.

Mrs. Barnet

Another of his Jewish dialogue partners was Mrs. Barnet of 13 Dudley Street; unfortunately, she cannot be identified in the census records at this address.

Wednesday, 2 October 1861
13 Dudley Street

1st front. Old M[rs] Barnet, a Jewess, was very glad to see me again & I have once more been permitted to speak to her of Jesus of Nazareth as the only name given under heaven whereby we can be saved; & that Jew or Gentile are all alike in the sight of Him who is no respector of persons.

13 January 1862

What is truth?

2nd front. Called upon M[rs] Barnet, an old Jewess, who is always very glad when I call, I urged upon her once more to accept Jesus of Nazareth as the Messiah & explained to her several passages from the old as well as the New Test[ament] she listened attentively but said "Nobody knows who is right, we think we are & you think you are, so nobody knows who is & I am no scholar so I shall die as I was born, a Jewess." I endeavoured to impress upon her that the Bible is the only rule to be guided by & that God has promised His Spirit, in answer to prayer, for to lead us into all Truth. left a tract.

A Dutch Jew: Mr. and Mrs. Emanual

Dudley Street.
6 January 1862.

A dutch Jew

85 Shop. A dutch Jew, did not seem best pleased with my visit at first, but after a few preliminary remarks he entered into conversation & I was permitted to speak to him of Jesus of Nazareth, as He who was promised to be the light of the Gentiles & the glory of his people Israel; I was listened to very attentively but found both Mr & Mrs Emanual very indifferent to their own, as well as to any other religion. left a tract.

Mr. and Mrs. Joseph

Except for the Emanuals, and possibly Mrs. Barnett, the other Jews with whom Oppenheimer had contact were London-born. Solomon Joseph, a 53-year-old clothier, and his wife Pricilla, aged 48, were the parents of Isaac, a 20-year-old who worked as a stockbroker's assistant, Esther, 18 years old, who was employed as a "feathermaker's woman," 15-year-old John, who worked as his father's shop assistant, and 12-year-old Henry, and 9-year-old Ann, both of whom were students.

23 January 1862
55 Dudley Street

55 shop; Called upon M[rs] Joseph a Jewess & was permitted to speak to her of Jesus of Nazareth the crucified & glorified Redeemer of Jews & Gentiles.

18 February 1862
55 Dudley Street

false interpretation of Scripture.
Tuesday 18.
55. Had another conversation with M[r] Joseph, a Jew, who told me when I explained to him that "without shedding of blood there is & can be no remission of sin" that this passage had reference to the circumcision. I endeavoured to convince him of the fal[l]acy of this interpretation by reading & explaining to him several passages from the old Test[ament] we parted good friends & he asked me to call again.

All four families with whom Oppenheimer conversed were owners of clothing shops and represent relative stability in Dudley Street. Three of the four were London-born. None of them appear to have been particularly observant; in this, they well illustrate the relative lack of interest in religion among many English Sephardic Jews.

OPPENHEIMER'S RELIGIOUS BACKGROUND

It would be most helpful to know more of Oppenheimer's own upbringing, as he appears to have been raised as a devout, Talmud-studying Jew—perhaps among the Perushim, who were devoted to Talmudic study. The Jews whom Oppenheimer encountered appear to have been Sephardim, originating in western Europe and representing a very different sort of Judaism than that in which he had been raised. The eastern European Ashkenazim, who were divided into two mutually opposed groups—the Hasidim and the Perushim—were relatively scarce in London at this time.[19] The LSJ normally concentrated its conversion efforts in Europe on the Ashkenazim and tended to disregard the Sephardic community, but the Sephardim—who in Britain tended to convert to Christianity for social reasons—were virtually ignored by the London Jews' Society. Robert Michael Smith makes the case that most of the conversions among the

Sephardim in Britain can be explained in terms of "The anglicanization of Sephardic Jews and their social assimilation into English society," the impact of intermarriage, and the lack of alternate expressions of Judaism. These "conversions" for social reasons would not have interested the evangelicals, for they would have seen them as creating mere "nominal professors" of Christianity. For the evangelicals, true conversion was a matter of both the heart and mind, and involved a total reorientation of the life of an individual. Adopting a Christian pose for social or economic advantage was of no interest to them.[20]

Oppenheimer's attitude toward these Jews fits well with his having a background among the Perushim, since they too disdained the emergence of a western "liberal" Judaism characteristic of the Sephardim. His comment, that "Mr. A[ngel] is called and calls himself a liberal Jew, which is plainly no Jew at all, for it is equally as far from real Judaism than it is from Christianity," expresses a sentiment that would be shared by many conservative Jews from an Ashkenazi background. Similarly, the Perushim would have been appalled by the fact that "Mr Benjamin knows but very little Hebr[ew]" and by the Emanuels being "very indifferent to their own, as well as to any other religion." The evangelicals were theologically much closer to the Perushim than to other expressions of Judaism.

It is clear that when dealing with Jewish believers, Oppenheimer advanced arguments that he had found persuasive in his own embracing of Christianity, reflecting the influence of the London Jews' Society. Oppenheimer's approach to the Jews he visited illustrates the standard evangelical emphases in proselytizing them during the nineteenth century: an appeal to Jesus as the one who has fulfilled Old Testament expectations of the Messiah, and the inconsistency of acknowledging him to have been merely a good man and an exemplary moral teacher (as with Mr. Angel, who acknowledged that Jesus was "no doubt a great man, but he was no more than other great men") while dismissing his claims to Messiahship. Oppenheimer never raises questions about the role that Jews would play in evangelical explanations of yet unfulfilled biblical prophecies.

VICTORIAN EVANGELICALS AND OPPENHEIMER'S JEWISHNESS

Before his training with the London City Mission, it is clear that Oppenheimer received his basic theological formation at Palestine Place, headquarters of the London Society for Promoting Christianity Amongst the Jews (LSJ).

22. PALESTINE PLACE, THE LONDON HEADQUARTERS OF THE LSJ

By the 1850s, the LSJ had seventy-seven missionaries and their dependents scattered at thirty-two different locations throughout Britain and across Europe and North Africa—from Ireland in the west to Jerusalem in the east. By the mid-1840s, the LSJ's donation income easily surpassed the combined incomes of both the London City Mission and the Church Pastoral-Aid Society. Palestine Place was located in Bethnall Green in London, only a few miles to the east of Dudley Street and St. Giles's Church. It was in effect a missionary compound in the heart of London for the purposes of evangelizing the Jews of Europe, North Africa and the Middle East. It came to include a church, the Operative Jewish Converts Institution (where Oppenheimer lived when he was employed by the LCM in 1858), and an "Enquirers' Home"—a dormitory for potential converts, where Oppenheimer probably lived for a time. In addition it had a Bible depot and a "Hebrew College." No curriculum of study has survived from the LSJ's "Hebrew College," which opened in 1840, but it is important to note that it represented a strain of robust evangelical Calvinism within the Church of England.[21]

We know that the dominant figure in the London Jew's Society was Alexander McCaul (1799–1863), an Irish clergyman who had proposed the establishment of a "Hebrew College" to the LSJ in 1839 and who became its first principal in 1840. Undoubtedly Oppenheimer and McCaul would have known each other. A staunch Calvinist, McCaul personified the Celtic fringe and its considerable influence on English evangelicalism in the mid-nineteenth century, holding together in his person two dominant themes that preoccupied many evangelicals: philosemitism and anti-Catholicism. On Oppenheimer's first visits to Mr. Benjamin, it was one of McCaul's tracts that he left, "...on the Jewish subject 'Can the Jew be saved.'"

OPPENHEIMER AND OTHER GERMAN JEWISH CONVERTS

Oppenheimer, although an obscure Jewish convert, begs comparison with three other German Jewish converts whose names would have been well-known to him, and two of whom we have already encountered: Joseph Frey, the founder of the LSJ, and Bishop Moses Solomon Alexander, the first Anglican/Lutheran bishop at Jerusalem. All three were German-born Jews who converted to Christianity while in their twenties.

Another German Jewish convert who was a contemporary of Oppenheimer's, and was probably better known to the Victorian public than Frey or Bishop Alexander, was the legendary Joseph Wolff (1795–1862). Oppenheimer may well have met Wolff through his close association with the London Jews' Society. Wolff, a Prussian Jew, had converted to Roman Catholicism before becoming an Anglican. By the 1830s, his was a household name in many English Protestant homes. An itinerant Jewish convert–evangelist like St. Paul before him, he was the embodiment of the evangelical ideal of apostolicity.

Wolff was an intrepid pioneer: From 1821 to 1826, he worked as a roving missionary in Egypt and the Levant. His reports from his first visit to Palestine in 1822 had raised hopes within the LSJ that a mission could be established in Jerusalem.[22] In 1828, Wolff essentially became an independent freelance missionary to the Jews. Larger than life, he was an amazing character: brash, energetic, and dogmatic, yet with winning ways. Lewis Way said of Wolff that he could "conciliate a pasha, confute a patriarch, travel without a guide, speak without an interpreter, live without food and pay without money ... a comet capable of setting a whole system on fire." He styled himself "Apostle of Our Lord Jesus Christ for Palestine, Persia, Bokhara, and Balkh" and exercised the ministry of an apostle as a messenger to Jews scattered throughout the Near East and Central Asia. Interest in the "Lost Tribes of Israel" had been rekindled by the writings of Claudius Buchanan (1766–1815), a pioneer Anglican missionary in India whose *Christian Researches in Asia* (London, 1811) did much to revive speculation about the identity of the ten lost tribes of Israel.[23]

In 1828, Wolff undertook the first of several missionary journeys beyond the Near East in search of the ten lost tribes, seeking evidence of Jewish communities in exotic eastern climes including Anatolia, Armenia, and Khorassan. At one point, he was enslaved by captors who deprived him of *all* his belongings; he arrived in Kabul in the nude after walking several hundred miles through Central Asia. Wolff was ever a publicist (some of his works were translated into German), and his missionary adventures proved to be excellent propaganda for the cause of Jewish missions.

Oppenheimer, of course, was an unknown lay worker who never achieved the fame or notoriety of Joseph Frey, Bishop Alexander or Joseph Wolff. Yet his life's path, the arguments he employed in talking with his fellow Jews, and his fervency in his newfound faith cannot be understood without acknowledging the impact of these other Jewish converts on British Christianity. In many ways, Oppenheimer's humble life and difficult work in the St. Giles' slum is a testament to their influence.

Notes

[1] This argument is developed in my *Origins of Christian Zionism* (Cambridge: Cambridge University Press, 2010), chapter 3.
[2] Quoted in Krupnick, "The Rhetoric of Philosemitism," In Walter Jost and Wendy Olmsted, eds., *Rhetorical Invention and Religious Inquiry* (New Haven, CT: Yale, 2000), p. 361.
[3] The genesis of the movement is often dated from 1675, with the publication of a work entitled *Pia Desideria* by Lutheran pastor and theologian Philipp Jakob Spener (1635–1705). Its organizational center was at the University of Halle in southern Prussia, where Spener, through the patronage of Frederick, King of Prussia, was able to establish a Pietist faculty of theology. Often aided by the patronage of the Calvinist rulers of Lutheran Brandenberg–Prussia in the late seventeenth and early eighteenth centuries, Pietism established itself as a major influence within the Lutheran Church. Halle trained pastors, who sought to imbue the German Protestant state church with their theology and practices.
[4] Christopher M. Clark, *The Politics of Conversion: Missionary Protestantism and the Jews in Prussia, 1728–1941* (New York: Cambridge University Press, 1995), 23.
[5] In Spener's view the unwillingness of Jews to convert to Christianity was understandable, given the blatant immorality and unchristian actions of professing Christians. Significantly, even crucially, Spener linked improvement in the life of the church with Jewish conversion.
[6] Clark, *Politics of Conversion*, 31.
[7] Christopher M. Clark, "'The Hope for Better Times': Pietism and the Jews," in Jonathan Strom, Hartmut Lehmann, and James Van Horn Melton, eds, *Pietism in Germany and North America 1680–1820* (Farnham, England, Routledge, 2016), 22.
[8] The SPCK began by aiding the Danish-Halle Mission in Tranquebar, sending Portuguese New Testaments for distribution. Then in 1711 it sent out a printer and a printing press; unfortunately the printer died before reaching India, but the press proved highly useful. A. K. Davidson, *Evangelicals and Attitudes to India 1786–1813* (Sutton Courtenay: Sutton Courtenay Press,1990), 31.
[9] Steinkopf's family connections were also important; his brother was a leading Pietist publisher and book retailer. (See E. Staehelen, *Die christentumsgesellschaft in der Zeit von der Erweckung bis zur Gegenwart* [Basel, 1974] and Obituary, *The Record*, 6 June 1859.) Steinkopf's predecessor at St. Mary's was Dr. Johann Gottlieb Burkhardt, a director of the London Missionary Society and its key link with the Basel network of German Pietists, which Steinkopf represented. It was quite natural that as pastor of St. Mary's, Steinkopf would take over this role from Burkhardt as the LMS link with the German Pietists. (See s.v. Jänicke, Johannes, in Donald M. Lewis, ed., *The Blackwell Dictionary of Evangelical Biography, 1730–1860* [Oxford: Blackwell, 1995].) Jänicke's younger brother, Joseph, had gone to India in 1789 as a missionary with the SPCK (dying there in 1800), but now

Jänicke sought to establish links with the London Missionary Society, and Steinkopf was the natural link. For further details on Steinkopf, see N. Railton, *No North Sea: The Anglo-German Evangelical Network in the Middle of the Nineteenth Century* (Leiden: Brill, 2000), 71–73.

[10] Frey offers his own account of his life to 1809 in Joseph Frey, *Narrative of the Reverend Joseph Samuel C. F. Frey, Minister of the Gospel to the Jews* (London: Gale and Curtis, 1809).

[11] They were to serve with Dr. Van der Kemp (1747–1811), who was originally born in Holland and obtained his medical education in Edinburgh; he underwent an evangelical conversion in 1791. He played a significant role in the founding of the Netherlands Missionary Society in 1797, a sister society to the London Missionary Society on which it was modeled. He had been in Cape Town with the LMS since 1799.

[12] The 1808 society was known as the "London Society for Visiting the Sick and Distressed and Instructing the Ignorant especially such as were of the Jewish nation."

[13] In 1816, the new directors dismissed Frey after it was revealed that he had had an affair with the wife of another convert. The revelation and dismissal did not derail Frey's ministry; he went on to a long career in Jewish missions in America. M. Sailman, *The Mystery Unfolded, or, An Exposition of the Extraordinary Means Employed to Obtain Converts by the Agents of the London Society for Promoting Christianity Amongst the Jews.* (London: printed by author, 1817). See also Eichhorn, *Evangelizing the American Jew* (Middle Village, NY: Jonathan David, 1978): 18–74, for details on Frey and his subsequent career in America.

[14] In the late 1810s, the LSJ turned its attention from attempts to evangelize Jews in England to the wider mission field of Europe and the Near East. Of the first fifteen missionaries sent abroad by the LSJ, eleven were Germans. Railton, *No North Sea*, 152. For a summary of the LSJ's expansion beyond England, see Yaron Perry, *British Mission to the Jews in Nineteenth Century Palestine* (London: Frank Cass, 2003): 7–11.

[15] Geoffrey Alderman, *Modern British Jewry* (Oxford: Clarendon Press, 1992), p. 3. Alderman sets the London Jewish population between 20,000 and 25,000. Cf. Colin Holmes who sets the number between 18,000 and 20,000. Colin Holmes, *Anti-Semitism in British Society,* 1876–1939 (London: E. Arnold, 1979), pp. 4–5.

[16] Holmes, *Anti-Semitism in British Society,* p. 6. Alderman points out that by the 1850s the late 18th and early 19th century image "of the Jew as a pedlar and hawker, was no longer grounded in fact" as Jews moved into occupations requiring craft skills. Alderman, *Modern British Jewry*, pp. 9–10.

[17] Colin Holmes, *Anti-Semitism in British Society,* p. 5. The Jews of London were concentrated in the East End and upwards of half of them were very poor, barely eking out a living. Geoffrey Alderman, *Modern British Jewry* (Oxford: Clarendon Press, 1992), 8.

[18] Robert Michael Smith, "The London Jews' Society and Patterns of Jewish Conversion in England, 1801–1859," *Jewish Social Studies* 43 (1981): 284–86.

[19] Hasidic Jews embraced a mystical version of Judaism affected by kabbalist teachings and followed the teachings of the Baal Shem Tov (the Master of the Good Name). Theirs was a warm, emotional expression of Judaism, and they eschewed the leadership of rabbis for that of the Tzaddik ("the righteous one"), a dynamic and charismatic spiritual leader. The second (and rival) Ashkenazi community was the Perushim ("Separatists"), sometimes

referred to as Mitnagdim ("Opponents"), following the teachings of Rabbi Elijah, the Gaon of Vilna. Unlike the Hasidim, the Perushim preferred Talmudic study to religious enthusiasm and ecstatic experience. In 1772, the Gaon of Vilna had declared the Hasidim to be excommunicated from the House of Israel. The tensions between the two Askenazi communities still exist today.

[20] Smith, "Patterns of Jewish Conversion," pp. 284–86.

[21] The Hebrew College opened on 7 May 1840 and was headed by Alexander McCaul, the key clergyman in the LSJ. See Dep. CMJ c. 16, entry for Special Meeting of Friday, Nov. 6, 1840, Item I, 802.

[22] Yaron Perry, *British Mission to the Jews in Nineteenth Century Palestine* (London: Frank Cass, 2003), 19.

[23] On Buchanan, see entry in Lewis, *Dictionary of Evangelical Biography.*

7

The "Unfortunates" Soil In Darkest London

> I am afraid, as respects the gross evils of prostitution, that there is hardly any country in the world where they prevail to a greater extent than in our own.[1]
>
> W. E. Gladstone, *Parliamentary Debates*, 1857

The Victorians spoke of prostitution as the "Great Social Evil," and the subject clearly fascinated them. Respected doctors wrote candidly on the subject, politicians waxed eloquent decrying its dangers, newspapers editorialized about it, and religious activists seemed pre-occupied by it. In 1860, the *Saturday* Review acknowledged that it was one of the most popular topics of discussion in mid-Victorian England—although not, it seems, in mixed company.[2]

THREE MODES OF ANALYSIS OF PROSTITUTION

Prostitution was not strictly illegal in nineteenth-century Britain, although "it was a stigmatised activity, socially unacceptable and surrounded by so many legal restrictions as to be illegal in all but name."[3] The police sought not so much to suppress prostitution as to try to keep it out of public view by limiting it to specific neighbourhoods, and they generally intervened only when prostitutes formed alliances with thieves.[4] Police could make life difficult for prostitutes if they proved uncooperative by prosecuting them for loitering.

However, in the 1830s and 1840s the prostitute came to be seen as symbolic of the dislocation caused by the Industrial Revolution, and thus closely related to the "Condition of England Question" discussed in chapter three. By the early 1840s, a new generation of writers were employing social research techniques to study the "Great Social Evil," and activist programs for amelioration were being proposed.

Linda Mahood, in her work *The Magdalenes: Prostitution in the Nineteenth Century*, has noted three paradigms used by scholars in their analysis of prostitution: the double standard model, the oppression model, and the problematization model. The first approach focuses on the idea that a "double standard" existed in Victorian society: sex outside of marriage was pardonable in men but unpardonable in women. The expectation of premarital chastity among middle-class couples, it is argued, forced men to turn to prostitutes for sexual satisfaction, thereby preserving the virtue of middle-class women. Once married, the double standard dictated that wives should ignore instances of their husbands' unfaithfulness. Underlying this view was the belief that "while sexual desire was virtually absent in middle-class women, it was rampant in men….."[5] An apology for this view was famously advanced by William Lecky in his notorious defense of prostitution: "Herself the supreme type of vice, she is ultimately the most efficient guardian of virtue."[6] The assumptions of the double standard model were regularly rejected in evangelical discourse.

The second approach is the oppression model, which sees the Victorian prostitutes as victims "forced into prostitution by destitution, poor wages, and lack of employment opportunities; conditions which were the consequences of exploitative class relations." This view is closely associated with the work of Josephine Butler in fighting the Contagious Diseases Acts. The difficulty, however, with this approach is that these women are thereby denied any personal agency and are considered as incapable of shaping their own history. Judith Walkowitz in her work *Prostitution and Victorian Society: Women, class and the state* attacks the oppression model, contending that these women were not passive victims, but rather were important historical actors who exercised their rational choice in view of limited options.

The third approach is that of problematization theory, which locates the discussion of these women in terms of the power dynamics of the social construction of language. Drawing on the work of Foucault, Mahood acknowledges the discourse on female inequality and oppression on the one hand, and the emphasis on women's agency on the other, and discusses the strengths and weaknesses of both. She sees the very use of the term "prostitute" as problematic, arguing that it was a term employed by middle-class observers to censure women for their "dress, behavior, physical appearance, or vocation."[7] It was a label in a discourse of social control that marginalized these women in an attempt to control them.

PROSTITUTION IN LONDON AND EVANGELICAL RESPONSES

Female prostitution was massively on view in the streets of nineteenth-century London, and in spite of the Victorian Age's reputation for sexual repression, "there is little doubt that there was widespread sexual license among respectable males even when Victoria and Albert were exhibiting the virtues of wedded bliss."[8] In 1842 the *London City Mission Magazine* provided its readers with detailed accounts of the ways in which prostitution operated in the metropolis,[9] and much to the chagrin of the Dean and Chapter of Westminster, it pointed out that twenty-four of the twenty-seven houses on its almonry property were brothels.[10] The higher concentration of prostitutes in London would appear to have "reflected the uneven sex ratios, the limited employment opportunities open to women, as well as the presence of a transient male population that formed a ready clientele for the prostitutes" in that city. Further, London was attractive to seasoned prostitutes from the provinces hoping to avoid police harassment and attract better-paying clients.

Police statistics kept between 1857 and 1869 on "known" prostitutes and brothels show a relatively high concentration of prostitutes in commercial ports such as London and Liverpool, in garrison towns like Colchester where they served the members of the largely "bachelor army,"[11] and in pleasure resorts such as Brighton. This pattern is also reflected in the data on death rates from sexually transmitted diseases.

All of the LCM agents were brought into daily contact with prostitutes, and within a few months of the mission's founding in 1835, it had considered adopting special means of reaching them.[12] In the early 1840s, evangelical interest had been focused on the problem with the publication of a series of *Lectures on Female Prostitution* by Dr. Ralph Wardlaw, a well-known Scottish evangelical.[13] The London City Mission made clear that its sense of moral outrage was more directed at the "great men and debauched nobility" who frequented London's many brothels than with the prostitutes themselves.[14]

Judith Walkowitz argues that evangelical ministers and medical doctors were in the forefront of early investigations into prostitution, although her use of the term "evangelical" is sometimes problematic and would probably more accurately be described as simply "Protestant."[15] The "evangelicals" she contends, condemned the double standard and upheld "the traditional puritan ideal of a patriarchal 'marriage of affections' consecrated in the home, a zone of intimacy and refuge from the competitive world of work and politics."[16]

It is the case, however, that the "seeking and saving" of such women was a central concern of nineteenth-century evangelicals. Much of the impetus behind this effort came from evangelical women who were willing to endanger their own reputations, respectability, and at times their own safety in pursuit of wandering females.[17] The LCM, however, declined to employ women as urban missionaries, hoping that its male workers would refer repentant prostitutes to homes and asylums run by evangelicals.[18]

One study by a city missionary appointed to work among the estimated 2–3,000 "fallen women" in Marylebone revealed that applications for "rescue" were chiefly received from older women fearful for their health, instead of from the majority aged sixteen to twenty.[19] The agent's work often was aided by the women directing the brothels, who were eager to encourage religious visitation when their charges were ill, in the hope that "an inmate so useless to herself should be persuaded to return home to her friends, or to enter an asylum."[20]

As will be seen in Oppenheimer's entries below, it was not unusual for a City Missionary to establish cordial relations with prostitutes in his district. R.W. Vanderkiste, a City Missionary who was a prolific writer on behalf of the London City Mission, described one brothel where he was welcomed:

> This den of infamy was situated in W---H---C---, T--- Street. It consisted of one small room on the ground floor, and parties might well be excused for remaining dubious, as to whether so small an area could have been so replete with pestiferous moral influence to the neighborhood, as this place unequivocally has been.

He also explained the key to his access with these women and detailed the manner in which he dealt with them:

> The fact is, I appeared to have a great influence *given* me over the proprietor of this wretched place and others, in consequence, perhaps of attention I had paid to one of their companions, who died in a very dreadful manner. They appeared to retain so grateful a sense of these attentions, that they could not insult me. It constituted one of the strangest sights in the wide world, to see me enter this place at night, sometimes alone—on one occasion my companion was ordered away; it was said to him, "you go, or else perhaps you'll have a knife put into you. He (me) may stop" —disturbing all kinds of wickedness and merely saying "I've

> come to read to you." Standing there in the midst of ferocious and horrible characters, reading the Scriptures, and explaining portions concerning our Lord and Saviour Jesus Christ, heaven and hell, and a prostitute holding the candle next to me. This young woman has since abandoned her evil course of life. Then would follow some discussion, one would say, "I don't believe there's no hell—it's in your heart, mister." Then some prostitute would bust out into indecent profanity, would be *sworn* at until she was quiet. Then I would go down on my knees in the midst of them and pray, waiting to see if the Spirit of God would act, (and the Spirit of God *did* act).[21]

The great innovation of this period was the development of evangelical-directed "rescue work," which sought to remove the prostitutes from their habitual haunts. Evangelical women volunteers roamed the streets and even visited brothels to seek the "lost sheep."[22] In 1859, a number of evangelicals associated with the London City Mission promoted an outreach to prostitutes known as the Midnight Meetings Movement, whereby large numbers of women were invited to attend free meals in designated restaurants late at night, following which a sermon was given that implored them to take the proffered assistance of a place in a "home" or "asylum."[23] These meetings attracted considerable attention in both the religious and secular press, and the pattern soon was adopted in other cities throughout Britain. This sort of approach remained popular throughout the century, although it was not regarded by all women rescue workers as an effective substitute for the visiting of the brothels themselves.[24]

WHO WERE THESE WOMEN? A PROFILE OF THE COMMON PROSTITUTE

Judith Walkowitz has undertaken to craft a social profile of the women in Victorian England who became prostitutes. She argues that the common prostitute "was not the innocent victim of middle-class seduction and betrayal; nor was she a mere child drugged and entrapped into prostitution by white slavers. Instead, her entry into prostitution seems to have been voluntary and gradual."[25] Most of these women were independent operators, working without pimps in a trade that in Victorian London was largely organized by women rather than men, participating in a strong female subculture. They dressed to indicate "an outward appearance and a more affluent style of life that distinguished them from other working-class women" and that signaled their way of "advertising themselves and attracting male customers."[26] They could be mutually supportive in times of distress, helping to pay for the proper funeral of a friend or covering bail for a peer who had been arrested. But this often proved to be an unstable support system. Theft from their peers was a constant problem, and violent battles over "pitch," or territory, were frequent.

Most were "ambivalent and defensive about their occupation," and their move into prostitution was more circumstantial than premeditated, reflecting the "local conditions of the urban job market."[27] In many ways, working-class prostitutes were unremarkable in their backgrounds: little set them apart from their peers, with most being "either natives of the city or recent migrants from the local countryside." They shared the cultural and religious values of their class, often even embracing conservative politics.[28] Walkowitz notes that "Most inmates of the Rescue Society of London had attended Sunday school and most could read and write 'tolerably well.'"[29] Alexander Flexner's memorable description of them remains apt: they were the "unskilled daughters of the unskilled classes."[30] Over half of them had worked as domestic servants or in other low-paid, low-skilled occupations such as dress-making, farm labour, shop work, domestic service and street selling. These occupations were low-paid or characterized by seasonal unemployment, or sometimes both.[31]

One characteristic that set them apart from many of their peers was that their family backgrounds were disrupted far more frequently than was common: Walkowitz notes that "an extraordinarily high percentage of prostitutes had lost one or both parents during the Victorian and Edwardian period," and there is evidence that "rescue-home reports indicated that many of the nonorphans came from broken homes where the father had deserted the family or where the parents were separated."[32] As Paula Bartley has observed, "... girls who lived at home with caring parents rarely became prostitutes unless the family faced starvation."[33] Further, in working-class families of this period there was "a consistent social undervaluing of daughters."[34] They were often expected to care for younger siblings so that the mother could work outside the home; they had less free time than their brothers, a narrower choice of occupations, and they were "fed worse than their brothers, not to speak of their fathers."[35] Often without the close family bonds that other women enjoyed, these women had fewer personal restraints. Prostitution seemed to offer attractive economic and personal advantages, although they soon discovered that prostitution "was a more hazardous and precarious occupation than they had anticipated."[36]

Most women who became prostitutes appear to have had their first sexual encounter about the age of sixteen, and it appears to have been extremely rare for a girl younger than sixteen to be working as a prostitute.

The danger of sexually transmitted diseases (syphilis, chancroid and/or gonorrhea) was ever-present. Often, one or more of these was contracted within the first year of active solicitation. Pregnancy was another concern, although the prostitutes' fertility rates may have been lower because of the high incidence of venereal disease that caused "sterility, miscarriages, and sickly children who died in infancy." Some sought to employ contraception, underwent abortions or turned to infanticide. Those prostitutes who did give birth often "boarded their children out" or "left them in the workhouse."[37]

OPPENHEIMER AND THE PROSTITUTES

At the time Oppenheimer began his work in London in 1858, the London City Mission had one full-time agent working amongst London's prostitutes.[38] Oppenheimer was no specialist in dealing with such women. Still, his assigned district included Monmouth Court, which seems to have been a haven for prostitutes: a narrow passageway that ran south from Dudley Street to Little Earl Street, constituting a very small portion of his district. He records eight encounters with prostitutes in his journal: one in Broad Street and one in Dudley Street, but six in Monmouth Court. The first such entry is related to his encountering three "young women," whom he describes as "apparently bad women" in Broad Street:

26 September 1861
10 Broad Street

Unfortunates.

10. 2nd back; found three young women apparently bad women (prostitutes) in this room, they behaved very well & listened attentively whilst I talk[ed] to them about the exceeding sinfulness of sin & the awful doom of the sinner. One especially a girl about 20 years old seemed very much affected. Each accepted a tract.

This arrangement of several prostitutes living together in a boarding house was typical. Apparently most lived not in brothels but with two or three other women, in low common lodging houses in areas such as Oppenheimer's "Dudley Street district." In fact, the number of brothels in London appears to have declined from 933 in 1841 to 410 in 1857.[39]

In 1857, Dr William Acton in his celebrated work *Prostitution Considered in Its Moral, Social and Sanitary Aspects in London and Other Large Cities: with Proposals for the Mitigation and Prevention of its Attendant Evils* estimated that London had about 8600 prostitutes, or one working prostitute for every 81 adult males[40]—although Acton acknowledges that he is only speaking of those prostitutes who have come to the attention of the police and allows that there were many more who were omitted from this estimate.[41] Paula Bartley has pointed out that estimates of London's female prostitute population at mid-century ranged between 5000 and 200,000; the discrepancies depended on who was collecting statistics, and how narrowly one defined prostitution.[42]

Oppenheimer's reception on Broad Street seems to have been respectful, with one woman clearly being impacted by his words. Their willingness to receive a tract from him would appear to confirm their literacy, something that they most likely would have acquired in a Sunday school. As Thomas Laqueur has observed: "If there was a single experience common to the children of an agricultural labourer in Bedfordshire, of a stockinger or handloom weaver in the Midlands, or of a factory operative in south Lancashire, it was attendance at a Sunday school. … by the late 1820s … outside the Metropolis, nearly every working-class child must at some time have attended one. They were instructed, largely by teachers from their own class, in reading, writing, religion, and occasionally other subjects for periods of four to six hours each Sunday over a period of, on average, four years."[43]

His second entry is at number 7, Dudley Street:

8 October 1861
Dudley Street

A sad case.

Tuesday 8.

Went with a young girl named McCarthy, to several institution[s] to get her in, but am sorry to say did not succeed in either. The poor girl is only 16 years old, has no parents or friends in England & unfortunately fell in with a girl of bad character who induced her to walk the streets with her, which she has done for the last three months & now as far as I can see she seems truly penitent & anxious to amend her life. I got her into the lodging house No. 75 Dudley St[reet] for the present & hope by next week to get her into a Reformatory.

The lodging house in question is the "Working Girls' Dormitory" discussed in chapter one. It would appear that by October 1861 it was now more a "refuge" for prostitutes than a "dormitory" for working women—the first stopping place for many women leaving prostitution. Ellen Ranyard explained to her readers in 1861, "Our rule is, that rent shall be paid daily by Missionaries or friends desirous to snatch those whom they bring there, from a life of sin, for the few days that may intervene between their rescue and placing them in a Refuge or Reformatory."[44]

In McCarthy's case, the pattern of involvement in prostitution seems to fit the pattern described above: not seduction by a social superior, but introduction to the trade by a working class peer. Oppenheimer's attempts to get her admitted to a home for prostitutes, and his failure to do so, suggest a scarcity of places to accommodate a large number of women wanting out of prostitution. Early in the nineteenth century, institutions known as penitentiaries had been the chief means of reform of prostitutes. Paula Bartley has argued that it was evangelicals who "advocated an alternative system of reform and tried to establish a home system rather than a penitential one"[45] reflecting "more sympathy towards them" than was shown by many Anglicans. The many Magdalen Asylums represent this trend; they offered such women a fresh start, "aimed to offer sanctuary and forgiveness rather than reproach."[46]

Oppenheimer's next entry related to prostitution is the only one in the journal that has a follow-up entry. In this instance he finds two women who were initially resistant to his message, but eventually one laments her situation, and blames her entry into prostitution on having been seduced while working as a domestic servant, although it is not clear whether the man was her employer or a working class peer. Clearly she is despairing of her situation:

> 28 October 1861
> 1 Monmouth Court
>
> *Two unfortunates. Future visit promised*
>
> Monday 28.
> 1 Monmouth Court. 2nd back. two young girl[s] (unfortunates) did at first seem not to be very favourable to my visit, but still were pretty civil, endeavoured to impress them with the terrors of the Lord &.c. both listened attentively & one the eldest seemed to be much affected & with tears in her eyes said, "I know, sir, I am ruining body & soul, but what shall I do, I have been seduced

whilst in service by decrees [sic] I have become what you see me now, I could not now get any place, my character & all is gone & I must put up with it there is no chance left &.c." The poor girl seemed to feel what she said & I could not but feel with her; promised to see her again.

The second recorded visit came about three months later, and in this instance the responsive woman is identified as Jane King. With her roommate absent, she complains of being deeply indebted to her and virtually under her control. She despairs of any hope of escape from her situation:

3 February 1862

1 Monmouth Court. February 1862.

A poor unfortunate girl.

Monday 3.
1 2nd back; found Jane King by herself, her companion being out, she seemed to be very much in trouble & told me she wished she was dead; "I know I would be worse off if I died as I am now but I am tired of my life;—it's all very well to look at us poor creatures & tell us that's our own fault, but I know better[.] I must suffer now for that wretch who seduced me; I got in it now & can't get out again; I owe ever so much to my companion & sometimes she will take my clothes off my back & tells me she would turn me out naked in the street;" I endeavoured again to persuade her to come away from her companion & give up her wicked life &c. but again without success. She told me not to call when her companion is at home for she told her that she would pay me outright well, but I told her I was not afraid of it.

Two days after his first encounter with Jane King, Oppenheimer records another visit in Monmouth Court, where he met thieves and prostitutes and a great deal of sustained resistance to his efforts:

30 October 1861
10 Monmouth Court

Bad characters.

10 This house is inhabited by all sorts of bad characters; prostitutes thiefs [sic] &c. but still I have been permitted to deliver my

message in 3 rooms, the rest refused me admittance to day; There is not a Copy of Scripture amongst any of the 7 families; most are Irish.

In early January he met two more prostitutes, again in Monmouth Court. They are the first women he notes as illiterate, which would indicate that they did not have the Sunday school background of so many other prostitutes. They also say they are from the country and are both orphans, which fits the profile of so many other prostitutes. The lack of any friends or relatives in London helps to account for their plight:

6 January 1862

6 Monmouth Court

Poor unfortunate girls.

second front; found two young girl[s] in the room (unfortunates) they did not seem best pleased with my visit but after a few minutes they seemed to be more inclined to listen & I was permitted to warn them to flee from the wrath to come; both are Country girls & neither can read; they told me that both their parents were dead & have no friends or relations in London.

In January of the new year he was called to the room of a violently ill 18-year-old woman. He was apparently familiar with her two roommates, whom he knew to be prostitutes:

15 January 1862
7 Monmouth Court

A sad case of a dying girl.

Was called to see a young woman who I was told was dying fast, went to N° 7 Monmouth Court top front room & found a girl, 18 years old, in most dreadful agony, crying & tearing everything to pieces; two other young women were with her & tried to keep her quiet in bed, the lat[t]er two I know to be bad girls who walk the streets & from which fact I judge that the sick girl is of the same unfortunate class. I endeavoured to speak to her, but she did not, or could not, answer me, for I could not get a word out of her, although she cried repeatedly to one of the young women "O Mary Ann I die, O I die Mary Ann." I was quite overcome with the sight I beheld, but used the opportunity and endeavoured to impress upon the living, the awful condition of the dying & I promised to call again.

The final entry in the journal related to a prostitute—again in Monmouth Court—is of his visit to a woman who was very unreceptive to his message:

> 3 February 1862
> 2 Monmouth Court
>
> 2 1st back; A woman of apparently bad character, was very abusive in her language when I told her the object of my visitation, but was permitted to give her a Solemn warning to flee from the wrath to come.

It is interesting that Oppenheimer's most characteristic way of describing these women is with the word "unfortunate." This seems to indicate a degree of sympathy and that he sees them as victims more than as dangers, revealing the sympathetic attitude of evangelicals towards these women that Paula Bartley has observed.

In fact, the evidence suggests that "most prostitutes were not seduced by men of the upper classes" but rather that far more "had been 'led astray' by other girls who had persuaded them to sell their bodies for money."[47] Most prostitutes were poor working-class women induced into the trade by their peers, and the great majority of their clients were men of the same under class.[48]

Bartley argues that as the century progressed, there was a gradual "shift from holding prostitutes responsible for prostitution to thinking of them as the victims of masculine sexual profligacy and social injustice."[49] This was particularly the view advocated by Josephine Butler, the evangelical who crusaded so powerfully for the repeal of the Contagious Diseases Acts. Her Ladies' National Association "upheld the human rights of the prostitute, even while disapproving of her occupation."[50] She argued that prostitution was first and foremost a social, rather than a sexual problem:

> for the lessening of this enormous evil it needs only that men of education should apply themselves earnestly to the much neglected subject of social economy; for this is not a question of natural vice so much as one of political and social economy.[51]

However, that said, the mission stood squarely against any moral double standard that found sexual license excusable in men but censured it in women. The sharp rejection of this standard seems to have been characteristic of evangelical attitudes. Certainly it was shared by many of the female reformers such as Josephine Butler, who "welcomed drunken whores into their homes but swore 'never to receive … any man, whatever his rank may be, who is known to be a profligate.'"[52] Prostitution affected women more profoundly than men, and in the view of Butler and others, women had to defend their sisters from male exploitation. Clearly, however, men such as Oppenheimer and the London City Mission that sponsored them also stepped forward to do their part, both in defending and in caring for exploited women. The soil of the unfortunates was not left ignored, untended or unprotected; these women were worthy of hearing the message that Oppeheimer brought.

Notes

[1] W. E. Gladstone, *Parliamentary Debates* (Hansard, 3rd Series, vol. 147, col. 853, 31 July 1857, accessed December 26, 2017, http://hansard.millbanksystems.com/commons/1857/jul/31/adjourned-debate.
[2] Paul McHugh, *Prostitution and Victorian Social Reform* (London: Croom Helm, 1980), p.17.
[3] Paula Bartley, *Prostitution: Prevention and Reform in England, 1860–1914* (London: Routledge, 2000), p. 4.
[4] Judith Walkowitz, *Prostitution and Victorian Society: Women, class and the state* (Cambridge: Cambridge University Press, 1980), p. 14.
[5] Linda Mahood, *The Magdalenes: Prostitution in the Nineteenth Century* (London: Routledge, 1990), p. 4.
[6] William Lecky quoted in McHugh, p. 17.
[7] Mahood, p. 14.
[8] Trevor Fisher, *Prostitution and the Victorians* (New York: St. Martin's Press, 1990), p. vii.
[9] *LCM Magazine* (Nov. 1842):161–67.
[10] Ibid., p. 211.
[11] McHugh points out that in the British army "marriage was restricted by regulation to about 6 per cent of enlisted men." McHugh, p. 18.
[12] *LCM Minutes*, Feb. 10, 1836.
[13] Ralph Wardlaw, *Lectures on Female Prostitution: Its Nature, Extent, Effects, Guilt, Causes and Remedy. Glasgow, 1842.* See *Evangelical Magazine* (Nov. 1842): 689–93. Wardlaw is one of the key evangelical spokespersons whom Walkowitz identifies. Walkowitz, p. 33.
[14] *LCM Magazine* (April 1840): 58–59.
[15] Walkowitz cites Viscount Ingestre as a key evangelical writer on prostitution but the Viscount was not known as an evangelical. Walkowitz, p. 41.
[16] Walkowitz, p. 33.
[17] F.K. Prochaska, *Women and Philanthropy in Nineteenth Century England* (Oxford: Oxford University Press, 1978), pp. 182ff.
[18] For an overview of such societies and their work see: "Female Penitentiaries," in *LCM Magazine* (Jan 1839): 6–15; and "Female Penitentiaries," *Quarterly Review* 28 (Sept. 1848): 359–76.
[19] *LCM Magazine* (Aug. 1856):173.
[20] Ibid., p. 175 .
[21] R. W. Vanderkiste, *Notes and Narratives*, pp. 281–82. For a study of Victorian efforts to rescue prostitutes, see Prochaska, *Women and Philanthropy*, chapter 6, pp. 183–221.
[22] Prochaska, *Women and Philanthropy*, p. 186.
[23] *LCM Magazine* (Oct. 1860): 281–96. Prochaska thinks that the idea for the Midnight Meetings originated with Theophilus Smith of the Female Aid Society. He apparently was unsuccessful with them in 1850, but by 1860 the time for his idea seemed to have come.

Prochaska, *Women and Philanthropy*, p. 194.
[24] Prochaska, *Women and Philanthropy*, p. 196.
[25] Walkowitz, p. 13.
[26] Walkowitz, p. 26.
[27] Walkowitz, p. 14.
[28] Walkowitz, p. 15.
[29] Walkowitz, p. 260, n. 9.
[30] Quoted in Walkowitz, p. 15.
[31] Paula Bartley, *Prostitution: Prevention and Reform in England, 1860–1914* (London: Routledge, 2000), p. 7.
[32] Walkowitz, pp. 16–17.
[33] Paula Bartley, *Prostitution: Prevention and Reform in England, 1860–1914* (London: Routledge, 2000), p. 10.
[34] Walkowitz, p. 20.
[35] Walkowitz, p. 20.
[36] Walkowitz, p. 21.
[37] Walkowitz, p. 19.
[38] *LCM Magazine* (June 1858): 152 ff.
[39] Walkowitz, p. 24.
[40] William Acton, *Prostitution Considered in Its Moral, Social and Sanitary Aspects in London and Other Large Cities: with Proposals for the Mitigation and Prevention of its Attendant Evils* (London: John Churchill, 1857), p. 19.
[41] He acknowledges that "The return gives, after all, but a faint idea of the grand total of prostitution, though it may be received as a conscientious approximation to the number of street-walkers." Acton, *Prostitution,* p. 17.
[42] Paula Bartley, *Prostitution: Prevention and Reform in England, 1860–1914* (London: Routledge, 2000), p. 2.
[43] T.W. Laqueur, *Religion and Respectability: Sunday Schools and Working Class Culture* (New Haven: Yale University Press, 1976), p. xi.
[44] Ranyard, *Life Work,* p. 264.
[45] Bartley, *Prostitution,* p. 26.
[46] Bartley, *Prostitution*, p. 31. For a description of the various reform institutions see Bartley, chapter 1.
[47] Bartley, *Prostitution*, p. 5.
[48] Mahood, p. 5. Mahood's view on this is supported by Finnegan's study of prostitution in the city of York in northern England, which demonstrated that prostitutes there were "generally working-class women" but that their 73% of their clients were from the same social class, thereby undermining the common view that prostitution generally involved middle-class males and working-class females. See also: Paula Bartley, *Prostitution: Prevention and Reform in England, 1860–1914* (London: Routledge, 2000), p. 5.
[49] Bartley, *Prostitution,* p. 5.
[50] McHugh, *Prostitution,* pp. 20–21.
[51] Josephine Butler quoted in McHugh, p. 21.
[52] *Parliamentary Papers*, "Reports from Commissioners, Report of the Royal Commission

upon the Administration and Operation of the Contagious Diseases Acts," 1871m 18m o, 447. Quoted in Prochaska, *Women and Philanthropy*, p. 185.

8

The Stony Ground
In Darkest London

Previous chapters have looked in depth at Oppenheimer's relations with the Irish Catholics, Jews and prostitutes in his district, seeking to provide background which helps to understand his approach to these three groups of people. There were other specific groups that can be identified and this chapter will look at some of these in order to better understand the different types of response to his visits, so that we may come closer to understanding both his experience and their experiences of him. Five different categories of response to his efforts will be examined in a systematic fashion: a) those overtly hostile to him; b) nominal Christians; c) infidels and skeptics; d) the indifferent; e) Sabbath-breakers. The next chapter will look at positive responses to his work.

Before embarking on such an analysis, more of the mindset of Victorian evangelicals has to be unpacked in order to appreciate the approach which Oppenheimer had been steeped in, particularly the obligation which many evangelicals felt in regard to their dealings with others. Harold Perkin in *The Origins of Modern English Society* in commenting on the impact of religion in this period observed that "Between 1780 and 1850 the English ceased to be one of the most aggressive, brutal, rowdy, outspoken, riotous, cruel and bloodthirsty nations in the world and became one of the most inhibited, polite, orderly, tender-minded, prudish and hypocritical."[1] The extent to which Evangelicalism was responsible for this moral revolution has long been debated by historians; Perkin makes a strong case that the evangelicals (both Anglican and Dissenting) while important, were not entirely responsible, as the secular Benthamite Utilitarians shared some of the responsibility. Related to these movements, of course, was the impact of the French Revolution on Britain. The old adage that "as the French became republican, the English became pious" has a good deal of truth in it. The French Revolution and its chaotic aftermath cast a dark shadow over the long nineteenth century. The fear of the social consequences of abandoning traditional Christian values and institutions loomed large in the Victorian mind; the French case was to many a good example of the chaos and upheaval that befell nations that turned their backs on their Christian heritage. A second anxiety that loomed large was Roman Catholicism which many English Protestants felt was responsible for the French Revolution in the first place: in their minds the intolerance of "persecuting Rome" bore much responsibility for the strong reaction against the intolerance of the Ancien Regime manifested in the Revolution.

But Perkin's observation about the nature of the moral revolution that took place in the first half of the nineteenth century can be seen in Oppenheimer's directness in confronting practices and attitudes which many nineteenth century evangelicals regarded as sinful—whether they be Sabbath-breaking, drunkenness, profanity, or more importantly, unbelief. In doing this, Oppenheimer was clearly doing what he had been instructed to do—point 5 in the LCM's instructions to missionaries is quite specific: "Point out, as occasion may require, their relative duties, and faithfully but prudently reprove open vice, such as swearing, intemperance, and the profanation of the Sabbath."

THE DUTY TO REBUKE

The role that this censorious criticism played in creating and sustaining the moral revolution that Perkin refers to needs to be understood in a larger historical context. It was undoubtedly the thing that made Victorian evangelicals most unpopular with their contemporaries. There is, of course, a long Christian tradition of such speech, particularly in Christendom where it was assumed that everyone in the body politic (excepting Jews) was, in some sense, Christian. In the Middle Ages wandering "preachers of repentance" often took this role upon themselves—denouncing people for their flagrant sins and calling for them to change their ways. Most famous, perhaps, was Girolamo Savonarola, the Dominican reformer in late fifteenth century Florence, who drew upon this tradition.

In the evangelical revival of the eighteenth century this theme re-emerged in the preaching of both John Wesley and George Whitefield. Early Methodist preachers often saw themselves in the role of modern day John the Baptists—who was known for his public rebuking of the Roman ruler, Herod, for unlawfully taking his brother's wife as his own (Mark 6: 17, 18).

Wesley spoke clearly of the importance of his followers "bearing testimony against sin" and insisted that Methodists had to "declare the whole counsel of God" to those whom they met. Wesley argued that his followers had a simple choice: either publicly condemn the sin they encountered, or by failing to condemn it, they were, in effect, condoning it. If one remained silent, reasoned Wesley, one shared in the unrebuked sin. Another New Testament passage cited was the apostle Paul's advice to Timothy "Them that sin rebuke before all, that others also may fear" (1 Timothy 5:20). A good deal of the anti-Methodist rioting in the 1730s and 1740s was related to such confrontations.[2]

Another aspect of this rebuking is the frequently repeated phrase which Oppenheimer used when he warned his listeners to "flee from the wrath that is to come." Here Oppenheimer is picking up the words of Jesus, recorded in Matthew 3:7 and Luke 3:7 ("who has warned you to flee from the wrath to come?") and Jesus' words recorded in John 3:36: "He that believes on the Son hath everlasting life: and he that believes not the Son shall not see life; but the wrath of God abides on him." Here are a few examples of Oppenheimer's emphasis upon the necessity of avoiding "the wrath that is to come:"

17 September 1861

68 Dudley Street

Indifference
Tuesday 17.
68 Kitchen, Called upon M[r] Evans who was again very talkative & approved of every word I said by "Yes" or "no", again I earnestly urged upon him to flee from the wrath of God, read several passages of Scripture &.c. but am sorry to say with seemingly no more success than on many previous occasions.

17 October 1861
60 Dudley Street

Public house.

60 Public house, distributed tracts at the bar to several men & women, the Public master likewise accepted one & I had a short conversation with him in which I was permitted to warn him to flee from the wrath to come, although he is a notorious character for using bad language, yet he has been pretty civil to me & shook

hands when I left him.

65 Dudley Street

A sad case of Indifference.

Tuesday 28.
65 top front. A. Dale, an Irishman, has been poorly for a long time; ["]don't attend a place of worship["] & has not done so for more than 10 years; ["]don't see the use of it, can be as good as other[s] who attend regular; has no Bible & would not read it; has to work hard if he can get it & has no time to read the Bible; Yes, of course must take time to die, but hopes to be all right; because God won't be so hard with poor people." Endeavoured to persu[a]-de him to flee from the wrath to come.

This theme of God's wrath is central in the writings of St. Paul, particularly in the book of Romans (1:18; 2:5; 2:8; 5:9) and in various places in other of Paul's letter and in the book of Revelation (6:16 "Fall on us, and hide us from the face of him that sits on the throne, and from the wrath of the Lamb"). The evangelicals were strongly Pauline in their theology and focused on Paul's insistence that the basic human condition is characterized by human rebellion against God which is the fundamental fact for him of the human condition: people are by nature opposed to God and his purposes; their most important need is to acknowledge this and to make their peace with him. (Hence Oppenheimer's frequent reference to "the one thing needful.") This perspective fits well with the Augustinian tradition in the Roman Catholic Church; Augustine, the fourth century theologian was as focused on human rebellion against God as were the evangelicals and was as insistent on the need for the grace of God in overcoming this alienation rooted in human rebelliousness.

OVERT HOSTILITY

This background helps to understand the degree of opposition that Oppenheimer faced as he sought to carry out his double task of speaking of God's love and warning of judgment to come. As has been seen in the chapter on Irish Catholics, Oppenheimer experienced much opposition from that quarter, but the Catholic hostility was generally verbal. Two instances of threatened violence are recorded by Oppenheimer but the people involved are not identified as Catholics:

Agent Rejected.

2nd back. Was refused ad-
mittance by a young man who
told me to go to the — & not
preach to him or he would let
me know what his creed was
he went on thus whilst I endeavoured to speak to him &
at last shut the door in my
face, & I could hear him swear
& curse whilst going down the
stairs.

23. OPPENHEIMER DIARY, 29 OCTOBER 1861

Tuesday, 29 October 1861

Monmouth Court

5. 2nd back. Was refused admittance by a young man who told me to go to the -- & not preach to him or he would let me know what his creed was, he went on thus whilst I endeavoured to speak to him & at last shut the door in my face, & I could hear him swear & curse whilst going down the stairs.

In another instance the hostility was clearly influenced by Dutch Courage rather than by Celtic anger:

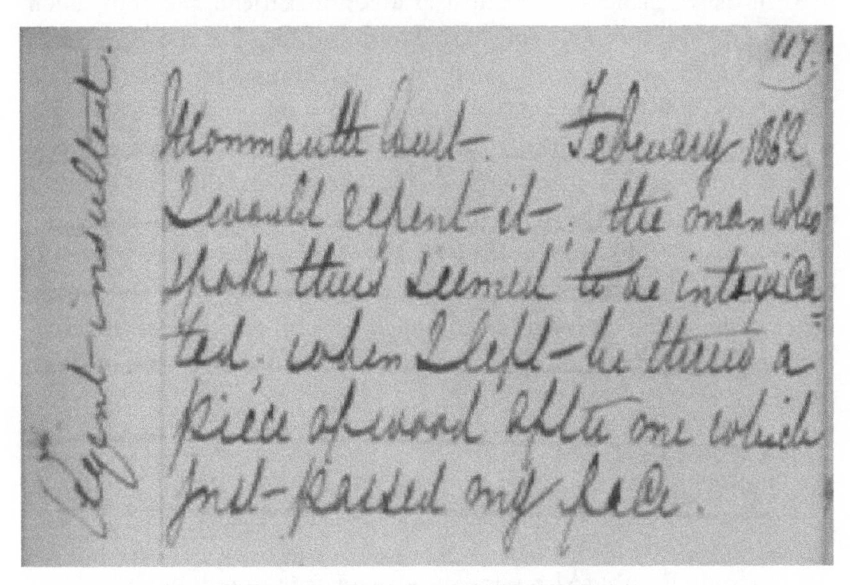

117

Agent insulted.

Monmouth Court. February 1862
I would repent it. the man who
spoke thus seemed to be intoxica
ted. when I left he threw a
piece of wood after me which
just passed my face.

24. OPPENHEIMER DIARY, 5 FEBRUARY 1862

Tuesday, 5 February 1862
Monmouth Court

Agent insulted.
8 shop. was refused admittance & told that if I come again I would repent it; the man who spoke thus seemed to be intoxicated; when I left he threw a piece of wood after me which just passed my face.

The very fact that the city missionaries were initially resisted because they were often seen in the same light as census gatherers and government officials—that is, as outsiders, meant that as they became familiar with the long-term residents, the hostility tended to subside. Incidents of hostility involving threats of physical harm seem to have occurred about once a month for Oppenheimer.

NOMINAL CHRISTIANS

Oppenheimer's journal demonstrates that although attendance at a church was a goal of his work, he did not view the habit of church going as an adequate measure of spiritual health. What evangelicals were anxious for was a wholehearted embracing of Christianity, characterized by a turning of one's whole life over to Christ, both for the forgiveness of sins and a life lived in daily reliance upon Christ as a personal friend and companion. The city missionaries were encouraged to discern whether those professing to be Christians in fact measured up to the evangelical understanding: did they both believe and behave? Or did they rely on their own merits and acts of goodness to justify them before a God who insisted that only the sacrifice of his own Son was sufficient to atone for the heinousness of humanity's rebellion against the Divine Majesty? Those were doubly guilty who professed to be religious and yet insisted that their acceptance with God could be established on their own terms. They rejected God's loving offer of forgiveness and had the effrontery to substitute their own efforts, their own self-righteousness. Such was the condition that Oppenheimer diagnosed of Mrs. Groves:

> 8 October 1861
> Dudley St.
>
> 34
> top front. Poor old Mrs. Groves is very much in trouble not having any work, she complained a great deal & I had some difficulty to avert the subject from things temporal to things spiritual, read the word and endeavoured to impress upon her to seek first the Kingdom of heaven &c. Mrs. G. is a regular attendant at church but is still far from the Kingdom of heaven.

INFIDELS AND SKEPTICS

Oppenheimer rarely encountered open skepticism toward Christianity or a somewhat thought-out attack upon it. The local skeptic was a shopkeeper who seems to have had plenty of occasions to sharpen his arguments in debate with Oppenheimer:

> Dudley Street October 1861.
>
> *Skepticism.*

71
shop. Mr Viney was glad to see me & I was again permitted to warn him to flee from the wrath to come; when I spoke of the fearful doom of those who neglect so great salvation &.c. he said "now do you think that God punish[es] all who don't believe what you call the gospel & if there is a hell do you think they will all go to hell; well you tell me you are sure of that because your Bible tells you so, but i tell you then that God must be very cruel & would act like a tyrant to send to hell more than half the human race, what did he send them in the world for if it [is] only for to damn them." Explained to him that God willeth not that any should perish in proof of wh[ich] he gave his son to redeem them, so that like the fall was universal, redemption is universal, but men will not accept that provision freely made, hence they are under the curse of the law, entirely of their own choice.

Hugh McLeod has noted that "confident dogmatism was not typical of the working class" in the nineteenth century and this observation seems to be born out in Oppenheimer's experience on his district. [3] Religious eclecticism tended to be the more typical stance, something that irritated both the militant unbeliever and the ardent Christian.

THE INDIFFERENT

Far more frequently the response which concerned Oppenheimer was simple indifference to his message. What is perhaps most surprising in these cases is his persistence and the willingness of those he addressed so frequently to hear him out. Some appear to have felt it necessary to justify their own actions to him, as was the case with Phoebe Terry, the 37 year-old wife of 40-year-old William Terry. At the time of the census in early 1861 they had two daughters, ages 13 and 6, and two sons, ages 10 and 4.

Dudley Street September 1861.

Indifference

Friday 6
28 2nd back. Called upon Mrs Terry who is still very indifferent to the things which are made for Peace. "Poor people can't do what they ought, my husband & I work hard, and don't taste a drop of drink from one week[']s end to another & we try to do our best to bring our children up well, they are all going to school; I know

that all this won't save us, but there are plenty of people who go to church & all that-; but who are much worse than we are, we don't like to profess what we are not." Read & explained the 3rd chapter to the Rom[ans] & endeavoured to impress upon her the solemn truth "without holiness no man shall see the Lord."

In spite of the solemnity with which Oppenheimer addressed her, the next time he visited he apparently found a welcome:

Dudley Street. October 1861.

Monday 7.
28 top back. Called upon M[rs] Terry; was glad to see me; has been in great trouble since I saw her last her husband being out of work; has not been to a place of worship for a very long time, don't know why but would be almost ashamed to go now & in fact she could not now because she has pledged all her clothes. has got a Bible & does read it occasionally; her children attend St. Giles school.- read & explained a portion of the word & left a tract.

Several months later Mrs. Terry appears to have become a mother once again:

Dudley Street. January 1862.

28 2nd back, Called upon M[rs] Terry, a respectable poor woman, endeavoured to persuade her to send her girl 11 years old to St. Giles school again, the poor girl used to go there some time ago but of late is kept at home to help her mother; she promised me to comply with my request as soon as her Baby is a few weeks older. Read the word & left a tract.

Mrs. Terry's initial statement "I know that all this won't save us" evidences her awareness of the missionary's line of argument about the futility of self-justification, although she insists on using that line of defense.

Others seem to have listened to the missionary because he lent a sympathetic ear and liked to tell him their problems and complaints while remaining unmoved by his arguments. His consolation was obviously not always to their liking:

10 February 1862 Dudley St.
Spiritual poverty.

32
1st front; found M[r] Blakehay in great distress on account of having

> lost all his little furniture for 22 shillings of rent which he owed to his Landlord; endeavoured to impress upon him that this world is not our home, & that trials & troubles are sent for the purpose of bringing us to our senses & leading us nearer to God &c. read & explained a portion of Scripture, but am sorry to say Mr B. remained unmoved to all I said & read, although he listened attentively.

From time to time, Oppenheimer endeavoured to shake people out of their lethargy with a solemn rebuke. His stress in his conversations was normally on the love of God and his concern for people as miserably stationed in life as those he visited, but Oppenheimer could be moved to warn people "to flee from the wrath to come." Such was his approach with one overly talkative woman:

> 4 September 1861 Dudley Street
>
> *Indifference*
>
> 18 Kitchen. Called upon Ann Barry, endeavoured to imprefs her with Divine truth but she is so talkative about the things of time, & so indifferent about the one thing needful, that nothing seems to make any impression upon her, read the word & gave her a solemn warning.

SABBATH BREAKERS

Evangelicalism in the Victorian era was very concerned with keeping Sunday as the Christian Sabbath and to Oppenheimer, Sunday trading was a flaunting of the revealed law of God and thus was something that he had to rebuke with the same forcefulness that he condemned prostitution and drunkenness. It is difficult of contemporary readers to appreciate how seriously many nineteenth-century Christians viewed "the desecration of the Sabbath." The following entry is typical of the response that Oppenheimer received to his pleas:

> Dudley Street. September 1861
>
> *Sunday trading.*
>
> Wednesday 18.
> 77 Shop. Had another conversation with Mr Riggs on the evil of Sunday trading & endeavoured to impress him with the

exceeding sinfulness of this particular sin, but like on many previous occasion he pleaded "necessity" as an excuse & notwithstanding my convincing him of the fallacy of it, he persisted to say that he was not worse than other people, & was determined to give up Sunday trading altogether, on some future day.

Others, however, were less receptive than Mr. Riggs and had to be told in no uncertain terms of the seriousness of their misdeeds:

Broad St. September 1861.

24 Public house. Distributed tracts at the bar to 7 men & 5 women, two refuse to accept them, the rest did accept each a tract & so did the Public master himself.

Sunday trading.

26
shop. Had another conversation with Mr Sullivan, an Irishman on the evil of Sunday trading, read a portion of Scripture, and endeavoured to impress upon him the exceeding sinfulness of sin & the reallity [sic] of that place where the worm never dieth & fire is never quenched; list[en]ed attentively but brought forward the usual miserable excuse "that because others do it["] he is compelled to do the same. After my urgent pleading with him to flee from the wrath to come, I left him with that solemn warning "Be not deceived God is not mocked for what a man soweth that also shall he reap."

The city missionaries do seem to have had some impact in their areas, with the City Mission's annual report regularly reporting on its agents' progress in this regard. Undoubtedly there were numerous other factors at work influencing Sunday closings, but the efforts of these lay agents is one that has seldom been stressed in past discussion of Sabbatarianism by scholars of the movement.[4]

Clearly there was much stony ground for Oppenheimer to contend with as he made his rounds on Dudley Street. The labourer may have been persistent, but his harvest was meager; much patience was needed if any gains were to be made. We now turn to the labourer's harvest.

Notes

[1] Harold Perkin, *The Origins of Modern English Society* (London: Routledge, 2002, 2nd edition), p. 280.
[2] John Walsh, "Methodism and the Mob in the Eighteenth Century," in *Studies in Church History*, ed. G. J. Cumming and Derek Baker, vol. 8, Cambridge, 1972, pp. 219–23.
[3] Hugh McLeod, "The Dechristianisation of the Working Class in Western Europe (1850–1900)," *Social Compass*, 27, no. 2–3 (1980): 194.
[4] The important role played by organizations such as the LCM is given no attention in works such as John Wigley's *The Rise and Fall of the Victorian Sunday* (Manchester: Manchester University Press, 1980).

Part 4

THE SOWER'S HARVEST

9

The Sower's Harvest In Darkest London

> And these are they which are sown on good ground; such as hear the word, and receive it, and bring forth fruit, some thirtyfold, some sixty, and some an hundred.
>
> Mark 4:20

Oppenheimer's manuscript journal accounts for only portions of the last eight months of his four-year stint with the London City Mission, as during this period he was incapacitated for weeks at a time by illness. Although he began his work with the City Mission as a single man, by the time the journal ends in May 1862, he was married with two small daughters. Marriage and family life must have been a great solace to a man who regularly encountered hopeless poverty and suffering among the people he visited from day to day. His own frequent illnesses during the eight months of the journal must have been a hardship for his wife and their growing family.

When one considers his length of service, the personal sacrifices involved, and the difficult conditions of his work, the long-term results must have appeared to him rather discouraging. Given the ignorance he encountered, the latent anticlericalism ingrained in the poor, and a strong resentment of the upper classes who dominated and controlled the churches, any attempt to win the allegiance of the people of his district was bound to be difficult. However, as has been seen, the difficulties that workers such as Oppenheimer encountered were undoubtedly magnified by their penchant for rebuking sin. Although evangelical doctrine taught that a person's good works or moral life could not save, the missionaries' insistence upon keeping a strict moral code seems to have led to confusion in the minds of the poor. To many of their hearers, Christianity undoubtedly seemed like a stern ethical system far beyond the reach of the average mortal. Later in the century, a city missionary summarized just such a view as typical of the working-class: "These people's idea of Christianity is 'Doing the best you can and doing nobody no harm.' They appear to think that if they don't get to heaven, there was little chance for anybody."[1] People may have listened and accepted tracts, but positive responses appear to have been limited.

Such responses as he found, Oppenheimer divided into two categories: "hopeful cases"—people who seemed to be on the verge of conversion—and those who had already made a commitment and whose faith needed strengthening. Earlier chapters have dealt with his interactions with Roman Catholics, Jews and prostitutes; this chapter will limit itself to positive responses from others in his district. Responses are clustered according to gender and marital status in the following order: married women; widows; single women; married men; single men; and families.

MARRIED WOMEN

Oppenheimer visited many married women, carrying his ministry to them without any specific reference in his journal to their husbands. Such was the case with Mrs. Watson, who had recently given birth but whose name does not appear in the census record:

> Dudley Street September 1861.
>
> Friday 13
>
> 59 1st front. Called upon Mrs Watson who lately confined; endeavoured to impress upon her her duty to give thanks to God for safely delivering her with a healthy Baby &. c. She seemed so very much impressed & was shedding tears; read & explained a portion of the word & prayed.

Another woman who was expecting a child was Mrs Bird, with whom Oppenheimer spoke in September 1861.

> Dudley Street. September 1861
> Monday 23.
>
> 87. top front. Called upon Mrs Bird & found that she has been

> confined with another Baby, is doing well & asked me to speak to her to be churched free of charge as she can't afford to pay & don't like to go out before she has been churched; explained to her the meaning of that rite of the church, & endeavoured to impress upon her to give thanks to God for her safe delivery & to go to Jesus our merciful Saviour & plead his merits for the delivery from the power of sin & Satan. offered up a prayer.

Mrs. Bird raises the matter of "being churched," by which she is referring to "the churching of women." This ancient practice in Roman Catholic and Anglican churches was a religious ceremony performed in church after the birth of a child. Its theological significance had shifted at the time of the Reformation, from one that emphasized the mother's defilement and purification to one of thanksgiving for the child and its safe delivery. The practice remained popular and was often regarded superstitiously at a popular level, where it was seen as a social occasion focused on the mother and her achievement.

Oppenheimer visited her again after her delivery. Mrs. Bird appears to have been somewhat devout as an Anglican, given her desire to have her infant baptized:

> Dudley Street. October 1861.
>
> Thursday 24.
>
> 87 top front. Called upon Mrs Bird who was very glad to see me; she attends now a regular place of worship & promises very fairly indeed, she desired me to day to speak for her to get her child of which she has been lately delivered, free christened wh[ich] I promised to do; read the word & offered up a prayer.

Oppenheimer seems to take at face value Mrs. Bird's desire for the child's baptism as a good thing and does not probe further.

A very different scenario was played out with Mrs. Thompson at 72 Dudley Street, presenting Oppenheimer with a grieving mother whom he sought to console with the Christian belief in the resurrection of the dead:

> Dudley Street. October 1861.
>
> *A Mother in sorrow*
>
> Friday 18
>
> 72 2nd back. Called upon Mrs Thompson whose little child 11 months old is lying dead, the poor woman seems to grief

> [sic] very much; endeavoured to impress upon her to prepare to meet her child in glory; read & explained a portion of the word & offered up a prayer. She seemed to be much impressed & I promised to call again.

The census record indicates that Mary Thompson was 40 years old and from Croydon, just south of London; she was the mother of an 8-year-old son, John. She is listed as the head of household, so she may have been a recent widow. Her occupation is given as an "army clothes worker." Her deceased child would have been born in November 1860.

The census record shows that Mrs. Sarah German was the 43-year-old Irish-born mother of a 3-year-old daughter, Eliza, and married to Thomas German, a labourer. From Oppenheimer's account, by 1862 the Germans had two children, perhaps including a newborn. Sarah German's illiteracy prevented her from reading Scripture, but she was able to attend a "cottage lecture"—that is, evening religious instruction in an informal setting at a local school.

> Dudley Street. January 1862.
> Thursday 30.
>
> *future visit desired.*
>
> 77 1st back; Called upon M[rs] German, a respectable poor woman who seemed to be impressed with what I read & said to her; —has a Bible but can't read, does not attend a regular place of worship, but promised me to attend the Cottage Lecture at St. Giles old school this evening.

A few weeks later, a second visit made clear a fuller picture of Mrs. German's situation:

> Dudley Street. February 1862.
>
> *Drunken husband.*
> *future visit desired*
>
> 77 1st back; Called upon M[rs] German who received me kindly, but complained very much of her drunken husband who abuses her very shamefully when under the influence of liquor; he can earn between 30 shillings & 2 a week, the whole of that sum he spends in drink & the poor woman must provide for herself & two children. Read & explained a portion of the word endeavouring to

impress upon the poor woman the duty & priviledge of prayer &c. offered up a prayer & promised to call again.

WIDOWS

> Pure religion and undefiled before God and the Father is this, To visit the fatherless and widows in their affliction…
>
> James 1:27

Oppenheimer encountered many widows in his district. A devout mother in the person of Mrs. Eliza Winterton appears to have been a widow: The census record lists her as the head of household in her room at 41 Dudley Street, where she lived with three sons and a daughter. She was 47 years old and originally from Coventry, although her four children were born in London. Her sons Thomas, William and Frederick were 19, 13 and 5 years old. Her daughter, also named Eliza, was 16 years old and ill in hospital in January 1862:

> Dudley Street. January 1862.
>
> 41 top front. M[rs] Whittenton [sic] was glad to see me & thanked me for visiting her daughter in the Middlesex Hospital, who is now quite well & at home again; both Mother & daughter attend the Bloomsbury Mission Hall & read their Bible.

(The reference to the Bloomsbury Mission Hall is important and will be discussed at the end of this chapter.) It is curious and perhaps significant that no religious interest is attributed to any of her sons.

She appears again in the journal in the following month, when Oppenheimer comes up with yet another way of spelling her name:

> Dudley St. February [1862]
>
> 41 top front. M[rs] Wittonten received my visit kindly & listened attentively to the word read & explained; the poor woman seems in [sic] to be earnest & sincere in her christian profession, reads her Bible & attends a place of worship. Offered up a prayer.

Like Mrs. Winterton, elderly Mrs. Wilson was devout. She was a Wesleyan Methodist and a widow:

> Dudley Street. October 1861.

Hope in Christ.

2nd back. Old Mrs Wilson was glad to see me, she said everybody had forsaken her in the world, she had no one who cared for her but she knew God would never forsake, Christ was her only hope & trust & having Him she could bear all her troubles, & trials, knowing that she shall soon be in that land "where the wicked cease from troubling & the weary are at rest;" Read & explained a portion of Scripture and offered up a prayer. M[rs] W. has seen better days but her husband[']s drinking habits, which by the way were the cause of his dead [sic], & sickness have reduced the poor woman to poverty; she is a member of the Wesleyan body and attends Queen St. chapel regularly.

Another older person who responded positively to Oppenheimer was 75-year-old Mrs. Elizabeth Nellums, who lived at 17 Dudley Street; Elizabeth Gutteridge was a 66-year-old lodger who resided with her. Both were English-born:

Dudley Street. October 1861.

Hopeful case.

Thursday 3.
17 top back. Called upon old M[rs] Nelms who was very glad to see me; has regularly attended St. Giles church since I saw her last twice on Sunday & once in the week; Can't read but prays to God for Christ's sake to pardon her sins & to give her His Holy Spirit & make her meet for the Kingdom of heaven. Read & explained part of the 3 chapt[er] to the Rom[ans] & offered up a prayer.

The very next day, Oppenheimer spoke with yet another elderly woman, Mrs. Carla. This is the only journal entry related to her:

Dudley St. September 1861

Trust in Christ.

Wednesday 4
18 2nd back. Old M[rs] Carla is still very poorly, spoke to her of death & eternity when she said "I trust in Christ & I prays to him every day of my life; I know if I goes to heaven it's only for what Jesus has done for me. I am very poor you see but am thankful for ever so little, for I know I don't deserve nothing, I have got a bad heart, But I trust & pray to Jesus for I have nobody

else to trust in; I read my Bible every day."

There are three entries related to another elderly widow, 77-year-old Mary Maycock at 44 Dudley Street, who lived with her 50-year-old daughter, also named Mary. Both were London-born, and both are listed as working as shoe-binders:

Dudley Street September 1861.

Hope in Christ

43. 2nd front. Called upon poor old M[rs] Maycock, who is very poorly at present, but am glad to be able to say, she has fixed her hope upon the rock of ages, & is humbly submitting herself to the will of Him who loved her & gave Himself for her. It is encouraging indeed & I have derived many lessons by visiting this poor woman & hearing her (crossed out) express herself, of the hope within her. Read the 23 Psalm and offered up a prayer promising to call upon her again next Saturday.

Dudley Street. [10] October 1861.

An old disciple.

43 Thursday 10. 2nd front. Called upon old M[rs] Maycock, who is rather poorly at present, she was glad to see me & expressed once more her entire confidence in her God & her Lord; read the 23[[rd]] Psalm & offered up a prayer.

Dudley Street. January 1862.

A happy christian.

Tuesday 21.
43 2nd front. Called upon poor old M[rs] Maycock, who was glad to see me; found her as usual very happy & content, the only regret she expressed was, that she can't get out to go to a place of worship, which she always did as long [as] she possibly could manage to walk; "My daughter reads the Bible to me every day & we keep all the tracts & read them over & over again; Yes I pray & my daughter prays too; I shall soon be gone I know[,] but I am not afraid[.] Jesus is my Saviour & I shall soon be with him & be happy." read the word & offered up prayer.

A month later Mrs. Maycock was in significant decline:

[February] 1862. Dudley St. district.

Thursday 13.

A communicant.

43 2nd front; found poor old M[rs] Maycock very ill; but am happy to say she knows & loves her Saviour Christ & is longing for the time when she shall see Him in heaven; read & explained the word & offered up a prayer.

Another elderly widow who gave Oppenheimer encouragement was Mrs. Oldham:

Dudley St. September 1861

Thursday 5.
Trust in God's providence

25 Kitchen; poor M[rs] Oldham, was very glad to see me again & I am happy to say that amidst her extreme poverty, & her husband being in a state of consumption, the poor woman retains her trust & confidence in Him who ordered all things according to the counsel of His own will; "It's very hard for me["], she said, ["]but God knows best what is for our good. I pray to him & he gives me strength to bear my trial &c." Read the word & prayed.

The elderly Mrs. Oldham does not appear in the census record, but she appears to be the mother of Catherine Johnson, whose husband Frances Johnson, a 48-year-old bootmaker, is listed as the head of household in one of the rooms at 25 Dudley Street. Frances was from Scarborough in Yorkshire; his 36-year-old wife Catherine was Irish-born. Living with them were a five-year-old son, Henry, and a three-year-old daughter, Betsy. In addition there was a 30-year-old Irish-born brother-in-law, Thomas Oldman, a shoemaker, and his 30-year-old English wife, Harriet, who is listed in the census as helping her husband in shoemaking, along with their 7-year-old son Richard. Rounding off the family grouping was a 12-year-old niece, Alice Cockling, and apparently Mrs. Oldham, the Irish-born mother-in-law of Frances Johnson and her unnamed husband, making a total of ten family members.

Four more widows seem to have been responsive to Oppenheimer's work, but there are no census records to further identify them:

Broad Street. October 1861.

A christian poor woman.

[26] 1st. back. Mrs Page an elderly woman, was glad to see me; "is always glad to see the Missionary or any other christian man; Yes I do love the Lord Jesus Christ; I know it well that if He had not loveth me first, I would never have loveth Him; I have my troubles & trials but I take everything God sends me is for my good, sometimes I murmur but I know it's my evil heart &.c." Read the word & prayed.

Dudley Street. January 1862.

Thursday 30.
80 2nd back; Poor old Mrs Piggons, who lately came there from some other part of the Parish; found her in a most distressed state, the poor old woman is very ill indeed & her two daughters, both widows, are without work. Endeavoured to impress upon them the privilege & the power of prayer to which they listened very attentively; when questioning the old woman of the hope within her she said: "Jesus, in Him I trust; He is my Saviour; He loves me in my poverty just as much as when I was better off; I pray to him & I know I shall soon be with Him["] &c. Is a communicant at St. Giles Church.

Dudley St. February [1862]

[35] 2nd back. poor old Mrs Hart was very glad to see me again & told me that since I saw her last & spoke to her of the power & privilege of prayer, she began to pray more that ever she had done before "it's true["], she said, ["]you told me that saying prayers was not to pray; I know now that it is not, I said my prayers for a great many years but now I know I never prayed before, but I began to pray now & I can't tell you what a comfort it is to me, I feel as happy as a queen; I read my Bible & I pray & don't have half the troubles I had before, for I know that Jesus my Saviour will take care of me &c.&c."; read a portion of the word & offered up a prayer.

1862. Dudley St. district.

[43] Dudley Street. February

Thursday 13.
1st back. Was glad to find poor old M[rs] Taylor reading her Bible, in the words [of] St. Phillipp [sic] of old[.] I addressed her by asking her "un[der]standet[h] thou what thou reads["]? when I took up her Bible, and explained to her part of the 5[th] chapter of St. Mark's gospel wh[ich] she has been reading.

INDIVIDUAL UNMARRIED WOMEN

The person most frequently mentioned in Oppenheimer's journal is Sophia Cannon, at 81 Dudley Street. The census record lists two households with the Cannon name at that address. One is of Sophia Cannon, an unmarried 30-year-old sempstress [seamstress] who had been born in London and is listed as head of household. The other household was headed by Thomas Cannon, a 25-year-old glass cutter, married to Maria, a 21-year-old sempstress, who was the mother of two children: Serephina, age 2, and Thomas J., aged 6 months. Like Sophia, Thomas and Maria were London-born. Missing from the record are Sophia's father and mother, who apparently lived at the same address.

Oppenheimer's first entry relates to his visiting Sophia in the City of London Hospital for Consumption and Chest Diseases, also known as the Victoria Park Hospital:

Thursday 12 [Sept. 1861]

Visit in a Hospital.

Went to the Victoria Park Hospital this afternoon to visit Sophia Canon, a poor girl from 81 Dudley St. who is in a decline; she was exceedingly glad to see me & I am happy to say, she is very happy & expressed her entire confidence in her Saviour for the salvation of her soul. —left her a few tracts & promised to see her again if God permit.

A week later, Oppenheimer visited Sophia's mother and recorded the following:

Dudley Street. September 1861
Friday 20.

81 Dudley Street

Promised a visit in a Hospital.

2nd fr[ont]. Mrs Canon told me that her daughter Sophia, who is in the Victoria Park Hospital, is sinking fast since I saw her last week; endeavoured to impress upon her the necessity of making her peace with God; read the word & promised if possible to visit her daughter again in the Hospital.

A second hospital visited occurred about three weeks later, on Thursday, 10 October:

Dudley Street. [10] October 1861.

Rejoicing in Christ.

Visited Sophia Cannon in the Victoria Park Hospital this afternoon, found her but very little improving, there is hardly any hope of recovery for she is to all appearance in a consumption, but am happy to say her mind is fixed upon Christ, she said to me to day, "I wish to get well again if it is God's will but if not I shall be the sooner with my Saviour" & when I asked her whether she felt any comfort now in believing in Jesus, she said "All is comfort to me now, Jesus is my all & I am happy in Him &.c." Promised if possible to visit her again.

Three months later Sophia was out of hospital, but neither her physical nor temporal condition had improved when Oppenheimer visited her at home:

81 Dudley Street January 1862.

Friday 3.
2nd back. Sophia Canon is still confined to her bed, but is happy in her Saviour. ["]My father is out of work["], she said, & ["]we are very bad off now, but I must do the best I can, I am not afraid I know my Saviour won't let me starve; I love Him more now than ever did before, I am happy in spite of all my pains & troubles["]. Read the word & prayed.
The final entry is four weeks later, at the end of January:

Thursday 30. January 1862.

Dudley Street.
81 2nd back; Poor Sophia Canon is still very poorly, & has

> been obliged to keep her bed again for the last two or three days; expressed again her hope & confidence in her Lord & Saviour Jesus Christ, in whom she enjoys peace & happiness; read & explained the 23rd Psalm & offered up a prayer.

It would appear from the death records that Sophia Cannon went on to live for another two years, her death being recorded in Lambeth in 1864.

A second frequently mentioned unmarried woman was 43-year-old Ann Tyler, who had been born in London but had been blind from birth. Oppenheimer found that in visiting her, however, she was the one who brought encouragement and joy to him:

> Dudley Street October 1861
>
> *Missionaries [sic] encouragement*
>
> Tuesday 15.
> 59 top back. Called upon poor blind Miss Tyler who was very glad to see me; read the word & offered up a prayer. Miss T. is one of those who know in whom they have believed, is it [sic] really very comforting for the Missionary to have such bright jewels in a district full of sin & misery, where he can go for a short space of time to hear from the lips of one surrounded by all the evil influence, what the Lord can & does do for those who receive the Lord Jesus Chr[ist] & love him as their Saviour & their all.

25. 1861 CENSUS RECORD FOR 59 DUDLEY STREET

Miss Tyler's closest friend was 27-year-old Mary Day from Lincolnshire, who was also blind from birth. She was married to 26-year-old James Day, who was employed as a gilder; they had two daughters, May and Elizabeth, ages 3 and 1. The census form says that it was James Day who had been blind since birth, but this seems to have been a clerical error. We meet Mary Day on Oppenheimer's next visit in January, 1862:

> Dudley Street. January 1862.
>
> Monday 27.

> *A happy christian.*
>
> 59 top back; Called upon poor blind Miss Tyler, who was very glad to see me; read & explained the 23rd Psalm & offered up a prayer. The poor blind woman is one of the happiest christians I ever saw & each time I visit her, I really feel that it does me good. front room. Mrs Day, likewise a blind woman, is still in an indifferent state of mind, through the influence of Miss Tyler, her friend, she has been induced to attend to the outward forms of religion, but is still, as far as ever, from the Kingdom of heaven.

Oppenheimer's persistence and supremely the influence of Ann Tyler began to work a change in Mary Day:

> Dudley Street. February
>
> Tuesday 18.
> 59. top front & back; Called again upon Mrs Day & Ann Tyler, both blind; read and explained the word to them & endeavoured to impress upon Mrs D. the Duty & privilege of prayer. Miss Tyler is a sincere & faithful christian woman who though blind, yet sees with the eye of faith Him who has loved her & given Himself for her.
>
> Dudley Street. [February crossed out] May 1862.
>
> 21? May 1862
> Visited only a few special cases to day was kindly received & the poor people were very much pleased to see me again; poor blind Ann Tyler of 59 Dudley Street told me that she had prayed for me twice every day ever since she heard I was ill & sent to the church several times to enquire after my health. I read & explained to her & Mrs Day who was present the 23rd Psalm after which we knelt down in prayer to the throne of heavenly grace.

The image of the missionary and two blind women, kneeling together in prayer in such a hovel, is hard to imagine when one contemplates Gustav Doré's image of Dudley Street.

INDIVIDUAL SINGLE MEN

Although Oppenheimer was a door-to-door evangelist, he was much more than that; he functioned in several ministerial roles in his pastoral care for the poor. He mentions visiting people in four local hospitals:

the Middlesex, the City of London Hospital for Consumption and Chest Diseases (also known as Victoria Park Hospital), the Brompton Consumption Hospital and the German Hospital. Here is a typical entry, related to his hospital visitation on the 18th of October:

> *Visit in hospital.*
>
> Visited 2 persons from my district in the Middlesex Hospital this afternoon, they were glad to see me & I was permitted to speak to them of the the [sic] great Physician of souls, both will shortly leave the hospital.

On one of these visits he encountered a young man suffering from "consumption"—the same ailment from which Sophia Cannon suffered—which was the common term for pulmonary tuberculosis:

> Friday 17. January 1862
>
> Visited a young man in the Brompton Hospital, this afternoon, he formerly used to live in my district, but left some sixteen months ago & went to live near Victoria Park where I saw him since several times; he was admitted into the above hospital being in a rapid consumption; he wrote me a letter from the hospital & requested me to come & see him; he was very much pleased with my visit & seemed to be impressed with what I read & said to him. he has hope in Christ & is happy & content. I left him a couple of tracts written by the Rev. J. C. Ryle, one "Do you pray" & the other "Are you an heir;" he was much pleased with them & requested me to send him a few more, or if possible to come & see him again.

Another man whom Oppenheimer visited was Mr Frost, who lived at 44 Dudley Street, but whose name may have been Forrist. Given that he describes him as an "old man," it may be that he is describing the father of John Forrist, age 43, who appears in the census record. The aged father, who may have lived with his son John, does not appear on the census record. John Forrist's wife was Bridget, aged 41; they had a 9-year-old daughter, Ellen. Both parents had been born in Ireland:

> Dudley Street. January 1862.
>
> *An interesting case.*
>
> 44. top front. An old man, named Frost seemed to be very

much affected whilst I read & explained to him part of the 53[rd chapter] of Isaiah; "Yes there was love["], he said, ["]God giving His Son to die for us poor creatures who are so wicked; I believe that he died for me, I pray to him & try to love him He knows; if he did not love me first I would never know anything of Him; I know I do a great many things I ought not to do, but I pray to Him & he pardons my sin &c" left a tract & offered up prayer.

Oppenheimer also found a much younger single man receptive to his visits:

Dudley Street. January 1862.

Future visit desired.

Friday 31.
84 1st front; found a young man very willing to listen to the message; used to attend a Sunday school when he was a boy; has still got a Bible which he had given to him as a price [sic] for regular attendance; has not been to a place of worship since last Christmas twelf [sic] month. has not got tidy clothes now which are fit to go in; knows God looks into the heart & not at the cloth[e]s; reads his Bible occasionally. I had a long talk with the young man, whose name is Tennet, & found him very teachable, he seemed to be impressed when I read & explained a portion of the word; & when I left him asked me to call again.

John Wharton, a 76-year-old Irishman, was married to Mary Wharton, who was 56 years old and also from Ireland.

Dudley Street. January 1862.

Tuesday 28.
67 2nd fr[ont] called upon Mr Warton who was glad to see me again, & I was permitted to read & explain to him a portion of the word & to offer up a prayer.

Dudley Street district. February
Wednesday 19.

Missionary encouragement.

Thursday 20.
67 top front; Mr Warton was glad to see me & listened attentively to the word read & explained; attends still regularly

St. Giles church & is a Communicant there "under God you are the only person in the world,["] he said, ["]to whom I have to be thankful for what I am now; Well I can't help to look upon you as the only one who has brought me to my senses, if it has [sic] not been for you I would have died in my sins, God knows that there is not a day now in all my life that I don't pray for you &c." offered up a prayer.

At the same address was the elderly Mr. Westhall. It would appear from the census record that he is probably the father of John Westall, the 49-year-old husband of Sarah, who was 48 years old. Living with them were four daughters and two sons, ranging in age from 12 to 26 years old, and apparently, John Westall's elderly father:

Dudley St. February 1862.

A christian's temptation.

67 shop; Called upon blind old Westhall & found him very poorly, but thanks be to God, he knows his Saviour & hopes presently to be with him in glory. — said to me to day "I believe & trust in Jesus God knows, but I am always troubled with such wicked thoughts, my heart is so bad I sometimes don't know what to do; Yes I pray & prayer is the only comfort I have; I know it is Satan who puts these wicked thoughts is my heart but I can't always very soon get rit [sic] of it & that troubles me so &c.—". Read the word and offered up prayer.

Another responsive elderly man was Mr. Cook. The first of three entries from the 3rd of September 1861 reads:

Dudley St. September 1861

I Know that my Redeemer Liveth

Tuesday 3
13 Top back. Called upon old Cook who said "Thank God I am again able to get out & to go to church, next Sunday if I am spared, & intend to attend the Lord's Supper;" he is still a great sufferer, but when I alluded to it he said "O my dear Sir, what would have become of me if God had not visited me with this affliction. I would have died like a fool, for I did not know Christ before I was afflicted but I now thank God I can say "I know that my Redeemer lives.'" Read a portion of the word and offered a prayer.

Early in October, Oppenheimer visited Cook again:

Dudley Street October 1861.

A Communicant.

Wednesday 2.
13. top back. Read the word & offered up prayer with poor old Cook, who, I am happy to say, is growing in grace & the the [sic] knowledge of Christ his Saviour.

The final entry related to Cook is from the 13th of January, 1862, reflecting prolonged absences on the part of Oppenheimer, due to the breakdown of his health:

Dudley Street. January 1862.

Monday 13.
13 top back; found poor old Cook in bed ill, but very happy & content in fact he never complained, although I know him to be very bad off, he told me to day that he is sure God will care for him "I like to keep out of the Workhouse as long as I can["], he said, ["]but if it is God's will that I should go in, I am willing; I can truly say that it was good for me to be afflicted, it has brought me to Jesus & I should be happy now even in the workhouse; I know he loves me & I never knew before as I do now what it is to have a Saviour, there is not anything like it I would not change with a Lord for I am as happy as if I was a King." Read the word and offered up prayer.

An apparently much younger person who was interested in Oppenheimer's message was James Lee at 49 Dudley Street. A Lee family is listed in the census record at this address, but the parents of the family are Edward and Susan Lee, who are listed as having a six-year-old son, William. Immediately adjacent to 49 Dudley Street was 52 Dudley Street, where another family by the name of Lee dwelt. This family was headed by Henry Lee, age 31, who may well have been the brother of Edward Lee next door (both were born in Middlesex). Henry had an 11-year-old son named James, who is likely the subject of this entry:

Dudley Street September 1861.

Missionary encouragement

> 49. Top front. Young James Lee was very glad to see me again & told me that he regularly attended a place of worship since he saw me last, & read his Bible every day; I am happy to say, the young man, seems now to be very anxious regard[ing] the salvation of his soul & seems to take great delight in reading the word of God, and attending the sanctuary of the Lord; endeavoured to impress upon him the necessity of asking for the Holy Spirit of God, for the right understanding [of] the word of God, as well as for to lead him on in the right path; read the word & offered up a prayer.

Five months later, Oppenheimer was able to record significant progress in his young protégé:

> February 1862
> Friday 14.
>
> 49 top front; young Mr Lee was glad to see me again & I am happy to say that he reads now his Bible & attends St. Giles church very regularly. Read & explained a portion of Scripture & endeavoured to impress upon him the necessity & privilege of prayer.

The last three instances are related to men who cannot be identified in the census records:

> Dudley Street January 1862.
> Friday 3.
>
> [78] 2nd back; persuaded a young man to read the Bible, he is very fond of reading & is as he expressed it a first rate scholar; He came there only a few weeks ago & I found that he has several books (novels) but no Bible & upon his promising that he would read it I gave him a nice copy which I had in my pocket. His name is Baker & I promised to call again next
>
> February 1862
>
> Wednesday 12.
> back room; found that poor Mr Leary has left this room, I endeavoured to find out where they went to but nobody could tell me; I had good hope concerning them.
>
> [February] 1862. Dudley St. district.
>
> Thursday 13.

48
1st front; found that poor old blind M[r] Law, has gone into the work-house, where I intend to visit him.

INDIVIDUAL MARRIED MEN

Oppenheimer records visits with a number of individual men, some of whom are unmarried, and some who are married but seem to be the sole focus of his attention, rather than their spouses. The first such case is that of Samuel MacKenley, a 40-year-old Scot, married to Ann MacKenley, who was the same age as her husband but born in the parish of St. Giles. They had three children living at home: a 20-year-old son, and two daughters, ages 17 and 14.

Dudley Street. January 1862.

Future visit desired.

Friday 10.
7 2nd front. Called upon M[r] Kenley; is still very indifferent [to] "the one thing needful" but more willing to listen to the message & I was permitted to read & explain to him part of the 1st chapter to the Romans & when I left him he asked me to call again, which he never did before.

A "hopeful case" was that of John Leighton, whom Oppenheimer visited on the first day of the journal's entries. The census record indicates that he was a 31-year-old baker from Norfolk, married to a 29-year-old wife who is identified only as "M.," and who worked as a shoebinder. They were apparently childless, but had a 52 year-old monthly nurse from Oxfordshire, Mary Bentley, living with them:

Dudley St. September 1861
Tuesday 3
Hopeful case

14 Called upon M[r] Leighton who told me that since I saw him last he has been reading the New Test[ament] I gave him, almost every evening when he came home from his work, and he has also been twice at St. Giles church at the Sunday evening services, & told me that he would go again next Sunday evening. Read & explained a portion of the word.

William Fidoe, born in Suffolk, was a 63-year-old bootmaker and husband of Jane Fidoe, also 63 years old, but from Surrey. Their 24-year-old son John was employed as a servant. He had been born in the parish of St. Giles. John was seriously ill but strong in faith, which was a significant encouragement to Oppenheimer:

1862. Dudley St. district.

Hope in Christ

Thursday 13.
43. Top front. Called again upon M[r] Fidoe who was glad to see me; his son John Fidoe is still alive but fast sinking & can't possibly last much longer; the poor young man is a great sufferer, apparently he has not had any sleep for months & months & is not able to keep anything on his stomach; —when I spoke to him of Christ & his hope concerning his immortal soul he said; "I trust I am all right, my hope is in Christ, I love him; I pray to him & I hope soon to be with him; I know he is the only Saviour & I think I can say that his blood was shed for me to wash away my sin & make me fit for heaven." —read the word and offered up a prayer.

Another married man whom Oppenheimer met was Henry Heigh, a 50-year-old tailor who had been born in the parish and was married to Mary, a 59-year-old bootmaker, also born in the parish. The entries related to him are interesting in that there is no mention of Oppenheimer interacting with Mary Heigh. It may have been that the husband worked at his tailoring at home while his wife was out working during the day. Heigh was a communicant in the Anglican church, but Oppenheimer did not yet consider him fully converted, although he was hopeful that he would soon come to appreciate what had been promised to him in his baptism:

Dudley Street October 1861.

A Communicant.

Wednesday 2.

13. front room. Called upon M[r] Haig, who is now thank God quite another man, not that he is converted to God, he is but an earnest inquirer after truth, and I have a fair hope that with God's blessing upon the reading of his blessed book M[r] H. will soon find peace & joy for his guilty conscience.

The journal records a second visit to Mr. Heigh some three months later, and Oppenheimer reports on the progress that has been made:

> Dudley Street. January 1862.
> *Future visit desired.*
> Friday 10.
>
> *Hopeful case.*
>
> 13 top front. Mr Haig was glad to see me, & I can see a great change in him for the better; he seems now to be anxious for my visits & is very attentive to the word read & explained to him, whilst sometime ago he would not even look at me, much less listen to the message. He told me to day that he reads his Bible everyday & from the questions he put & the answers he gave me I have every reason to look upon him as a sincere & anxious inquirer after truth. May the Lord by His Spirit lead him into all truth, for his dear Son Jesus Christ's sake.

A particularly distressing case was that of the Heywood family at 78 Dudley Street. Launcelot Heywood was a 41-year-old boot-maker, married to 38-year-old Esther Heywood. The census record indicates that they had five daughters and one son, ranging in age from 2 to 15, although Oppenheimer tells us that by September 1861 they had another child. Also living at 78 Dudley Street was 31-year-old Joseph Keats, who may have been Esther Heywood's younger brother. He is listed as head of household in another room and shared the room with a 23-year-old brother, as well as two nephews ages 13 and 18. All were London-born. Esther Heywood, however, was suffering from mental illness:

> Dudley Street September 1861
>
> *A very distressing case.*
>
> Thursday 19
> 78 top fr: Mr Haywood was very glad to see me again & told me that his poor wife is getting worse every day, her mind being affected & he has to watch her very closely, lest she does some fatal act, either to herself or some one else. After I had been in the room for some minutes she entered seemingly very pleased to find me there, she spoke in a[n] incoherent manner, saying that her neighbours were all talking about her & telling each other that she was not born in wedlock &.c. she was very unhappy seeing that

she was surrounded by enemies, but "God is my friend" & they will all be rewarded &.c. —seeing that she is really in a state of mind not fit to be talked to about spiritual things, I endeavoured to impress upon her not to mind what her neighbours say & to keep herself quiet &.c. she took it very calmly & promised to do so. — The poor man has 7 childr[en] I prayed.

Four months later, Oppenheimer visited again:

Dudley Street January 1862.

Communicant.

Friday 3.
78 top front. Called upon M[r] Haywood, who was glad to see me again; he has been very poorly lately, but am happy to say he seems to grow in grace & the knowledge of Christ his Saviour. Attends regularly St. Giles church & is a Communicant.

In one of the very last entries in his journal, Oppenheimer reports that Esther Heywood had been incarcerated in the insane ward of the workhouse but seemed to have made a remarkable recovery:

Monday 12. May 1862.

27 Poor M[r] & M[rs] Haywood 1st front were particularly glad to see me, the lat[t]er has only come home from the workhouse last week w[h]ere she had been confined for more than a month in the insane ward, but she seems to have quite recovered again; read & explained a portion of Scripture & offered up a prayer.

The final entry related to married men is that of Mr. Shean, who cannot be found in the census record. He was another subject of Oppenheimer's hospital visitation:

[February] 1862. Dudley St. District.

54 Monday 17.
2nd front; poor M[r] Shean died last Friday in the Middlesex Hospital after a long illness; I visited him there several times & have reason to believe that my visits have been attended with the blessing of the Almighty; read & explained a portion of the word to the poor widow & endeavoured to impress upon her to "prepare to meet her God" she shed tears when I offered up a prayer & expressed her thanks before I left for the interest I took in her poor husband.

FAMILIES

Most of Oppenheimer's ministry was focused on individuals, as it was rare to find both husband and wife at home during the day, when he undertook his visits. However, early in the journal he records encountering a young unnamed couple who were open and receptive to his message:

> [27] Broad Street. September 1861.
> Monday, 30 [September]
>
> *An interesting & hopeful case.*
>
> top back. found a young couple who received me very kindly, found them very teachable & willing to listen to the glad tidings of salvat[ion] when I read & explained to them the 3rd chapt[er] of St. John & dwelt more especially upon the necessity & nature of the New birth, the husband remarked "Yes I know that if we would think more about it & remember what a[n] awful thing it is to die unprepared, & to go to hell afterwards for ever, I am sure there would be more people living a better life as they now do, but most of them don't know their danger, it's as you say their heart is so bad & wicked that they live in sin & don't know the end of it; it's quite true that I know I have [not] thought quite as much as I ought about it myself, but I shall try to do so now &.c." Promised to call again.

Another young couple, the Tanners, were similarly receptive when Oppenheimer visited them a week later:

> Dudley Street. October 1861.
>
> Monday 7.
> 28 Dudley Street
>
> *Promised a copy of Scripture.*
>
> 2nd back. A young couple named, Tanner, received me kindly; found them very teachable, the husband, a cobbler can read a little, has not Scriptures but would like to get a copy would read it. Read & explained a portion of the word & promised to procure a New Testament.

Another young couple in Monmouth Court offered Oppenheimer a similar welcome:

Monmouth Court January 1862

Tuesday 7.

Future visit desired

2 1st front; A young couple received me very kindly & I found the husband to be an interesting & teachable man, he told me that a few years ago he was very well to do & did not think he should ever come into such a state as he is at the Present; & when I asked him what effect that change produced upon his mind & whether it did lead nearer to God &c. he answered "it certainly made me think more of God than I did before, but I came to the conclusion that God don't interfere in our little matter, for if he did how is that sometimes the drunkards & worst men are better to do than an industrious, sober man if he try ever so hard &c." I read to him several passages of Scripture bearing on that subject, especially the Conclusion the Psalmist came to on this matter. he asked me to call again.

An unnamed Wesleyan couple attended the Great Queen Street Methodist chapel and received Oppenheimer warmly:

Dudley Street. January 1862.

25 2nd back; found a young couple recently come there, both husband & wife seemed pleased with my visit; the former I found to be a nice, teachable young man, who told me that he reads his Bible & attends Queen's Street chapel, being a Wesleyan, read & explained a portion of the word & offered up a prayer.

Similar to this couple were the Smiths, who were Baptists rather than Wesleyans:

Dudley Street. May 1862.

An interesting young girl; future visit desired.

7 I visited Smith & had an interesting conversation with both him & his wife and their daughter. I very seldom find anyone at home except Mrs S. but to day I found them all there; they received me kindly & listened attentively to the word explained. I liked

> very much the appearance of their daughter, a girl 15 years old who goes out to work at the book folding; she seems to delight in reading her Bible of which she is very proud as having received it as a present for regularity at the school; they attend a Baptist chapel & speak very highly of the Minister there, of the name of Wilkins; left a tract & promised to call again.

The minister in question would appear to have been James Wilkins (1796 -1874).

Richard Woodword, age 62 and a porter, lived with his wife, 54-year-old Mary Woodword, at 55 Dudley Street with their 15-year-old daughter Jane, and Thomas Young, a 54-year-old lodger who was employed as a printer. All were born in Middlesex. They appear to have been the couple whom Oppenheimer refers to as Woodall:

> Dudley Street September 1861.
>
> *We take God by His word.*
>
> Friday 13
> 55. Top front. M^{r} & Mrs Woodall were very glad to see me & said that not withstanding their great poverty, they were perfectly content & fully assured that God would provide for their daily wants, the poor old man said "I will tell you Sir what we do, we take God by His word, He say that we should pray & ask Him every day for our daily bread, so we do Sir, we pray every morning & evening, & we get it in some shape or other. We put our trust in Christ & I know he will save us, He died for us & He is a friend of the poor however poor we are, if we believe in him & pray to Him he will save us, won't He?["] — Read & explained a portion of the word & offered up a prayer.

Oppenheimer records one further visit with them in January 1862:

> Dudley Street. January 1862.
>
> 55 top front. M^{r} & Mrs Woodall were very glad to see me & listened very attentively to the word read & explained; attend a place of worship regularly & read their Bible; offered up a prayer & left a tract.

Another couple who were receptive to Oppenheimer, but who are not listed in the census record, were the Clarks who lived at 81 Dudley Street.

The impact of his work is seen in the husband's now joining his wife in church attendance at St. Giles and in Bible-reading:

Dudley Street. September 1861

Missionary encouragement.

Friday 20.
81. top front; Called upon old Mr & Mrs Clark; both are now attending regularly a place of worship; the poor woman expressed herself thus "I am quite happy now, O dear we never went to church before you visited us & my husband did not never read the Bible, but now he reads to me & goes with me to church; O yes we pray to Jesus, I can't say much, but I always says that short prayer you told me, I know it now by heart &.c." When I asked her whether I should read a chapter she said "O yes dear I likes you to read to me & to pray."

About a month later, Oppenheimer's interactions were with the husband who recounts the change that had come over him in the previous year:

Dudley Street October 1861

Missionary encouragement

Wednesday 23.
81 top front. Called upon poor old Mr Clark, was glad to see me; "is very poorly & lost the sight of one eye entirely, but can still read his Bible; don't expect to live much longer for I feel I am sinking fast; thank God I am now more prepared to die than I was this time a year [ago]; Yes I am truly thankful that God did not take me away unprepared, if I think of it now I see what a fool I was not to think if it before; if God had[n]'t sent you I would have gone on & never would have thought what was to become of my soul, but now thank God I am thinking of it all day & I read my Bible & I prays that God would pardon all my life long sins & I goes to St. Giles church twice upon Sunday, with Missus [sic] she always goes with me,["] &.c: read the word & offered up prayer.

Oppenheimer's last recorded interaction with them was three months later, and it is evident that Oppenheimer had been catechizing Mr. Clark in that he "examined" him on his understanding of the doctrine of the atonement:

Dudley Street January 1862.

Communicant.

Friday 3.

81 top front. Old Mr. & Mrs Clark received me kindly; I am happy to say both are now very regular in their attendance upon the means of grace; he reads his Bible everyday & has entirely given up to work on the Lord's day. I examined him to day on the most important doctrine of the gospel "the Atonement" & was very much pleased with his answers.—Read the word & offered up a prayer.

Another couple who were impacted by Oppenheimer were named Watts:

[59] Dudley Street October 1861

Missionaries [sic] encouragement

Tuesday 15.

Sick case.

1st front; found M[rs] Watts very poorly & her husband out of work; endeavoured to impress upon them the necessity of seeking the Kingdom of heaven, read & explained part of the 3rd ch[apter] of St. John and left a tract, both seem to me impressed & desired me to offer up a prayer.

OPPENHEIMER AND MISSION HALLS

The reference to the "Bloomsbury Mission Hall," in the section regarding widows, is important. Only one other reference to that mission hall occurs in the journal:

Dudley Street. January 1862.

Thursday 23.

52. 2nd front; called upon M[r] Leader who is still very indifferent, although he attends regular[ly] at Bloomsbury Mission Hall; endeavoured to impress upon [him] the awful end of those who know the will of God & don't do it; left him with the solemn warning "be not deceived God is not mocked."

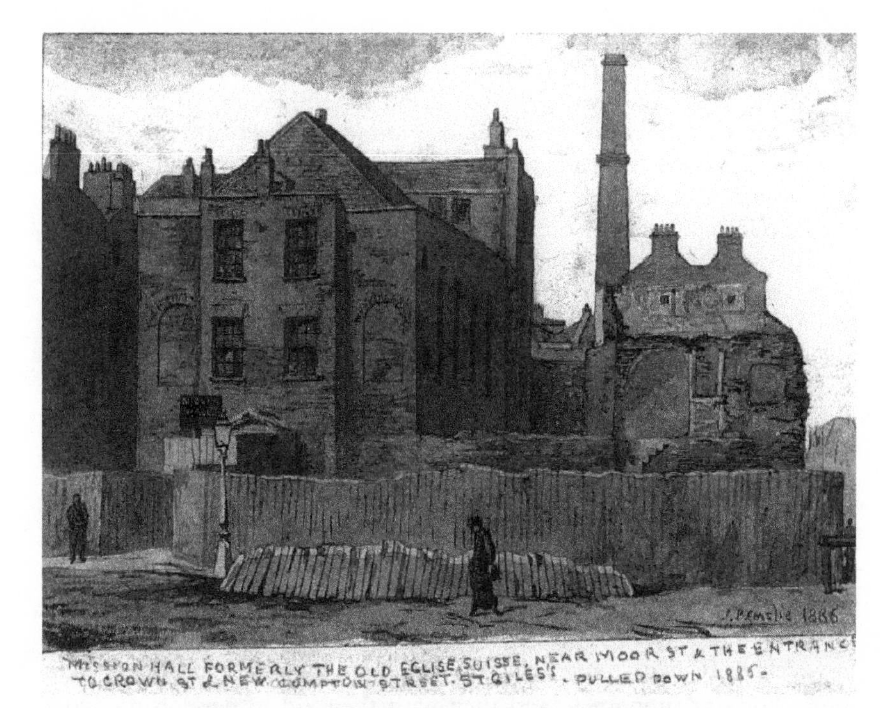

26. BLOOMSBURY MISSION HALL
The Mission Hall was located at the south end of Dudley Street at the intersection with Moor Street and Crown Street. Until 1855 the building had housed the "Old Eglise Suisse." This is a sketch of it before it was demolished in 1885.
Source: London Metropolitan Archives - SC/PZ/HB/01/215

The "Mission hall" phenomenon apparently emerged about mid-century, slowly growing in importance as centers were created for reaching those who never would darken the door of a church. Built by city missions, concerned individuals, denominational and nondenominational societies, and by individual congregations, they became an important part of the machinery by which evangelicalism gained access to these inner-city neighbourhoods. At the end of the century, social researcher Charles Booth—the famous author of *Life and Labour of the People of London* (9 volumes, 1892–97)—observed that "we find London dotted over with buildings devoted to this work. In the poorer parts especially, in almost every street, there is a mission; they are more numerous than schools or churches, and only less numerous than public houses."[2] He further acknowledged that all of this worth of work was "interwoven with that of the Society known as the 'London City Mission.'"[3] Regardless of who carried out the work, it was essentially the same in Booth's view:

> The amount of work done from these shabby centres is, however, in the aggregate enormous. In character it differs little. All the missions, of whatever description, or denomination, or lack of denomination, take up very similar ground. They set out to preach the Gospel, to teach and train the children, to influence and guide the mothers, to visit the homes and relieve poverty. They bring help in sickness and comfort in distress. They all seek to inculcate temperance, and most aim at being centres of social relaxation and enjoyment, while underlying all is the desire to lead man to God. And all alike acknowledge that if this is not accomplished nothing is accomplished. The heart must be touched.[4]

The mission hall movement was a clear admission that the churches were the preserve of the middle classes; such halls were far more widespread in the United Kingdom than in North America, a fact that undoubtedly reflects the strength of the British class structure. The city mission, in the long run, had to shift from its overwhelming concern with conversion to emphasize consolidation and pastoral care. Booth himself commented toward the end of the century that "A [city] missionary who had a hall in which he regularly preaches on Sunday evening, tends to gather round him a body of supporters, and then with their aid to develop the work along ordinary missionary lines."[5] Although they were never allowed to abandon their visiting roles, city missionaries eventually came to function as working-class pastors for the flocks that they had gathered.

However, this shift occurred well after Oppenheimer had finished his time as a city missionary. His role was both evangelistic and pastoral, and during his work, the City Mission had mission halls of its own nearby. Oppenheimer's work was pursued in conjunction with them, and with independent halls like the Bloomsbury Mission Hall.

******

Sower, sowing, seed, field and harvest. We have looked at each of these in turn, and considered the effects of Oppenheimer's work on different sorts of soil. His journal has brought into focus the bleak world pictured for us in Gustav Doré's dark sketch of Dudley Street. Doré draws the visual image, caricatures the drab people, captures our imagination as we frame what life there was like for those who eeked out their livings on that street. But Oppenheimer personalizes the rookery as he names its inhabitants, records their voices, and introduces us to their cramped quarters and poverty-constricted lives.

Perhaps most remarkable about the diary is how it shows Oppenheimer's amazing persistence in the face of such squalor and dreariness, smell and noise, hostility and rebuffs—not to mention the trial of his on-going health challenges. On the last two pages of the diary, in the entries dated May 1862, one can easily see how his writing deteriorates due to his weak and unsteady hand. In such times of illness Oppenheimer must have questioned his usefulness, wondering why so many people in "Christian Britain" were indifferent to the message that he as a Jew had embraced at such great personal cost, or why some were downright hostile and only a few were genuinely welcoming. He may have questioned whether he was partly to blame for his lack of success. Was his thick German accent a barrier to understanding? Was his German heritage a hurdle for him relating to his listeners? Was his Jewish background a help or hindrance in speaking with Gentiles? Or was the soil just so hardened and infertile that these factors mattered little?

Many questions come to mind that cannot be answered from the material at hand. But his small notebook opens to us a world lost to us, a world of poverty, of hope, of seed sown, of harvest gathered. Whether Oppenheimer's efforts were a waste of four years of a life in a hopeless task is not for the historian to answer. Any such assessment would depend on one's estimate of the seed he sought so faithfully to sow.

Notes

[1] Quoted in Hugh McLeod, *Class and Religion in the Late Victorian City* (London: Croom Helm, 1974), pp. 49–50.

[2] Charles Booth, *Life and Labour of the People in London* (London: Macmillan, 1902), 3d series, vol. 7. p. 270.

[3] Ibid.

[4] Ibid., p. 273.

[5] Ibid., p. 289.

Bibliography

Primary Sources

Newspapers and Periodicals

The Book and Its Mission
Evangelical Magazine
London City Mission Magazine
Quarterly Review
Scripture Readers' Journal
The Irish Monthly
The Record
The Times

Archive Sources

Bodleian Library, University of Oxford
Additional Manuscript c. 290
"The Principal Clergy of London classified according to their opinions on the great Church questions of the day, prepared for Mr. Delane, Edtr. of *The Times,*" 1844.
MSS Dep. Church Mission to the Jews, The Bodleian Library, Oxford. C. 16, C 63.
Greater London Public Record Office
Ranyard Bible Mission Manuscripts, Council Minutes
Greater London Archive
Settlement Records
London City Mission, 175 Tower Bridge Road, London
Hand list of City Missionaries
Minute Book of the London City Mission Committee, 1935–1860
St. Giles'-in-the-Fields Church, London
Manuscript Journal of Joseph Oppenheimer, City Missionary

Unpublished Theses

Ervine, W. J. C. "Doctrine and Diplomacy: some aspects of the life and thought of the Anglican Evangelical Clergy, 1797–1837." Ph.D. thesis, Cambridge University, 1979.

Gilley, Sheridan W. "Evangelical and Roman Catholic Missions to the Irish in London, 1830–1870." Ph.D. thesis, Cambridge University, 1970.

McIlhiney, David Brown. "A Gentleman in Every Slum: Church of England Missions in East London, 1837–1914." Ph.D. thesis, Princeton University, 1977.

Published Primary Sources

Acton, William. *Prostitution Considered in Its Moral, Social and Sanitary Aspects in London and Other Large Cities: with Proposals for the Mitigation and Prevention of its*

Attendant Evils. London, John Churchill, 1857.
Bayly, Mary. *Ragged Homes and How to Mend Them.* London, James Nisbet, 1859.
_____. *Workmen and their Difficulties.* London, James Nisbet, 1861.
Beames, Thomas. *The Rookeries of London: Past, Present and Prospective.* London, Thomas Beames, 1852.
Bickersteth, Robert. *On the Physical Condition of The London Poor.* London, privately printed, 1855.
_____. *A Charge Delivered to the Clergy of the Diocese of Ripon at his Triennial Visitation.* London, James Nisbet, 1861.
Booth, Charles. *Life and Labour of the People in London 3rd Series, Religious Influences.* Vol. 2 London, Macmillan, 1902.
_____. *Life and Labour of the People in London, 3rd series, Religious Influences.* vol. 7 London, Macmillan, 1902.
_____. *Labour and Life of the People.* vol. 1, East London, 3d ed. London, Macmillan, 1891.
Cooper, Anthony Ashley. *Moral and Religious Education of the Working Classes: the Speech of Lord Ashley, M.P., in the House of Commons on Tuesday, Feb. 28, 1843.* London, J. Oliver, 1843.
Frey, Joseph. *Narrative of the Reverend Joseph Samuel C. F. Frey, Minister of the Gospel to the Jews.* London, Gale and Curtis, 1809.
Greenwood, James. *Low-Life Deeps and the Strange Fish to be Found There.* London, Chatto and Windus, 1876.
Gurney, J. H. *The Lost Chief and the Mourning People.* London, privately printed, 1852.
Hodder, Edwin. *The Life and Work of the Seventh Earl of Shaftesbury.* London, Cassell and Co., 1893.
Mayhew, Henry. *London Labour and the London Poor.* 2 vols. London, G. Woodfall, 1851.
Ranyard, Ellen H. *The Bible Collectors: or Principles in Practice.* London, n.p., 1854.
_____. *The Missing Link: or, Bible-Women in the Homes of the London Poor.* London, Nisbet, 1859.
_____. *The True Institution of Sisterhood: or, A Message and Its Messenger.* London, Nisbet, 1862.
_____. *London and Ten Years Work in It.* London, Nisbet, 1868.
_____. *Nurses for the Needy.* London, Nisbet, 1868.
_____. L.N.R. [Ellen Ranyard]. *Life Work: Or, The Link and the Rivet.* London, Nisbet, 1861.
Roberts, Henry. *Home Reform: Or, What the Working Classes May do to Improve their Dwellings.* London, London Society for Improving the Condition of the Labouring Classes, 1852.
_____. *The Dwellings of the Labouring Classes, their Arrangement and Construction.* London, London Society for Improving the Condition of the Labouring Classes, 1854.
_____. *The Improvement of the Dwellings of the Labouring Classes through the Operation of Government Measures by those of Public bodies and Benevolent Associations, as well as by Individual Efforts.* London, Ridgway, 1859.
Sailman, M. *The Mystery Unfolded, or, An Exposition of the Extraordinary Means Employed to Obtain Converts by the Agents of the London Society for Promoting Christianity Amongst the Jews.* London, printed by author, 1817.

Vanderkiste, R. W. *Notes and Narratives of a Six Years' Mission, principally among the Dens of London.* London, Nisbet, 1852.
Wardlaw, Ralph. *Lectures on Female Prostitution: Its Nature, Extent, Effects, Guilt, Causes and Remedy.* Glasgow, J. Maclehose,1842.
Weylland, John Matthias. *Round the Tower: or, the story of the London City Mission.* London, S.W. Partridge, 1875.

Secondary Sources

Alderman, Geoffrey. *Modern British Jewry.* Oxford, Clarendon Press, 1992.
Bartley, Paula. *Prostitution: Prevention and Reform in England, 1860–1914.* London, Routledge, 2000.
Bebbington, D. W. *Evangelicalism in Modern Britain. A History from the 1730s to the 1980s.* London, Routledge, 1989.
Best, Geoffrey. (1992). Evangelicalism and the Victorians. In A. Symondson (Ed.), *The Victorian Crisis of Faith* (pp. 37–56) London: S.P.C.K., 1997.
Chadwick, Owen. *The Victorian Church.* 2 vols. London, A. & C. Black, 1966.
Chen, C. "Missionaries and the early development of nursing in China." *Nursing History Review,* 4 (1996): 129–49.
Clark, Christopher. *The Iron Kingdom: The Rise and Downfall of Prussia, 1600–1947.* Cambridge, MA, Harvard University Press, 2006.
Cox, Jeffrey. *The English Churches in a Secular Society: Lambeth 1870–1930.* Oxford, Oxford University Press, 1982.
Davidson, A.K. *Evangelicals and Attitudes to India 1786–1813.* Sutton Courtenay, Sutton Courtenay Press, 1990.
Denny, Elaine. "The second missing link: Bible nursing in 19th century London." *Journal of Advanced Nursing* 26 (1996): 1175–82.
Dyos, H. J. "The Slums of Victorian London." *Victorian Studies* 11, no. 1 (Sept. 1967): 5–40.
Englander, D. (1988). The Word and the World: Evangelicalism in the Victorian City. In G. Parsons (Ed.), *Religion in Victorian Britain* 2 *Controversies* (pp. 18–23). Manchester: Manchester University Press.
_____. (1998). Anglicanised not Anglican: Jews and Judaism in Victorian Britain. In G. Parsons (Ed.), *Religion in Victorian Britain,* vol 1 *Traditions* (pp. 253–73). Manchester: Manchester University Press.
"Father Kelly in his Prime." *The Irish Monthly,* 38, no. 443 (May, 1910): 262–67.
Fisher, Trevor. *Prostitutes and the Victorians.* New York, St. Martin's Press, 1997.
Gilbert, A.D. *Religion and Society in Industrial England: Church, Chapel and Social Change, 1740–1914.* London, Longman, 1976.
Gilley, Sheridan. (1973). Catholic Faith of the Irish Slums, London, 1840–70. In H. J. Dyos and Michael Wolff (Eds.), *The Victorian City: Images and Realities* (2: 837–53). London: Routledge and Kegan Paul.
_____. "English Catholic Charity and the Irish Poor in London, 1700–1840." *Recrusant History* 11 (1971–72): 179–269.
_____. "The Roman Catholic Mission to the Irish in London, 1840–1860." *Recrusant*

History 10 (1969–1970): 121–45.

_____. "Protestant London, No-Popery and the Irish Poor, 1830–1860." *Recrusant History* 10 (1969–70): 210–30.

_____. "Protestant London, No Popery, and the Irish Poor II 1850–1860." *Recrusant History* 11 (1971–72): 21–46.

_____. (1972). Papists, Protestants and the Irish in London, 1835–70. In G. J. Cuming and David Baker (Eds.), *Studies in Church History: Popular Practice and Belief* (259–66). Cambridge: Cambridge University Press.

Green, David R. "People of the Rookery: A Pauper Community in Victorian London," Occasional Paper No. 26, London: University of London King's College, Department of Geography, June 1986.

Green, David R. "The St. Giles Rookery: a slum in Victorian London," Occasional Paper, London: University of London King's College, Department of Geography, October 2009.

Holmes, Colin. *Anti-Semitism in British Society, 1876–1939.* London, E. Arnold, 1979.

Kitson Clark, G.S.R. *The Making of Victorian England.* Cambridge, MA, Harvard University Press, 1962.

Laqueur, T.W. *Religion and Respectability: Sunday Schools and Working Class Culture.* New Haven, CT, Yale University Press, 1976.

Lees, Lynn H. (1969). Patterns of Lower-Class Life: Irish Slum Communities in Nineteenth-Century London. In Stephan Thernstrom and Richard Sennett (Eds.) *Nineteenth Century Cities* (359–85). New Haven, CT: Yale University Press.

Lewis, Donald M., ed., *The Blackwell Dictionary of Evangelical Biography.* 2 vols. Oxford, Blackwell, 1995.

_____. *Lighten Their Darkness: The Evangelical Mission to Working-Class London, 1828–1860.* Westport, CT, Greenwood Press, 1986.

_____. (1990). 'Lights in Dark Places': Women Evangelists in Early Victorian Britain, 1838–1857. In W. J. Shiels and Diana Wood (Eds.) *Women in the Church, Studies in Church History* (415–27). Oxford: Basil Blackwell, 1990.

_____. (2016). 'A Sisterhood Powerful for Motherhood': Ellen Ranyard's 'Biblewomen' and 'Biblewomen Nurses'. In Marilyn Button and Jessica Sheetz-Nguyen (Eds.) *Victorians and the Case for Charity: Essays on Responses to English Poverty by the State, the Church and the Literati* (159–83). (Jefferson, NC: MacFarland and Co., 2013).

_____. *The Origins of Christian Zionism: Lord Shaftesbury and Evangelical Support for a Jewish Homeland.* Cambridge, Cambridge University Press, 2009.

McHugh, Paul. *Prostitution and Victorian Social Reform.* London, Croom Helm, 1980.

McLeod, Hugh. *Piety and Poverty: Working-Class Religion in Berlin, London and New York 1870–1914.* London, Holmes & Meier, 1996.

_____. "The Dechristianisation of the Working Class in Western Europe (1850–1900)." *Social Compass* 27, no. 2–3 (1980): 191–214.

_____. (1973). Class, Community and Region: the religious geography of nineteenth century England. In Michael Hill (Ed.), *A Sociological Yearbook of Religion in Britain* 6 (39–42). London: SCM Press, 1973.

_____. *Religion and Society in England, 1850–1914.* New York, St. Martin's Press, 1996.

_____. *Class and Religion in the Late Victorian City.* London, Croom Helm, 1974.

Mahood, Linda. *The Magdalenes: Prostitution in the Nineteenth Century.* London,

Routledge, 1990.

Malcolmson, Patricia E. "Getting a Living in the Slums of Victorian Kensington." *London Journal* 1, no. 1 (May 1975): 28–55.

Paxton, Jeremy. *The Victorians: Britain Through the Paintings of the Age.* London, BBC Books, 2010.

Pelling, Henry. *Popular Politics and Society in Late Victorian Britain.* London, Macmillan, 1968.

Perkin, Harold J. *The Origins of Modern English Society.* London, Routledge and Kegan Paul, 1969.

Perry, Yaron. *British Mission to the Jews in Nineteenth Century Palestine.* London, Frank Cass, 2003.

Pope, Norris. *Dickens and Charity.* London, Macmillan, 1978.

Prochaska, F.K. *Women and Philanthropy in Nineteenth Century England.* Oxford, Oxford University Press, 1978.

Railton, Nicholas. *No North Sea: The Anglo-German Evangelical Network in the Middle of the Nineteenth Century.* Leiden, Brill, 2000.

Scotland, Nigel. *Squires in the Slums: Squires and Missions in Late Victorian England.* London, Tauris and Co., 2007.

Smith, Robert Michael. "The London Jews' Society and Patterns of Jewish Conversion in England, 1801–1859." *Jewish Social Studies* 43 (1981): 275–90.

Thomas, Keith. *Religion and the Decline of Magic.* New York, Scribner, 1971.

Turton, Jacquelin. (1999). Mayhew's Irish: the Irish poor in mid nineteenth-century London. In (Eds.), Roger Swift and Sheridan Gilley, *The Irish in Victorian London, The Local Dimension* (122–55). Portland, OR: Four Courts Press.

Walkowitz, Judith R. *Prostitution and Victorian Society: Women, Class, and the State.* New York, Cambridge University Press, 1980.

Walsh, John. "John Wesley and the Urban Poor." *Revue Française De Civilisation Britannique* 6, no. 3 (1991): 18–30.

_____. (1992). Methodism and the Mob in the Eighteenth Century. In G. J. Cumming and Derek Baker (Eds.), *Studies in Church History* 8 (213–27). Cambridge: Cambridge University Press, 1972.

Werly, John N. "The Irish in Manchester, 1832–1849." *Irish Historical Studies* 18, no. 71 (March 1973): 345–58.

Wolffe, John, ed., *Evangelical Faith and Public Zeal.* London, SPCK, 1995.

Yeo, Eileen and E. P. Thompson. *The Unknown Mayhew.* New York, Schocken Books, 1972.

Young, G.M. *Portrait of an Age.* London, Oxford University Press, 1936.

Index

CPSIA information can be obtained
at www.ICGtesting.com
Printed in the USA
LVHW03s0123220618
581307LV00003B/3/P

9 781573 835640